Body and Story

Body and Story

The Ethics and Practice of
Theoretical Conflict

Richard Terdiman

The Johns Hopkins University Press
Baltimore and London

© 2005 The Johns Hopkins University Press
All rights reserved. Published 2005
Printed in the United States of America on acid-free paper

Johns Hopkins Paperbacks edition, 2006
9 8 7 6 5 4 3 2 1

The Johns Hopkins University Press
2715 North Charles Street
Baltimore, Maryland 21218-4363
www.press.jhu.edu

The Library of Congress has cataloged the hardcover edition of this
book as follows:
Terdiman, Richard.
Body and story : the ethics and practice of theoretical conflict /
Richard Terdiman.
    p. cm.
  Includes bibliographical references and index.
  ISBN 0-8018-8068-8 (alk. paper)
  1. Theory (Philosophy). 2. Postmodernism. 3. Enlightenment.
4. Diderot, Denis, 1713–1784. Religieuse. 5. Language and
languages—Philosophy. 6. Reality. I. Title.
B842.T47 2005
128—dc22   2004012071

ISBN 0-8018-8543-4 (pbk. : alk. paper)

A catalog record for this book is available from the British Library.

Contents

Preface

There are many theories, and they differ. Often they just pass by each other silently; they leave one another quietly alone. But not always. *Body and Story* tries to illuminate what happens when they clash.

Like any conflict, the collision between theories can be dramatic and exciting. But besides the excitement, what do such collisions produce? Positivist constructions of science might claim they produce *knowledge*. Such views imagine we confirm or disconfirm a theory by subjecting it to a "crucial experiment"—in effect, to a collision with the data.[1] But this protocol doesn't work for theories that deal with culture. When such theories clash, the consequence of their confrontation is rarely the collapse of one paradigm or the proof of another. Notwithstanding the other's challenge, the competing models rather go on. This persistence might seem perverse; certainly it is puzzling. Why don't false theories in the human sciences quail before the evidence? *Body and Story* wants to suggest what we might say about such disputes and about their outcome.

Confrontations between theories of human activity or understanding *do* seem uncommonly refractory to resolution. Nothing seems capable of "falsifying" a theory about culture. A theory may go out of fashion, and people do pass on to other views. But as Lévi-Strauss argued decades ago, even the most archaic myth *does* explain things. The notion of knowledge's "progress" (and the coincident codicil that bad ideas get washed out) is worth thinking about again. Why does it seem to have so little pertinence for the understanding of human beings and doings? And why does the relative indeterminacy of knowledges in contention with one another have so much? Scholars in humanities fields have not been good at explaining to colleagues in the sciences, or even more consequentially to the larger public, why we pass our time worrying about questions that people might have thought the ancients had already settled. Why do our disputes go on and on?

1. See Popper, *Conjectures and Refutations.*

I want to reconsider some of these questions in the "human sciences." I try to do this reexamination through a strategic reduction. I selected two conflicting theories (or theory-families) and I make them collide. So *Body and Story* stages a clash. But it doesn't expect resolution. The questions it aims to ask are, what can we say about a world in which *multiple* theories, even *contradictory* ones, have explanatory or interpretive traction? How can the world allow divergent, even contrary or incommensurable conceptions of itself? What is the epistemology, what are the pragmatics of such an irresolute or inconclusory structure of knowing? And what are the ethical consequences of this irresolution?

These questions are daunting. They arise in an attempt to think through how we might understand a world in which discourses, theories, modes of conceptualization *always* conflict, *always* differ—to the point that the mock-heroic "theory wars" of the past few decades come to seem the model for a much longer history, almost an ontology or a destiny, of paradigmatic contention. In reflecting upon the seemingly intractable confrontation of models, I have tried to think through, again, what *models, commensurability,* and *difference* mean to begin with.

The theory paradigms I chose to work with and to set against each other are Enlightenment "materialism" and Poststructuralist "textualism." Each of these models seeks to describe the way thought and thought's apparent "other" relate. In the modern period these models have been fundamental resources for understanding human beings and behavior. Questions of language and its function; of representation and its meaningfulness; of the ability of thinking to comprehend the world—such conundra receive answers in each theory, but the answers mutually repel. The world one theory presumes seems discontinuous with the other's world, as if the world itself had mutated or multiplied before theory's gaze. The confrontation of contradictory models lays down a challenge to our understanding. I hope my examination of this conflict can focus attention not only on the intrinsic strength and range of either theory taken on its own terms but on the challenge to it which arises in its immanent clash with a fundamentally antagonistic view. My concern lies most of all with this challenge.

This book assumes that theory-clashes can't *just* be understood abstractly, from far above them, as some sort of theoretical meta-phenomenon. Theories conflict—but the devil is in the details. Just *which theory,* and *where* does the clash articulate itself, concerning just *what,* with just *what* consciousness of paradigmatic alternatives? We must try to inhabit the specific paradigms in presence, dig down into their assumptions, their assertions—and their contradictions and irresolutions. So *Body and Story* tries to reconsider and reassess each of the two theory-families that the book brings into confrontation. It bases its discussion on specific texts. But necessarily for each theory it projects a kind of Weberian "ideal type," a synthetic version that seeks to reveal the theory's presuppositions and implications and, by the same process, the sources of the snags and kinks that occur when it rubs against another paradigm.[2]

If *Body and Story* had been a period study about the Enlightenment or about Postmodernity, it would have treated these moments in the history of thinking differently than it does. But I seek not so much to *position* as to *counter*-position them. That means that my perspective is comparatist. I emphasize elements of the assumptions and practices of these paradigms with a view toward exploring how, against appearances, these could relate to apparently incongruent features in the other. So for me the stakes in *Body and Story* do not lie in reinterpretation of either the eighteenth or the late twentieth century but in using these periods and their discourses as case studies of theoretical disparateness or contrariety.

The Enlightenment portion of the book goes into more detail about the theoretical issues and models in that period. It's probable that beneath the familiar story of Philosophical rationalism and of the Encyclopedists' effort to mock and destabilize the delusive certainties of Old Regime authoritarianism, nonspecialist readers may not be familiar with finer-grained complexities that make Enlightenment thinking exceed and complicate the image usually given of it. This is important because (as I will argue) the representation of the Enlightenment in a number of twentieth-century theoretical texts (from Adorno to Lyotard, from Althusser to Derrida) is itself strategically reductive. If we construe the Enlightenment through the lens of the notorious Postmodern allergy to it, the eighteenth century becomes too easy to bring down. Like Candide in his simplicity, it almost seems to become a mockery of itself. I want to restore some of its refractory complexity and credit both its explicit assertions about how to understand the world and its reflective puzzlements about its own conceptions.

I pursue these questions beginning in an analysis of one of Diderot's novels, *La religieuse* (*The Nun*). My interpretation seeks to open out from the explicit issues in the novel—thematic conflicts, doctrinal uncertainties, political

---

2. On the "ideal type," see Weber, *Economy and Society*, 1:18–22. Weber makes it clear that the formulation of such an "ideal" version of a theory or phenomenon necessarily entails the consequence that "it is probably seldom if ever that a real phenomenon can be found which corresponds exactly to one of these ideally constructed pure types" (1:20).

perplexities, gender confusions—toward a framing of questions on a different level. This is the level of the relationship between *language*—symbols and signs, discourses and practices; and material, non-fungible, vulnerable *human bodies*. So in this book *La religieuse* becomes the site and origin of analyses and speculations about Enlightenment thinking on the connections between language and what exceeds it.

The consequentiality of bodies has dropped out of Postmodern theory. The connections between language and bodies which fascinated Diderot are inhibited or even tabooed in most Poststructuralist theory. Not that Lyotard or Derrida don't care what happened to bodies in the bloody twentieth century. Of course they care. The issue is whether their theoretical paradigms have good ways of *talking* about this consequentially, of making it resonant. So my treatment of Poststructuralist "textualism" does not seek to represent its diversities (say, between Althusser, Lyotard, Derrida, Nancy, Deleuze, Foucault, and Certeau) in detail. Rather, for the purposes of the confrontation I stage between such thinking and Diderot's, my "textualist" ideal type seeks to capture the salient characteristics that form the horizon of Poststructuralist thought.

This is a speculative attempt. The world's diversity doesn't make for convenient packaging. If we mostly attend to the "comparison" side of the venerable high school dialectic of "compare and contrast," things can get homogenized past the point of usefulness. Obviously, we can construct a meta-level on which *any* two things become commensurable. The question is whether such an exercise is productive for understanding. On the other hand, if in our taxonomy we attempt to seize the finest-grained differences that make one theorist's thinking distinct from another's, or track the internal incoherences within the writings of a single theorist, then we will find ourselves afloat on a sea of disconnected particulars, and their meaning will elude us in direct proportion to the microscopic character of our attention to them.

Thought is always reductive. The world won't fit into our heads or within our theories. We always choose, select, and—quintessentially—we always *ignore*. I've tried to make my reductions helpful by keeping in mind that my account is not meant to be absolute, by holding on to the double angle of comparison and contrast, and by emphasizing elements that could make these operations productive.

I'm trying to write a story about how some people and some influential theoretical strains of thought have framed the relationship between language and bodies. I believe my assertions have a sound philological and empirical basis. But I don't vie with the specialists in my two periods because my objective diverges from theirs. My perspective in *Body and Story* can only be redeemed if it illuminates paradigmatic choices about the ways in which it is possible to conceive the realms of signs, communication, representation, corporeality, and materiality—and, if possible, to reconfigure in a more productive way the *divorce* to which these notions have generally been consigned for more than a hundred years of theorizing.

The idea for this book originated nearly forty years ago in an essay I wrote on *La religieuse* in Georges May's graduate seminar on Diderot at Yale University. Much has changed in the academic world since then, but my gratitude for the ethical intelligence that Georges May demonstrated in his scholarship has only grown. A year or so before he died, Professor May read a draft of *Body and Story* with a generosity and rigor that brought me back to his classroom. Let me begin by thanking this enlightened man.

Catherine Gallagher's influence on the Enlightenment portion of this book will be evident to anyone who has read her book *Nobody's Story*. She read an early draft of some of this material, and she gave me the benefit of her knowledge of the period, of cultural history more broadly, and of her intelligence. Julia Simon invited me to present some of this material at Penn State, and she read the Diderot material with care and perspicacity. My gratitude to her is great. Keith Baker read early versions of the eighteenth-century material in this book and helped me with historical grounding in a period that he knows as well as anyone. Through the intensity of his engagement with and challenge to my perspective here, my colleague Hayden White has honored me. His critique has been a gift of friendship, and it has helped me clarify things in this book. The perspective I take in this book owes most of all to my six years of conversation with Michel de Certeau, whose practices of ethics and particularly of toleration join with the lucidity of his intelligence and the intensity of his curiosity to make him a model for thinking in our period.

Monika Greenleaf helped me find the source of the quotation from Catherine the Great at the head of chapter 3. Richard Rorty was a challenging interlocutor concerning theoretical issues during our year together at the Stanford Humanities Center. Ross Chambers gave invaluable advice and encouragement, as he has always done. I'm honored by his friendship. My colleague Karen Bassi helped to determine the nuance in quotations from Aristotle. Madeleine Dobie was generous in assisting with some problems in eighteenth-century vocabulary. Dan Selden helped with several matters. Michael Ryan provided insight into Derrida's relation to Marx. Allan Stoekl helped with locating material concerning Bataille and Adorno which appears in chapter 8.

A number of students and former students gave me considerable assistance as this project evolved. With the energy and intelligence of his critical and historical perspective, Rob Halpern has kept me thinking hard for several years. Yu-mi Yang helped me understand eighteenth-century novel theory. Robert Buch introduced me to the Rilke quotation that appears at the head of chapter 1. Gabriel Brahm helped me locate the source of the epigraph from Richard Rorty in chapter 3. Michael Smith located a needed reference to the work of Merleau-Ponty. Leigh Fullmer found a quotation from Philip K. Dick which I needed. Sasha Santee helped considerably with nuancing translations from French.

I want particularly to thank three students who served as my research assistants, Johanna Isaacson, David Namie, and Melisa Preud'homme-Silver. More intelligence and diligence one could not hope for.

Current and former staff members of the McHenry Library at the University of California, Santa Cruz (UCSC) helped me with the generosity that is a hallmark of their service to the scholarly community. I want to thank, in particular, Beth Remak-Honnef, Lee Jaffe, Margaret Gordon, and Alan Ritch.

As she always has, Betsy Wootten helped in ways too numerous to count. Her intelligence and efficiency made work easier. I thank her most sincerely.

Neera Badhwar was a good friend through the composition of much of this book. Her philosophical intelligence has challenged me continuously.

The Cultural Studies Colloquium series at UCSC invited me to present some of this material. I thank the Center for Cultural Studies and its codirectors, Gail Hershatter and Chris Connery, for the invitation, and I thank the participants for the stimulating discussion. I've also presented some of the material in this book at the University of Pennsylvania, Pennsylvania State University, the University of Pittsburgh, the University of New Mexico, and the University of California, Berkeley. I thank everyone who worked to make these talks productive. I'm grateful to the people who saw *Body and Story* through production. My thanks to Michael Lonegro for shepherding the book's acquisition process at Hopkins; to Elizabeth Gratch for careful copyediting; to Juliana McCarthy at the press who superintended the manuscript through the editorial phase.

Some material drawn from my discussion of Diderot in this book appeared under the title "Political Fictions: Revolutionary Deconstructions in Diderot," in the special issue of *Yale French Studies* on "Fragments of Revolution" (no. 101 [2001]: 153–70). This issue was edited by Howard Lay and Carrie Weber, and I am grateful to them for inviting me to participate. Some material in chapter 6 is drawn from my essay "The Marginality of Michel de Certeau," in *South Atlantic Quarterly* 100, no. 2 (Spring 2001): 2. My thanks to these journals for permission to use this material in *Body and Story*.

Mistakes, alas, remain. They are my doing, and they belong to me.

Body and Story

Difference in Theory

Il n'y a pas de hors-texte.   —DERRIDA, *De la grammatologie,* 227

There is no "outside-the-text." —DERRIDA, *Of Grammatology,* 158; trans. modified

La mort est un hors-texte.   —CERTEAU, *L'écriture de l'histoire,* 321

Death is an "outside-the-text."
                              —CERTEAU, *The Writing of History,* 316; trans. modified

History is *not* a text.   —JAMESON, *The Political Unconscious,* 35

The body at work . . . is not one text among many.
              —SPIVAK, "Limits and Openings of Marx in Derrida," 110

The world doesn't wait for theories in order to happen. That's why theory is a problem. The Owl of Minerva—Hegel's evocative icon for thinking's endeavor to comprehend the world—is flying as fast as it can.[1] But the philosophical bird is always belated and behind. This is because thought regards and reacts to an "other" that is *not* just more "thought." Thinking's object exists in a modality different from language. If this wasn't the case, wouldn't we be able to change the world we think about as quickly as we can transform our ideas or edit this sentence? There's always a phase-change between the referent of our thinking and thinking itself. That translation or transmutation is always laborious. It takes time and work.

Even after we devise a model for comprehending the obscurities that confront us, how can we be sure we have the "right" one? How much credence

---

1. "As the idea [*Gedanke*] of the world, philosophy appears only after objective reality completes its formative process [*Bildungsprozess*] and has been accomplished [*fertig gemacht*]. . . . When philosophy paints its grisaille [*Grau in Grau*], it has the shape [*Gestalt*] of a life grown old; and with the gray-on-gray life cannot rejuvenate [*verjüngen*], only comprehend [*erkennen*]. The owl of Minerva begins its flight only at the coming of dusk" (Hegel, *Hegel's Philosophy of Right,* 13; trans. modified).

should we give to the theory we select, and how should we deal with its competitors? These are big questions for anyone who struggles with understanding. For theories regularly and sometimes spectacularly disagree. In the world of human beings and doings there is none whose "truth" is uncontested—so self-evident, so uncontroverted and incontrovertible, that it has risen from the level of doxa to the level of certainty and maintained itself there, world without end. Contention and counter-discursivity define theory's mode of existence. Such characteristics—theories' belatedness, their interrelatedness with other theories, their inherent uncertainty—both found and confound our efforts at understanding. They raise the problem of what practical stance we should take toward "theory-uncertainty." And we need to think through the *ethical consequences* of such contingency.

This book is about the situation into which thinking is put by these characteristics that delimit it. Despite being tardy and chancy, theory is indispensable. The world doesn't passively give up its secrets to whoever comes along. Theory is our fundamental tool for responding to this problematic silence. We ask, how are things different from the way they seem to be? What tools beyond immediate inspection can we use to understand what confronts us? Both materially and epistemologically, we work on the world to understand it better. Theory is thus first a matter of pragmatics, of what seems to work. Rather than the abstraction or abstruseness that people frequently attribute to it, theory is the most *practical* of our cognitive and epistemological practices. The problem is that *multiple* theories seem to work.

So *Body and Story* explores a theory about theory: about the way that the work of understanding gets done, about the sorts of outcomes it enables, and about the differences and the difficulties that arise as we seek to model the world. Reality exhibits no settled truth, manifests no unassailable essence of people, things, or institutions. There are always several theories claiming to account for any social or cultural phenomenon. This interpretive multiplicity demonstrates how inherently problematic understanding is. But how should we understand the diversity itself? How should we think about the fact that people think *differently* even about fundamental things?

As my preface suggested, *Body and Story* seeks to answer such questions by working out and working with a model of its own. Rather than taking on theory as a whole, I try to manage the theory problem through a tactical reduction, by bringing two prominent and foundational theoretical models into contact with each other. These are Enlightenment "materialism" and Poststructuralist "textualism." My initial plan was pretty simple. I wanted to map the differences between these two theories. They disagree about fundamental elements and assumptions. I intended to lay out their convergences and divergences. I hoped this would clarify the stakes that underlie and stimulate each model, the defining choices each makes in the effort to open the world to explanation. Comparing two theoretical paradigms that deal with the same problems but from different perspectives seemed like a useful clarifying task. A tableau of convergences and divergences between the models in question could help to illuminate their underlying assumptions, their methodological distinctions, their strengths, and their areas of blindness.

Ah, the seductive clarities of binarism! The project proved naive. The paradigms I chose resisted my cataloging and clarifying operation. Comparing things requires them to be commensurable in salient elements. But my models appeared to repel and refuse interrelation, to decline commensurability. In fact they sought to annihilate each other. It was not that they focused on divergent aspects of the world or talked about dissimilar things. Different tools do different work, and such pragmatic diversity presents no deep challenge. But these tools were designed for the same job. My paradigms invoke the same registers of life; they speak about the same elements of existence. Yet when brought into contact, no negotiation between them seems possible—or only the anathemas they pronounce against each other. How to bring into conversation dicta as antinomic as Hegel's "The Truth is the whole" and Lyotard's "Let us wage war on totality"?[2]

Such formulas, and the models they sustain, so resolutely disavow and fend each other off that one begins to wonder how they could occupy the same universe. So my question about the Enlightenment and Postmodernity transformed itself into a larger question: what is the function of "theory" when theories *contradict* each other? What is the universe that such paradigms inhabit as sworn enemies? Counter-position turned out to be more complicated and more precarious than it first appeared. The confrontation of two theories raised questions about the enterprise of theory itself.

The difficulty we have in confronting two divergent or contradictory theories—these or any others—might help us understand some formative patterns in thinking. Or, to put this more operationally, we need to ask how we can under-

2. Hegel's "Truth" could also be translated as "True" ("Das Wahre ist das Ganze"). Hegel, *Phenomenology of Spirit*, preface, 11, sec. 20, trans. modified; Lyotard, "Answering the Question: What Is Postmodernism?" 81–82.

stand contradictory theories, how we might devise ways to foster our grasp of them and open them to reflection and critique. The answers to such questions are particularly pertinent in the face of the multiform reality we confront in an increasingly heteronomous and variegated world, a world in which the conflict of theories is omnipresent, positively pandemic.

In culture things are never simple. The taxonomy of cultural objects is never stable, never neat. Theories don't take the form of an abstract array of binary options distributed in a tableau of *positive* or *negative*, *yes* or *no*. The world of competing theories is not primarily a *combinatoire*, even if the positions that models take do tend to fill up available choices. The story of theory is more complex. The element missing in a *combinatoire* is the same one absent from any two-dimensional structuralist array: *time*. History, with its crucial and ineluctable determinations, is what makes understanding theory and the relationship between theories more complex than it first appears.

The synchronic is too *thin* to catch the complications of theoretical relationships well. Theories aren't monads—detached, abstract, determined only by a need for internal coherence and consistency. Understanding the relationship between theories is not just a matter of logic. To understand, we must foreground the diachronic, because the interdeterminations that theories exert upon other theories are fundamental elements in their formation, their functioning, and their meaning. Theories never take shape ex nihilo. Each is complicated by the choices that other theories are making and have already made. Theories are always reactive to the range of paradigms that are already active. In the very fact of their divergence or denegation they embody an acute consciousness of what contradicts or differs from them. Theories *know* their competitors and their antagonists.

Today it is a commonplace to characterize the world as a space in which differences abound. We are supposed to respect them. Indeed, sometimes we so solemnly respect their dissimilarity from our own views that an "essentialist" position arises, maintaining that there can be no cognitive connection between them whatever—that the diversity between our situation and others' is not inter-comprehensible. Whether we accept that proposition or not, in the contemporary globalizing world *disagreement* is omnipresent and increasingly normalized. It resembles on the macroscopic level the situation of contrariety which manifested itself between the theoretical positions I first thought to bring into contact with each other in this book.

Then a fundamental question arises. Is there just *one* world that such antinomic paradigms seek to grasp? Or is there *more* than one? For, if not the latter, how could two irreconcilable explanations or theories *both* have the capacity to illuminate things? This book wants to investigate that complex of questions. Contrariety between the Enlightenment's materialist and referential credo and Postmodernity's denegation of the extra-textual has certainly not dropped out of what I want to investigate. It is the testing ground for what I will explore. But the contradiction between my models is as much the *means* and *mode* of exploration as it is the objective.

What are the *pragmatics*, what are the *epistemologies*, what are the *ethics* appropriate to a world in which the foundational ways we conceive our own behavior and that of others, our fundamental forms of intellection and interaction, seem irreconcilable? One might be tempted to say that there are as many worlds as there are theories constructing them. Such a solution would neatly turn the trick.[3] But common sense pulls against such a solution.

Despite heterogeneity and even contrariety everywhere we look, we appear to have a forceful intuition that the quantity of "worlds" in the world must be a number of a very low order. We seem to sense that, in some form, coherence and comprehensibility underlie the world's rich variegation. This might be true of the theory world as well. *Body and Story* tries to understand what kind of universe—freighted in its fundamental structures of cognition and epistemology with apparently irreconcilable differences—this world might be. The book tries to frame a question about how we might best think about a world of contrariety and operate within its multifariousness.

So, my investigation invokes two specific models, but it does not worry them simply for their own sake. I seek to describe their assumptions, their operations, and their implications—particularly (because of its relative distance from us and the apparent disfavor in which it is held today) the Enlightenment member of the pairing. Enlightenment theories of language, representation, and materiality deserve reexamination. They are very capable models. Often they have been oversimplified, even distorted, by later, sometimes invidious or tendentious characterizations. Even the common name for this family of

---

3. This is not just gratuitous coquetting with ideas. "Possible worlds theory" has long had a respected place in philosophy. The notion began with Leibniz's monadology, in which each separate world is sui generis, but "possible worlds theory" has flourished in twentieth-century logic. A radical subset of it ("extreme realism") holds that all possible worlds are on a par; that there is no distinction sustainable between the "actual" and the "possible." See Lewis, *On the Plurality of Worlds.* Lewis's title was meant to echo Bertrand de Fontenelle's celebrated *Entretiens sur la pluralité des mondes* (1686; *A Plurality of Worlds*, 1688), a series of dialogues whose objective was to theorize the scientific and the ethical consequences of the Copernican planetary system. See Craig, *Routledge Encyclopedia of Philosophy*, s.v. "Possible worlds."

paradigms—"Enlightenment rationalism"—oversimplifies and domesticates it. But understanding theories—in themselves and in their conflicts with other models—needs to work against the tendency to simplify them and their internal perplexities in order to be "clear." Such clarity can be too cheaply bought. It is liable to produce a cartoon of the model, sometimes ironed flat to the point of enfeeblement.

Despite the fact that reductionism is a condition of any explanation or description, my objective has been to avoid such damaging simplifications. Our models are always smaller than what they seek to elucidate—or else they would be useless to us and impossible to carry around. Here I want to allow the internal complications that are sometimes caricatured *out* of accounts of theoretical paradigms to retain their untidy and unsettled dissonances. This is because I believe that through such unresolved, unsutured snarls and tangles, *history* enters the story we can tell about them. I want to argue that detection of the competing and unresolved tendencies that underlie any given cultural object is a model for uncovering the historical potential in our discourse about theory itself.

I won't presume to define *history*. But one of history's charges or potentials is to figure the hidden untidiness and the internal incongruity of cultural objects that, once they are "finished," would rather like us to believe that they have achieved the crystalline coherence of logic. Such purity contravenes our quotidian experience of the unresolved messiness of life. History is a witness to that disorder. It registers that our ideas and our experiences don't all come or come together at once. They, and we, are the integration of many times and many confusions. But that integration (unlike the mathematical one) can never heal all the dissonances and differences in what it seeks to contain. Some muddle always remains unfused.

The temporal protraction and the possible *errance* in the development of a thought is something that all writers know when they return to their texts for another crack at perfecting them. But writers also know well that the struggle for coherence often, rather, produces its contrary. Such secondary and posterior remodeling forms a miniature paradigm for the way in which, in a seemingly self-coherent and contemporaneous text, strands with provenances from different epochs of the text's own history, with impulses pulling toward different assumptions, with the potential for divergent implications, all commingle or cohabit. The same is true in any theory.

In turn such internal multifariousness and variegation is a microcosmic ver-

sion of the external differences—between individuals, groups, cultural formations, theoretical paradigms—to which thinking about culture has become
more and more attentive in the past few decades. This is why going *deep* into
texts is so necessary and, potentially, so productive. But deep reading is poly-
morphic. The traditional mode of *explication de texte* seeks to find in texts'
wholeness the beauty of forms that it apprehends, to disclose their principle of
unification and celebrate their triumph in achieving it. But against such organi-
cist assumptions there is a divergent or contrary strain within the paradigms of
deep reading. This is "ideology-critical" or "deconstructive" interpretation. Its
objective is rather to detect and display the dissonant, unresolved elements of
an utterance or a text and to trace them to a diversity of determinations, to the
existence of extra-textual dissonances or contradictions to which we can then
attribute their formation.[4]

So *Body and Story* takes the two theoretical paradigms it counterposes against
each other as examples of a broader phenomenon of disagreement and conflict
in theory. The book does not attempt to bring apparent contraries into some
unification that had somehow previously gone unnoticed. The problem of how
to deal with difference, disagreement, contrariety, remains daunting. In the
face of the theoretical incompatibility with which my initial analysis collided,
I began to wonder what could allow experience to open to contradictions and
contrary models without itself becoming incoherent or incomprehensible or
spawning a myriad of possible worlds in which every theory would benefit from
a referent conveniently reserved for its own use alone.

The models whose relationship I had set out to explore underlie fundamental efforts at comprehending the world. But how can the world allow this to be
the case? As ideal types, these models appear to represent dual options for
seeing things. But they don't seem to obey logic's law of non-contradiction—
the principle holding that a proposition must be false if its contrary is true. The
trouble is that both of these contraries, both of these theories, *work*. Each appears to cancel the other; their respective epistemologies, ontologies, politics,
and ethics seem irreconcilable. Despite this, they are not disabled. The incompatible analyses they generate still foster and further understanding.

The Postmodern member of my theoretical pairing has many adherents

---

4. In diverse ways such modes of reading can be found in the work of a number of social and cultural theorists and critics. See, for example, Adorno, *Minima Moralia*; Adorno, *Negative Dialectics*;
Macherey, *Theory of Literary Production*; Derrida, *Writing and Difference*; Derrida, *Margins of Philosophy*;
and Derrida, *Dissemination*.

today. They are persuaded and they feel enabled by Poststructuralism's renunciation of referentiality and by the alternate focus upon "textuality." I will try to suggest the reasons for their allegiance. But today persistence of the Enlightenment alternative is less obvious. You might think that the Enlightenment version of the issue had been canceled out by history. Does anyone still credit the model the philosophes devised to rattle and subvert the irrationalities and abuses of the Old Regime? But, despite widespread denigration and denegation of the Enlightenment paradigm over a long period, I will try to show how influential it still remains and in what guises and disguises.

The Enlightenment believed fervently in what we call "representation" by language. The philosophes bet their politics upon such a conviction. Postmodernism subverts that view so radically that we often say it repudiates the notion of representation to begin with. But I will try to show that this simple mutual repudiation is more intricate than it seems. For Enlightenment theses regarding referentiality and language—often reproduced in much empirical and practical analysis today—are not just randomly divergent from their Postmodern counterparts. The two paradigms are related as overdetermined counter-discourses whose contrariety does not simply occur in a mode of arithmetic negation—one saying yes, the other no.[5] This is not just the case because Postmodernism seeks to renounce what it believes are the naive and credulous theses of Enlightenment thinkers. *It is because the Postmodern view of the problem was already in contention in the Enlightenment period itself.*

This is the surprising phenomenon I want to examine in my paralogistic claim that the Enlightenment "discovered" Postmodernism (see chap. 5). Not only do these two periods contend with each other, but each bears the trace of the other within itself and seeks to assimilate what, simply viewed, appears unassimilable. So there is a relationship of mutual imbrication and indebtedness in the condemnation that each of my paradigms pronounces against the other. This subterranean attraction to the contrary is one of the things about the world of theory which this book will try to illuminate.

I begin by examining the notions whose tension animates my argument. *Body* and *story. Materiality* and *imagination. Fiction* and *lies. History* and *theory. The Enlightenment* and *Postmodernity. Rationalism* and *textualism.* These are the polarities that orient and worry this book's reflection.

5. I discussed the counter-discursive relationship in Terdiman, *Discourse/Counter-Discourse.*

The book tries to operate on three nested levels. On the most local of these registers—microscopically, as I might put it—*Body and Story* is concerned with a moment in the history of modernity. I want to bring the problem of "fictionality" into contact with the Enlightenment's tensed attention to materiality and corporeality. And I want to speculate on the reasons why *bodies* (as the most privileged constituents of the "material" realm) captured such attention in the period. I will try to frame an analysis of a cultural transition beginning in the Enlightenment which transformed the way the *body-story* connection was thought about and practiced. Enlightenment reflections in this moment of transition are important because the conceptual structures by which the eighteenth-century philosophes sought to understand the problem of *representation* which was becoming acute for them remain consequentially so for us.

Moving up one level toward greater generality—call it mesoscopically—*Body and Story* argues that the tensions we experience in conceiving the notions of *fictionality* and *textuality* fundamental to the cultural experience of Postmodernity can be illuminated through a reexamination of their early formation. Thus, a second preoccupation of *Body and Story* is a conflicted but compelling connection between contemporary Postmodernity and Postmodernity's prehistory in the eighteenth century.

Finally—on the most macroscopic level—this book will urge a way of practicing and thinking about cultural theory and methodology which seeks to reframe and to undermine the virulence of conflict between theories, of the last decades' "theory wars." I want to project a paradigm of relationship between seemingly antagonistic theoretical approaches or orientations. I want to suggest ways in which apparently incompatible theories can speak to each other and make sense of each other.

History and *theory* thus form fundamental poles of my analysis, and their association adds itself to and inflects the other pairings in *Body and Story*. But history and theory themselves don't easily or self-evidently cohere. In recent decades we have grown accustomed to theorizing history. But *historicizing theory* has been less attended to. Yet the historicization and de-absolutization of theory offers a way of construing what we really *do* with it which might foster its capacity for helping us understand cultural production and activity.

Jean-François Lyotard once remarked that theory is "thinking without proper names."[6] The aphorism's economy is admirable. Theory seeks generality and

6. In a seminar taught around 1978 at the University of California, San Diego.

regularity; specificity subverts its objective. To the extent that the proper name—
or any concrete particularity—invokes the unassimilable contingency that theoretical thinking resists or seeks to transcend, the tension between specificity
and generality would appear to be irreconcilable. This may be one of the dynamics fostering the rigidification and the absolutization of theoretical positions which has characterized so much academic squabbling in the contemporary period. But this structure of apparent repulsion between the impulse to
seize specificity, emblematically in *history*, and the search for generality, a cardinal element in the *theory* enterprise, might productively be reconstrued.

In considering these issues in *Body and Story*, I want to allow some Enlightenment speculation on related issues to *decenter us* and thereby open up our constructions of—or confusions concerning—these problems to a willfully anachronistic reading, an interpretation of cultural representation at the turn of the
twenty-first century generated from powerful reflections in the eighteenth.
Poststructuralism has fundamentally destabilized whole continents of cultural
and analytical assumptions that were current in the period preceding its intervention. The result is that intellectuals today face a seemingly irreconcilable
theoretical dilemma. It appears as if we either have to sign on to Poststructuralism or fight it like the devil. There have been older contentions of this kind. We
might think of the one that in the 1940s divided Marxian and Freudian interpretations in such an airtight and hostile way that it appeared the choice of one
approach virtually foreclosed the other.

This is a bad situation for theory to find itself in. *Body and Story* seeks to
construct a different understanding of how theories relate to each other and
how they solicit or command allegiance. I suggest that a movement away from
conception of theories as antagonistic or bipolar contraries, and toward one
that sees them as situated, motivated, and modulated choices, will be more
productive for comprehension.

I take up my argument on the first of the levels I alluded to earlier, the
problem that in the period of the European Enlightenment interweaves fictionality, corporeality, and an inflection in the theory and practice of representation. I center my examination on the period's most interesting and complex
reflections on this issue, in the work of Denis Diderot.

How might we relate to Diderot today? One thing is clear: Diderot is still a
star. Modernity and Postmodernity have been dazzled by him. We have seen
our contemporary preoccupations uncannily anticipated in his effort to work
on and work out the problems of his own period. Any reader of *Jacques le*

fataliste recognizes instantly how the antic textual practices Diderot was experimenting within that text foreshadow familiar Postmodern textual moves in Borges, Cortázar, Calvino, and Pynchon. A double relation, of technical inheritance and of shared cultural problematic, links eighteenth-century reflection on fiction and verisimilitude to worries in our own time about representation, language, and textuality.

But contemporary fascination with Diderot suggests that we need to rethink our relationship to the Enlightenment, particularly in the face of its depreciation in influential quarters today. To what in the Enlightenment is Postmodernism allergic? My claim will be that important origins of cultural puzzlements today, and insight about their difficulties, lie in the eighteenth-century incipience of our modern, democratic, capitalist, increasingly language- and exchange-oriented society. But whole realms of contemporary theory don't want to think about that. Whence the anathema concerning "Enlightenment reason" which has characterized several influential strands of conceptual reflection over the past fifty years or so.

In culture or social existence nothing comes into being unproblematically. Nor is anything ever abandoned without disruption. These stresses are diagnostic. But incipience has its privilege. For the analyst it offers advantages in two related areas. First, in the period of its early institutionalization a sociocultural form leaves traces of its functioning which, as its domination later solidifies, become harder to detect. Only with time and ideological work do social practices integrate themselves into the network of the culturally normalized, the self-evident, the socially transparent. Early on, their "fit" is rougher, their functioning less seamless and more contingent. The "guarantee" provided to them by the system of dominant ideology fails to provide them with blanket protection. When we examine their transitional period, we can re-detect the configuration of that which has since become organized as invisibility.

Second, the early penetration of a new cultural form or practice typically produces explicit—indeed, sometimes violent—movements of resistance: counterhegemonic tactics, counter-discursive practices, which assist us in perceiving the nascent form's configuration *before* it becomes absorbed into doxa. However functional it may later be destined to become, in the early phases of its constitution as a social practice, it cannot fail to be disruptive in some way. Its configuration is readable through the disturbances it causes. Such counter-discourses map points of stress within the social system which accompany the slow institutionalization of the new. The attempts to critique or resist or negate these emerging practices and discourses define their operations with a clarity that later, when they have become consolidated, will be harder to achieve.[7]

On the historical side *Body and Story* thus seeks to tell a story about the struggle and the perplexity that occur when culture changes—particularly when the change in question involves one of the cardinal registers through which people make sense of the world. In this case that register is the functioning of representation. The specific Enlightenment mutation I will be examining made literary fictions into an intelligible category for a broad range of people in the West. I seek to recapture the drama, but also the complication, of this change.

In our world of virtuality today the capacity to deal with fictions seems intrinsic to experience. But this was not always so. *Fiction* was once a controversial attainment. During that period of incipience writers and readers wrestled with the forms of cognition and imagination which fictionality proposed to make available to them. The most thoughtful of them even worried about what in culture might be *threatened* if "fiction" became an accustomed form of narrative practice and representational imagination.

I want to go back to a point when the socialization of fiction was still a contested process. My argument is that the stakes in such moments of contestation have significance for the evolution of the processes and capacities at issue. Culture never really "settles" anything. It comes to terms with its conflicts in a shifting and precarious negotiation of the unresolvable. This suggests that the problems of one period almost always project themselves, disguised and only seemingly pacified, into subsequent moments. That is what I want to claim about the practices of fiction—or, to put it in terms of our contemporary version of the conflict, about the pragmatics of textuality.

The first of the seemingly irreconcilable pairings that motivate this book is the one I call "body and story." What most people may notice first about this binary is the incommensurability that for a century now has made *representation* a central enigma in theoretical reflection. *Signs* and *things* appear to us as antinomic categories, disjunct from each other. They feel and they function in what seem irreconcilable ways. The lability that characterizes imagination and language-use collides with the dense materiality of the corporeal; the untrammeled "flight of fancy" stands over against the cumbrous inertia of the flesh. With the modes of their existence so disconnected, how can we get from things

---

7. On the privilege of incipience, see Terdiman, *Discourse/Counter-Discourse*, 120–21.

to words or back to things again? The refractory nature of the task of fitting signifiers to referents—when reflection over the past century or so has underlined how little they have in common—defines modernity.

Mallarmé is a canonical theorist of this separation. According to one of his celebrated images, we may write about palaces, but the stones our words refer to will never fit between the pages of our books.[8] Mallarmé's figure projects the complication of our experience of extra-textual materiality. The map is never the territory; the language we use is always separate from what it designates or describes. In the movement from Modernism to Postmodernism we have increasingly taken this separation not only as unbridgeable but as unrationalizable, even as meaningless. But if words don't simply refer to things, are they just plumb cut off from each other? In the contemporary period we have tended to treat the rift between them as an unbridgeable chasm, as if no circulation or mediation was possible between these realms. Such a view—*il n'y a pas de hors-texte*—has become the foundation of the metatheory of "textualism" that has dominated the past few decades of literary and cultural theory.[9]

But what we might call Newton's third law of cultural theory always prescribes that there will be a reaction to any action. That is happening now. For more than a generation of cultural criticism and theory we have been exploring the heady lability of language and of thought. The impulse to do so was well founded, and we came by it honestly. It based itself in and it carried forward the project of liberation which, since the Enlightenment, has been a pervasive aspiration in the Euro-American world and well beyond it.[10] But this thinking about thinking has tended to project our aspirations for freedom into reductive conceptions of thought and of freedom themselves. The issue—framed since Marx's resonant eleventh thesis on Feuerbach as the dialectic between theory and practice—is not new. In this sense Marx, here a principal legatee of the Enlightenment itself, would stand as the counter-term to Postmodern notions of thought's incommensurability with an unattainable and uncognizable realm of material entities and practices.

Marx was ferocious in contesting earlier Idealist versions of this Kantian dilemma—as, for example, in this passage from *The German Ideology*: "It is possible to achieve real liberation only in the real world and by real means. . . .

8. Mallarmé, "Crise de vers," 366.

9. "*There is no 'outside-the-text.*'" The dictum is from Derrida, *De la grammatologie*, 227; English trans., *Of Grammatology*, 158.

10. See Terdiman, "On the Dialectics of Post-Dialectical Thinking," 111–20.

'Liberation' is a historical and not a mental act, and it is brought about by historical conditions."[11] But Modernity and, even more intransigently, Postmodernity have scanted reflection on the *constraints* that make the realization of freedom arduous. The tendency has privileged thought's autonomy over its mystifying but powerful fetters.

The character of criticism and theory over the past three or four decades suggests that the entire enterprise has been about *difficulty*: in the hermeneutic strain, the arduousness of interpretation; in the structuralist strain, the complexity of signifying relationships; in the Poststructuralist, the irreducibility of slippages, disseminations of meaning, and other instabilities that make understanding feel constantly at risk. Such difficulties have seemed delicious, and the cultural disciplines have made their fortunes from them.

Body and Story seeks to attend to a different kind of difficulty: the brute and often brutal difficulty of materiality. This difficulty materializes as the resistance to our projects, desires, and dreams which recurrently confounds us in our quotidian and our historical experience. This is the challenge to human hopes which John Berger captured in a phrase he borrowed from the peasants of central France which he used as the title of *Pig Earth*. Anyone who has ever tried to move a reluctant mule or hog knows in her or his body the sort of obstinacy this graphic figure seeks to evoke. This is the world of crushing weight and overpowering friction, of countervailing will and downright intractability. It is what makes what most people call "real life" seem more *real* than words can easily convey.

The former strain of analytical or interpretive difficulty has drawn attention away from this other sort of arduousness—from what we might term referential difficulty or, perhaps even better, the *difficulty of referents*. Their resistance reimmerses us in our finitude and frailty. This is the difficulty that human culture over millennia has sought to depict, to understand, and whenever possible to lessen.

No doubt there is a relationship between these different sorts of difficulties. But, however interdetermining these registers may be, their links and resonances often seem disconnected. The side of dumb necessity and unforgiving burden can appear nearly inaudible today—in the advanced West at least. We need to rebalance this relationship and return attention to what remains *refractory* in thinking, language, and culture. Today a language-centered perspec-

---

11. See Marx and Engels, *German Ideology*, 44. For the *Theses on Feuerbach*, see 615–20.

tive often seems hegemonic. But this was not so in the Enlightenment period, which I want to pose as a cultural and intellectual counter-frame to help us denaturalize fundamental assumptions of our own time. After two hundred years of an epochal effort to achieve liberation from it and from its servitudes, materiality—brute reality—still weighs us down, still determines our possibilities. Let us imagine how to recapture the notion of such constraint.

Part I / The Consequentiality of Bodies

CHAPTER ONE

The Nun Who Never Was

Farai un vers de dreyt nien.
[I'm going to make a poem out of absolutely nothing.]
　　　　　　　—WILLIAM IX, Duke of Aquitaine, *Lyrics*, 24

Qu'il est facile de faire des contes!
[Damn, it's easy to make up stories!]
　　　　　　　—DIDEROT, *Jacques le fataliste*, DFPV 23:25

Something happened to the way that readers responded to texts in the late
eighteenth century.　—DARNTON, *The Great Cat Massacre*, 251

Daß man erzählte, wirklich erzählte, das muß vor meiner Zeit gewesen sein.
[That people told stories, really told them, must have been before my time.]
　　　—RILKE, "Die Aufzeichnungen des Malte Laurids Brigge," 6:844

They cannot tell stories because they do not believe the stories are true.
　　—WOOLF, "How It Strikes a Contemporary," *The Common Reader*, 244

Fictions and *bodies*. A simple conjunction appears without effort to link these
two terms. But their relation has seemed uncommonly difficult to Enlightenment and post-Enlightenment imagination. Dual ontologies resonate here, the
mutually determining and simultaneously incommensurable modes in which
language and materiality exist.

The representational world is intriguingly different from the referential one.
But we are not obliged to think of this difference as a dire fate or an irrevocable
fracture. It can be conceived in the image of a slowly revolving contention with
each party to the argument framing fundamental perceptions and cognitions
but in a way that resists the other's insights. Since the Enlightenment period
each of the positions in this argument has been alternately inhibited or enabled: now one, now the other suffering denegation in order to preserve the
appearance of stability which the other projects.

The dissonance has thereby been managed. But for our efforts to make sense of Enlightenment theory of representation and its relation to contemporary paradigms today, the tension *between* these terms is more significant than the manner in which, over several centuries, it has been handled in cultural perception and practice. The stress between these two models for understanding the world and our activity in it—the world of *fictions*; the world of *bodies*—defines a border across which the negotiations of Modernity and Postmodernity situate themselves.

I want to explore some paradigms in Enlightenment thinking in the second half of the eighteenth century about what a fiction is and what it does. The period's concern with narrative arose because its culture confronted thinkers and writers with some new and unsettling story patterns—patterns that simultaneously put the making of fictions on the agenda and raised troubling questions about their meaning and their use. Diderot will be my testing case for these issues and, within his work, his novel *La religieuse*.

All stories tell two tales: their accustomed referential narrative; and a second, embedded account of their own generation, their conditions of possibility and practice. Enlightenment texts, Diderot's in particular, speculate intricately about the meaning of this second, self-reflexive narrative that they bear within themselves. Why do they worry so intently and so intensively about how stories *work*, about the realm and range of narrative origin, functioning, and effect? What in the Enlightenment period made these questions urgent? What produced the need not only to tell that second story but to focus so insistently upon it that sometimes in Diderot's tales, self-referential interrogation swamps referential narrative?

The course of true narrative never runs smooth. Stories are made of the difficulties people have. They arise in the problems or contradictions in human existence: *no trouble, no tale*. In the mode and through the time of narrative, stories work upon the conflicts that constitute and simultaneously stress lives. This work of representation, hypothesis, projection, and fantasy is their cognitive and imaginative function. To read a story is to engage with a conflict drawn from, and phantasmatically projected back upon, the referential world.

What is at issue in Diderot's fictions is the entailment that links *representation* and *agency*, the basis of any narrative pragmatics as of any politics. One of the central problems in his tales turns out to be narrative itself—experienced as an uncanny, unsettling social and cultural practice. Both *La religieuse* and *Jacques le fataliste* worry storytelling in radical ways. They interrogate and destabilize the ontology of fictions. It's not obvious why this should have seemed a necessary operation in the period, still less an urgent one. From what in experience did its urgency arise?

Modernist narrators have taught us to admire texts in which writers appear to have anticipated our own contemporary fascination with what I termed the "second" narrative that is folded within any tale. The interpretive contract between writers and readers prescribes attention to the structural, thematic, and linguistic characteristics of narratives, particularly those that foreground the conflicts that generated the story's cultural or personal urgency to begin with. We have learned to value those narratives in which we perceive significant and purposeful transfer of attention from the level of the tale to the level of the telling.[1]

With Diderot the habits of such auto-referentiality were not yet focused with the single-mindedness we identify with later-nineteenth-century formalisms and, even more, with their Modernist literary and critical progeny. Diderot's narrative practice is highly self-conscious. But his attention to the organization and the functioning of storytelling in his texts does not simply anticipate, still less duplicate, the blithely transhistorical and depoliticizing modernist presumption that all writing is really just writing about writing itself.

On the contrary, Diderot's preoccupation with the question of narrative had conjunctural determinations. Enlightenment culture was preoccupied with narrative practices and possibilities because of a complex of unmanaged uncertainties within the culture itself, and particularly in its mode of producing, reproducing, and potentially transforming its structures and its meanings. The formal and narratological preoccupations of Diderot's stories are not first-order aesthetic concerns, despite interpretations of them based upon the assumptions of "experimental" or avant-garde narratives nearer to our own period. Rather, they arise in the turbulent cultural preoccupations that grew out of and reciprocally implicate the patterns of experience and apprehension through which the Enlightenment framed its self-understanding. The fundamental problem being worked upon in these Diderot stories is the vexed relationship between language and bodies, between thought and materiality.[2]

---

1. This distinction parallels—and anticipates—Roman Jakobson's well-known characterization of poetic language as language defined by a "focus on the message for its own sake"; by what Mukařovský called the "foregrounding of the utterance." See Jakobson, "Closing Statement: Linguistics and Poetics," 353; and Mukařovský, "Standard Language and Poetic Language," 19.

2. Since Foucault put them there, "bodies" have been on the contemporary critical agenda—to

Il faudra me représenter.

[I will have to be present. / I will have to be represented.]

−DIDEROT, *La religieuse*, DFPV 11:145

Diderot's *La religieuse* is a hybrid, heteroclite, self-divided text. It is made up of two discontinuous parts. The novel is cast in the mode of memoir, as a first-person autobiographical narrative composed by a runaway nun named Suzanne Simonin. It recounts her forced religious vows, the misery she experienced in the convent, her fruitless efforts to have her vows annulled, and her eventual escape from the cloister. Diderot worked on this narrative for more than twenty years, longer than any other text in his corpus.[3]

But Suzanne Simonin's account of her suffering does not stand alone. It has always been accompanied by a second text in the form of a frame or preface, purporting to explain the unusual circumstances in which the novel itself came into being. This framing text is conspicuously different from the authorial and editorial introductions that open many eighteenth-century novels. Such exordia regularly pledge the veracity of the tale to follow. But the preface to *La religieuse* does the opposite: it proclaims the text's mendacity. In doing so, it tells some unexpected truths about how the book came to be created, and it raises important questions about how stories work.

The preface was originally composed not by Diderot but by his friend and collaborator, Baron Melchior Grimm (*DFPV* 11:15). It was published in Grimm's periodical *La Correspondance Littéraire* in March 1770, ten years before the text of the novel itself appeared. Following its initial appearance in 1770, Diderot reworked it over at least a decade. Then it reappeared with the odd title "Preface-Annexe" at the time of the serial publication from 1780 to 1782 of Suzanne's purported autobiographical account—the novel we call *La religieuse* proper— also in *La Correspondance Littéraire* (see *DFPV* 11:3–23).

The disparate components that make up the hybrid *La religieuse* were the product of a hoax that the preface explained. In 1759, following financial reverses and an intensification of his religious piety, the Marquis de Croismare, a member of Diderot's and Grimm's circle, decided to leave the corruptions and

---

the point where the tendency has already been somewhat cruelly satirized. Suddenly, in critical theory bodies are everywhere. For the parody of such theoretical body-chic, see Ellmann, *Hunger Artists*, 3–4. But the fact that such critical consideration has become a trend hardly makes bodies negligible, as Ellmann's book eloquently suggests. The issue of bodies and of materialism in Diderot is not new. It has not been examined, however, from the perspective I take upon it here: the question of how the existence and, particularly, the *limitations* of real bodies influence and reframe the conception of language and the writing of imaginary narratives.

3. See May's "Introduction," in Diderot, *La religieuse*, in *DFPV* 11:3.

expense of Paris and retire to his country estate in Normandy, near Caen. Croismare's comrades in the capital missed him, and they wanted to induce him to return. Beginning in early 1760, they devised a plot to do so. They concocted a young woman, Suzanne Simonin, and they contrived a poignant story for her. The fictive Suzanne had supposedly escaped from her convent, and she implored the Marquis's assistance in saving her from the authorities on her trail.[4]

In the eighteenth century monks or nuns who left their cloisters were in grave jeopardy. Ecclesiastical vows were irrevocable and enforced by royal power. Once recaptured, an escaped nun would have been forcibly returned to the convent she had fled. There she could expect physical punishment and psychological retribution at the hands of her sisters. As the conspirators framed it, the fictional Suzanne Simonin's situation was thus perilous. Suzanne claimed to have tried a lawsuit to get her vows annulled, but she was unsuccessful. Despite this defeat, she had not submitted to royal or ecclesiastical authority nor abandoned her desire to quit holy orders. When she lost her made-up lawsuit, the made-up Suzanne fled her convent.

The hoax was organized with care. Plaintive letters detailing her plight, purportedly written by Suzanne and by those who had given her asylum in Paris, were sent to Croismare at his country estate in Caen. Croismare seems to have swallowed the story the conspirators had cooked up for him. His letters back to Paris concerning the matter were themselves published in the preface. They were earnest and solicitous, and Croismare took pains to urge the greatest caution in order to avoid exposing Suzanne's whereabouts to the authorities who were supposedly searching for her.

But, if this flickering oscillation between the real and the delusive were not enough, Diderot began to wonder whether Croismare had tumbled to the plot. He wrote to one of his fellow conspirators, Madame d'Épinay, to say that, with friends like his—inveterate mystifiers just as he was himself—he always needed to be on his guard against the possibility of being double-bluffed. Years later, revising Grimm's preface after its original publication in 1770, Diderot asserted that, of all the plotters, he had been the one with the greatest doubts about whether Croismare had been playing the fraud back against them from the start. The evidence will always be inconclusive. But it is reasonable to believe that Croismare remained (as they say in the espionage world) "unwitting" con-

---

4. This plot had its foundation in real circumstances. Two years previously, in 1758, Croismare had tried, ultimately without success, to help a real nun who was seeking to have her vows annulled. This woman, Marguerite Delamarre, had made her appeal from the Paris convent of Longchamp. But after a lengthy lawsuit she lost her case, and she was forced to remain in orders for the rest of her life.

cerning the deception until, a number of years later, the conspirators revealed it to him themselves (*DFPV* 11:5–7).

My use of the espionage term *unwitting* here is deliberate. Most people conceive of the spy world as defined by *concealment*. But there is another side to the falsification of identity. In relation to the kind of textual conjuring operation that Diderot and his co-conspirators were engaged in, there may be no closer parallel than the ginning up in espionage and intelligence work of a chimerical world, made entirely out of signs and traces and intended to counterfeit the real one to the point of substituting itself for it entirely.

The title of this chapter, "The Nun Who Never Was," mimics that of a intriguing story from World War II which might throw some light on the Enlightenment's problem with fictionality. *The Man Who Never Was* recounts the artifactual life and death of one of Suzanne Simonin's successors in the uncanny family of nonexistent people.[5] In April 1943 the body of Major W. Martin of the British Royal Marines washed ashore on the Spanish coast at Huelva. Among the major's effects were letters he was transmitting from General Sir Archibald Nye, vice chief of the Imperial General Staff in London, to General Alexander at Eighteenth Army Group headquarters in Tunisia. The letters suggested that the initial Allied invasion of Europe would target not Sicily (control of which was felt by the Allies to be essential to any further operation in southern Europe) but, rather, Sardinia and Corsica.

The textual accompaniment to Major Martin's corporeal appearance in Spain included love letters from his fiancée, used London theater ticket stubs, and all the appropriate accoutrements of a believable life. The objective of this contrived biography was to induce the Germans to concentrate their defensive efforts far from the real target of the invasion. Of course, the major had never existed. The operation order that crafted him out of nothing began as follows:

1. *Object*

To cause a briefcase containing documents to drift ashore as near as possible to Huelva in Spain in such circumstances that it will be thought to have been washed ashore from an aircraft which crashed at sea when the case was being taken by an officer from the U.K. to Allied Forces H.Q. in North Africa.[6]

---

5. See Montagu, *The Man Who Never Was*. Particularly pertinent for my purposes here is chap. 6, "The Creation of a Person." It begins: "From quite an early stage Major Martin had become a real person to us."

6. Montagu, *Man Who Never Was*, 37.

With the delusive briefcase came a corpse—with the *story* came a *body*. In this sense Major Martin's ontology differs from Suzanne Simonin's—she never had a body to begin with. But, despite the physical carcass of the pseudo–Major Martin (which did not actually fall from a plane but was released from a British submarine off the Spanish coast), just as with Suzanne, everything in the fiction was painstakingly contrived and constructed. *Legend* is the espionage term for the construction of such a delusive identity and history. The etymological and epistemological resonances of the term itself point us directly to the connection between bodies and stories.

The history and practice of espionage is rich in analogues of the textual operation that Diderot and his friends were mounting to deceive the Marquis de Croismare. One of the significant features of such accounts is the "finally it can be told" flavor that (if we believe Diderot's and Grimm's preface) also accompanied the conspirators' revelation to the Marquis later on of their plot to attract him back to Paris. This temporal delay is worth a moment's reflection. Why wait to reveal a plot? Because stories have material consequences. Like materiality and unlike fictions, the resistant reality of human time doesn't just give itself over to unconstrained slippage, play, and transformation. This initial concealment of the deception (whether Diderot's or the British army's) then its subsequent revelation provide another register of the relations that tie the phantasmatic lability of stories to the more refractory world of bodies.

In such operations the play of representations quickly turns labyrinthine. Anthony Cave Brown's *Bodyguard of Lies* is a history of the deception operations by the British during World War II. The book could only be published thirty years after the end of the war.[7] And in a piquant metadiscourse even avowed fiction can get into the act. In Joseph Finder's spy novel *The Moscow Club* the following passage appears: "James Angleton, the legendary CIA chief of counter-intelligence, had once borrowed a phrase from T.S. Eliot to describe the business of espionage and counter-intelligence as a 'wilderness of mirrors.' That it was. The truth was often concealed behind a reflection of a reflection of a reflection."[8] This specular projection of a virtuality with no reality behind it, this double *mise-en-abîme* juggling literature and materiality and worrying intri-

7. Brown, *Bodyguard of Lies*. The title refers to Churchill's remark that in war truth must be accompanied by a bodyguard of lies. Publication of *The Man Who Never Was* after the war occurred with less delay but only because it was becoming clear to British authorities that the story was going to come out anyway.

8. Finder, *Moscow Club*, 234. See also Martin, *Wilderness of Mirrors*. The Eliot quotation is from "Gerontion"; see *"The Waste Land" and Other Poems*, 21.

cately about who in these delusive representations was outwitting whom in the mirror-game, is diagnostic because of the limitless slippage enabled once we are in a realm of substitution. Once *language* represents *bodies*, then bodies can be conjured up, named, clothed, characterized, and even killed off, however you like.

We look for what is grounded, for what will not lend itself to wanton exchange, replacement, simulacrum, and falsification. In a world of language this nostalgia for stability of meaning is never satisfiable. But by no means does this signify that it is fruitless. Despite the exhilarating sense of liberation which conjuring with texts may induce, we're not really so casual about our reliance on the well-foundedness of communication. To take an immediate, if unpretentious, example, convention holds that the documentation in a scholarly publication such as this book will refer to real sources, accurately cited. We rely on such representation being veridical. If I then say that one of the footnotes in this chapter is imaginary (which is in fact the case), most readers will feel a violation of trust. Such trust is not negligible. The phenomenology of such reliance is one piece of evidence signifying that theories of radicalized textualism may not be able to capture fundamental aspects of how existence feels and how we live it.

In this sense the world of intelligence or espionage is the counter-frame for the world of corporeality. In fiction and theater we know we are being gulled. In most "nonfiction" writing, including academic criticism, we presume truthful scholarship. But in intelligence work *bodies exist to lie*. What is corrosive in the spy world is that communication depends upon a violation of the representational contract that is unilaterally decided and intended to be undetectable. When people learn that they are being deceived in the spy world, the consequences can be destructive. Bodies engaged in the deception of espionage so betray their *embodiedness*, they so want to achieve mendacity, that they decorporealize entirely and become *figures* of bodies. Such subversion of the nominal taxonomy dividing fiction from nonfiction establishes the spy's existence as a cardinal *Mischwesen*, an "intermediary being," between corporeality and language. Such mediatory terms help us to see the resonances of the supposedly stable entities between which they mediate. The effect is both to enrich and to complicate their opposition.

In *La religieuse* Diderot was trying out or trying on this uncanny flickering *between* materiality and language. We could think of the novel, then, as an exploration of the freeing of language in a field of constraining bodies—an experiment not only with the liberating play of signifiers but also, and crucially, with the constraining force of materiality. In the celebration of pure semioticity that strands of Poststructuralism have sought to promote or, at the other end of the reduction, in the false immediacies of naive Realism, that dialectic is veiled or abrogated. But, as over against these polar truncations, Diderot wants to make the case *hard*; he wants to focus on the *work* that is necessary for such vertiginous phase-changes between nominally disconnected ontological orders. He is fascinated and troubled by the energy released in such transmutations, an energy that, when such releases occur, must be lodged somewhere new. For this bodies serve as a privileged ontology, for, unlike meanings, they cannot be instantaneously superseded. And, unlike meanings, they can absolutely and consequentially *die*.[9]

Bodies are my code for this resistance to semiotization. We may agree that everything is a sign. But some things carry their semioticity *resistantly*, unwillingly. They do not glide insouciantly into mutation; they rather seem captured in some ontological version of inertia or of gravity. They do not float; they are not free; they seem borne down in a material enactment of the constraint that defines them as what they are and pulls them, and our experience with them, in a direction contrary to that figured by language's lability.

Language requires bodies. Materiality enters language as the quiddity of the signifier. Language needs bodies' grounding; it needs the character of *being exacting* that bodies impose. But this dialectic isn't self-imposing for conceptualization. It is possible to lose track of it, whereupon these constraining modalities can float out of mind. This is a liberation as Poststructuralism often projects it, but it is also a loss. This dialectic fascinated and troubled Enlightenment writers in their reflections about language and bodies.

We can restore some of the richness and complication in the relationship between sign and referent which preoccupied Diderot in his fictions by examining a widespread intuition concerning representability. It suggests a construction of the problem significantly divergent from the Postmodern doxa that conceives the incommensurability of *word* and *thing* as a divorce and on this basis concludes that mediation between them is impossible.

9. In his seminar on *The Purloined Letter* Lacan makes this point in a thoughtful—if seemingly uncharacteristic—reflection on the refractoriness of bodies. He writes that the singular materiality of bodies arises from the fact that, unlike language-objects, they cannot survive dismembering. See Lacan, "Le séminaire sur 'La lettre volée,' " in *Écrits I*, 24.

The intuition in question concerns the languaging of epochal catastrophe. It has become notorious in our period, most typically concerning representation of the Holocaust.[10] In such performances something like an ethical *respect for bodies* at times counters the capacity by which signifiers seem to disseminate uncontrollably—by which, in our Postmodern conceptualization, they can appear to float free. The "Holocaust deniers" are the outliers that test such general conviction. Nobody thinks that anyone could dissolve the Holocaust by saying it never happened. But while we remain within the hypostatization of "language *as* reality" which has been dominant for decades now, it is harder to frame a theory that can effectively resist the mutability of language and give the lie to the Holocaust deniers.[11]

Derrida is often identified as our period's most forceful exponent of language's free play. Of course, that does not mean he believes that in meaning anything goes—despite frequent and insistent attributions of such a view to him and his work. In terms of history and politics Derrida has indignantly repudiated the Holocaust deniers. The question is whether his theory of language and representation can capture the basis for this resistance to their heinous historical views.

For this reason it is important to see in Derrida's more recent work a moving hesitation about subscribing to the limitless dissemination of language's figurality and thereby *mis*-representing the imperiled reality of human bodies. Consider this brief but striking passage in Derrida's dedication of *Specters of Marx* to the assassinated South African revolutionary leader Chris Hani: "One name for another, a part for the whole: the historic violence of Apartheid can always be treated as a metonymy. . . . *But one should never speak of the assassination of a man as a figure.* . . . A man's life, as unique as his death, will always be more than a paradigm and something other than a symbol. And this is precisely what a proper name should always name."[12] The passage (particularly the powerful modals *can* and *should*) reads as if Derrida was on his way to a critique of his earlier linguistic absolutism.

A similar inflection can be found in the "Discours" that Derrida presented

10. On the question of representing the Holocaust, see, among many other volumes: Vidal-Naquet, *Assassins of Memory*; LaCapra, *Representing the Holocaust*; and *Probing the Limits of Representation*.

11. On the Institute for Historical Review and the most notorious of the deniers—Robert Faurisson, Ernst Zündel, David Cole, and others—see Shermer and Grobman, *Denying History*. On the general question of denial, see Vidal-Naquet, *Assassins of Memory*.

12. Derrida, *Specters of Marx*, xv; emph. added.

when the University of Silesia in Poland awarded him an honorary doctorate of humane letters in 1997. Speaking to the Polish scholars assembled for the ceremony, speaking particularly of what Poland has meant and means for Europe, Derrida said:

> In the history and landscape of Europe, Poland occupies a privileged place. In this century, your nation has endured, traversed, overcome the greatest possible number of ordeals, which were above all European ordeals, ordeals for Europe, for the body and for what is often called the idea, the soul, or the spirit, of Europe. Twentieth-century Poland: in no other European nation, I'm speaking carefully here, can one identify, in a comparable space and in the rapidity of a similar chronology, at such a high degree of condensation, a more concentrated figure, a more wrenching metonymy, a graver and more serious metaphor of everything that has happened to modern Europe. Of her disasters, her resistances, her insurrections and resurrections. To recall these times by speaking about metonymy and metaphor is not to reduce your nation to being a figure of Europe: *it is the very body of the Polish people* which suffered, literally, and with them the bodies of all people.[13]

Derrida's humanism here sounds like Enlightenment reflection.[14] Of course, denying the figurality of something calamitous is a familiar rhetorical move. But in my interpretation of these passages, more than that is going on. Derrida is reaching for a representation—beyond the simply pious or *bien-pensant*—which would reestablish and honor the possibility of the very mediation between language and bodies which (in the United States at least) Derrida's work has often been taken to repel.[15]

13. Derrida, "Discours," in *Jacques Derrida*, 116; emph. added; my trans.

14. Derrida acknowledged the connection with the Enlightenment explicitly in his lecture. Speaking of deconstruction as an attempt to transform fundamental structures, he says, "This concern with critical independence belongs to the *Lumières*, to the Enlightenment, to the *Aufklärung*, to the *Illuminismo*, to the *Oswiencenie* of our period" ("Discours," 124). On Derrida's "humanism," see Rorty, "Remarks on Deconstruction and Pragmatism," 14.

15. This is a perspective toward which Derrida has been reaching since the early 1980s. He put it this way in a dialogue he had in 1982 with the Irish philosopher Richard Kearney. Deconstruction, said Derrida, is an "openness toward the other"; "the critique of logocentrism is above all the search for the other." Deconstruction asks "whether our term 'reference' is entirely adequate for designating the 'other.'" "The other, which is beyond language and which summons language . . . is perhaps not a referent in the normal sense which linguistics have attached to this term." To say so, he claimed, "does not amount to saying that there is nothing beyond language." See "Deconstruction and the Other," 123–25. One might say that it is in the work of Michel de Certeau that this tentative adumbration of what lies *beyond* the dictum asserting the vacuity of the "hors-texte" is most fully developed.

Suspicion concerning language's capacity to convey truth is as old as Plato.[16] We can't *resolve* the crux about representation—indeed, this is the point of my book. But I want to urge that we reconceive the separation of language from materiality in such a way that the incommensurability to which I refer, and upon which many contemporary theorists base a linguistic absolutism, is no longer conceived as a non-negotiable disjunction and transforms itself into a *relationship*—vexed and difficult, to be sure, but a relationship nonetheless. This move reconceives difficulty, seeing it not as theoretical impossibility but as practical, analytical refractoriness—like the refractoriness I attributed earlier to bodies in their resistance to semiotization. Then the bipolar disjunction that since Saussure has been figured as unbridgeable could be reconceived as a space of problematic mediation—of difficult or restricted *flow* or *passage*, rather than absolute blockage.

That some things (the Holocaust, a person's death, *bodies themselves*) resist representation puts time, thought, and work back into the process of conception and sublates into a cognizable narrative both naive notions of unproblematic mimesis, on the one hand, and exclusivist ideas of linguistic exceptionality or absolutism, on the other. Like many narratives, this one registers the drama of difficulty. But it points toward denouement or convergence, rather than ending in a blank and empty theoretical impasse. This replaces the logical antinomy between word and thing with a projection of their fraught, problematic, but indispensable relation. After all, words and things, stories and bodies, do inhabit the world *together*.

These problems bring us back to *La religieuse* and its reflections upon the fraught linkages between language and bodies. Diderot's novel embodies its own problems. Consider the text's metanarrative concerning its own history in the preface. Perhaps the preface is *itself* just a sophisticated hoax. Most critics believe the exchange of letters it reproduces arose in a real attempt to fool the real Marquis de Croismare into returning to a real Paris and only evolved later into the text of Suzanne Simonin's fraudulent autobiography composed by Diderot as a fictitious self-description and self-justification that the delusive Suzanne

16. See *Republic* 602d; or *Sophist* 235a. These issues are discussed by Hobson, *The Object of Art*, esp. chap. 1. Plato never doubted such capacity across the board but attributed it only to *figuration*, as Diderot observed (*Salon de 1767*, 6e site, *DFPV* 16:215). Subsequently, Nietzsche extended this suspicion of figuration to *all* language, plausibly arguing that a language without figuration is inconceivable. See Nietzsche, "On the Truth and Lies in the Nonmoral Sense."

was supposed to have written and sent to their distant but veridical friend Croismare. This fictitious autobiography forms the largest portion of the text-complex of *La religieuse*. But perhaps as a literary fake Diderot and Grimm concocted the Croismare story *itself* for the *Correspondance Littéraire*. Then the preface, too, would have been entirely fabricated—just as fancifully and just as delusively as Suzanne's supposed autobiography—and the joke would be on us. Given the inherent underdetermination of texts and the irreducible uncertainty of representations, there is no way to tell for sure.

But that's the point. Radicalizing the mystification in this way changes little. At the level of fantasy or imagination *projecting* the material consequences that a story like this one would have had on a reader like Croismare is indistinguishable from a concrete attempt to induce such consequences elsewhere. The issue is how to produce with language a practical result under a certain set of conditions: a conjuring with the power of texts. Whether we cook up a plot in our minds or actually put it into effect, whether I try to fool Croismare or fool you, the crucial point is the knowledge that we have internalized of textual pragmatics—the reading we make of how reality responds to representations. Whoever the hoax was meant to dupe, what this text was bringing into focus for Diderot was the realization that, because it is not bodily, no text can ever tell you whether it is veridical or not.

But, if texts can hoax us, then anyone who relies on them can become the victim of their power. Not just other people but us—beginning with writers such as Diderot himself. For how (as Diderot realized when he began to worry that Croismare might actually be seeking to dupe *him*) could anyone be insulated from the uncertainty inherent in representations? The most unsettling element of the transaction arises when, in the face of a text's capacity for deception, we try to sort out the problem of agency and seek to imagine how we could separate the roles of con man and mark, how we can stabilize our own activity in using language without being used by it in our turn. Then it becomes clear how precarious are our protections against being victimized by the very contrivances we fabricate to persuade, how uncertain it is that we can evade implication in the fictions—the deceptions—which we project for others while conceiving that we can manage not to be cozened by them in our turn.

This structure of potential reversal is a critical one because all cultures rely on tools—material or representational—to do their work. But tools always bear the danger that their instrumentality can turn back against us. The instrument we use constrains our perception and our practice. Put more broadly, any mediation between an agent and a task has the potential to take over determination of the relationship between them. This truth—that, as Emerson put it, "things are in the saddle and ride mankind"—is unsettling.[17] Such structures dominate our consciousness and our agency in ways that all of Modernity has been seeking to comprehend.

More highly segmented, stratified, and differentiated economies produce these experiences. Such subversion of agency had already become apparent in the Enlightenment period. In one of the articles he wrote himself for the *Encyclopédie*—"Bas" ("Stocking Weaving")—Diderot described the eerie process of inversion of control between worker and machine.[18] The perception became a fundamental element in radical critiques of the increasingly pervasive capitalized and rationalized organization of the socioeconomy. Under capitalism, Marx wrote, "it is not the worker who employs the instruments of his work, but rather the reverse, the instruments of work employ the worker."[19]

These insights concerning the reversal of agency in the labor process are an emblem of how, under the conditions of modern social and economic production, our control of process can capsize and of the concomitant decay of the humanist ideal of individual sovereignty which is their theoretical complement. Such structures affect categories of experience such as *will*, *intention*, *project*, and *work*. In turn, all of these implicate an individual's or a culture's understanding of itself. Consequently for the experience and the representation of human activity, the effects of such inversions of control are profound. In *La religieuse* Diderot was exploring these complications as they arose in the foundational instance of language and of texts.

Diderot's novel enacts double mode of representation. One mode emerges from a world of imaginative fiction; the other implicates real people and real bodies. The odd analytical privilege of *La religieuse* arises in the collision between these two registers. Diderot and his friends thought they were using the text as a tool to get their friend Croismare back to Paris. But, as in "Bas," their tool took over the transaction and played it back against them in a way that Croismare probably never was seeking to do. In this complication the novel discovers its issue. It materializes in the way that in its narrative and pragmatic

---

17. Emerson, "Ode, Inscribed to W. H. Channing," 50–51.

18. See "Bas," *DFPV* 6:78. Diderot makes a parallel point about the control by machines in another of his articles, "Art," *DFPV* 5:505. Jacques Proust has provided a remarkable study of the rhetoric and bearing of "Bas" and its relation to Diderot's more explicitly literary works in "De l'*Encyclopédie* au *Neveu de Rameau*," 273–340.

19. See Marx, *Capital*, 1:548; trans. adapted.

situation *La religieuse* seeks to practice the problematic negotiation that I considered briefly in my introduction. The novel brings the sign/referent antinomy that many today have claimed severs these two entities from each other into an experimental situation in which their divorce *can't happen*. The letters are fake; Croismare is real. They shouldn't meet up anywhere. But they do.

On the Paris end of the plot things proceeded as a quintessential and at times hilarious con game. But on Croismare's side the experience must have been different. The conspirators were laughing out loud, but what of their friend in Normandy? It would be hard to believe that Croismare was not affected by the story of fear, flight, and suffering narrated in the letters supposedly written by Suzanne Simonin which he was receiving from Paris. This disjunction between the hoaxers and the hoaxed is structured like a perverse version of dramatic irony, paralogistically transferred from the world of stage representation to the more consequential world of genuine referentiality. But what happens when real people are treated like characters in a fiction? Such a mutation locates the textual and social perplexity produced in and uncovered by *La religieuse*. That the world of texts and the world of reality are separable seems clear enough. But texts can make them intersect. Then something like an ontological category mistake arises—and, because of it, an unsettling ethical and practical conundrum.

The conspirators lived concretely and analyzed carefully the disjunctions such a structure projects. Concerning their experience, the preface tells us: "We spent our suppers amidst bursts of laughter reading letters which must have been making our good Marquis cry" (*DFPV* 11:30).[20] There is an unnerving edge to this amusement. For, while Suzanne was only a phantasm, the tears she presumably elicited were real for the Marquis. In such a situation, from the privileged position of the conspirators privy to the division between what was real and what was fabulation, the unsettling power of representations becomes unmistakable. In any deception there is a risk of cruelty; in any fiction the potentiality of pain is inherent. *Representations can hurt*. But where and how does this performative capacity arise? where and how does it exercise its effects?

Such representational structures implicate not just fictions but *bodies*. The status of language is never indifferent in any society, nor is the relation between words and things given once for all. Consider the epistolary novel, the closest generic analogue to the letters between the conspirators and the Marquis which

---

20. Translations of Diderot's texts here are my own.

Grimm printed in his preface. At the moment the Croismare plot was being hatched, the epistolary form was pervasive. As fashionable and influential examples, think of Richardson's *Clarissa*, so admired by Diderot, or Rousseau's *Nouvelle Héloïse*, about which he was considerably more critical.[21] But there is an obvious difference between these texts and the letters in the Croismare affair. The epistolary novel stages an exchange between imaginary characters.[22] But Grimm's preface is peculiar. It fuses together texts fully as fictive as those, or as novels are generally thought to be, with others—Croismare's letters—written by a real person, in genuine expectation that his addressees, and the anxious subject of their correspondence, were likewise real and consequential.

This odd heteroclite status offers a perspective on the situation of fictionality in Diderot's practice and in his period. Based upon its odd mélange of fictive representation and authentic referentiality, we might conceive *La religieuse* as a transitional form, in effect a conceptual missing link, between two experiences and understandings of narrative. When from our contemporary perspective we try to understand the connection between fictional representations and real corporeal or emotional effects, we run into a difficulty. Modernism has so dissolved us into texts that the material or referential world slips toward invisibility. Such denegation of the extra-textual is familiar. But it blinds us to aspects of the functioning of narrative to which Diderot and other writers in his period were finding themselves attentive. In particular we have learned to bracket

21. *La nouvelle Héloïse* and *La religieuse* were nearly simultaneous. *Julie, ou la nouvelle Héloïse* went on sale in Paris in January 1761, but previous versions of the novel had been circulated among Rousseau's acquaintances and had been sent or read aloud by Rousseau to Diderot as early as 1758. See Pomeau's introduction, xx–xxiii, xxvi. Rousseau's debts to *Clarissa* are well known (xxvi–xxvii), as is the extraordinary success of Rousseau's own text. It established his popularity (xxiv). Richardson died in July 1761; Diderot, who had famously "broken" with Rousseau in 1758, published his *Éloge de Richardson* in January 1762, in part to unmask Rousseau's borrowings from Richardson (Pomeau, intro., xxvii). Diderot's critical opinion of *Julie* was perhaps reflected in the negative review of the novel published in Grimm's *Correspondance littéraire* (Pomeau, intro., xxv).

22. As Rousseau emphasized in the second paragraph of his preface to *La nouvelle Héloïse*: "Is this entire correspondence a fiction? Gentle readers, what difference does it make? It is surely a fiction for you" (Rousseau, *Nouvelle Héloïse*, 3). See also the second preface to the novel ("Préface de Julie, ou Entretien sur les romans," *Nouvelle Héloïse*, 737–38), in which the alternatives of factual veracity or novelistic verisimilitude are considered in greater detail. I will return to this second preface later. On the dual prefaces, see Darnton, *Great Cat Massacre*, 228–31. Darnton emphasizes Rousseau's effort to define a reading of his work which would destabilize the literary conventions of the upper-class *beau monde* and recover the truths of simplicity and honesty. This distinction surely was designed in part to justify the publication of a novel by a writer so famously associated with the systematic *condemnation* of "literature"—a position that had been associated with Rousseau's writings from the *Discours sur les sciences et les arts* (1750) to the *Lettre à d'Alembert* (1757). It displaces the question "truth or literature?" into another question about conventionality or originality.

affect in cultural representations, as if the stakes in fictions were no more than formal. But the tears to which Grimm's preface recalls us exceed the effects that Modernism has schooled us to expect or to understand. The pain they evoke is essential to comprehending Diderot's engagement with the radicalization of fictionalizing which is the essence of *La religieuse*.

It is important to distinguish these genuine experiences of tears from those represented *within* fictional narratives. Of the latter, in his discussion of Prévost's *Manon Lescaut* (1731) Auerbach says: "In the literature of the eighteenth century tears begin to assume an importance which they had not previously possessed as an independent motif."[23] But the importance of tears in the Enlightenment extends *beyond* the space of fictions to their effect upon real people in real situations. Grimm's preface to *La religieuse* narrates the conspirators' recognition that Suzanne's misfortune was being taken seriously by her would-be benefactor—indeed, was weighing upon his heart—and, consequently, that the moment was approaching when inevitably their fraud would be unmasked. Clearly, the partition between fiction and materiality could not stand up indefinitely. At some point Croismare would arrange and expect direct contact with this woman who did not exist. Only one resolution was then possible for the representational blind alley down which the conspirators had laughingly marched. Diderot determined that the fictional Suzanne would have to die (preface, 30), and, after a lingering illness, the letters to the Marquis killed her off (63).

But at this point Grimm's narrative of the consequences of the plot goes on to a perplexing observation: "One fact that is not among the least remarkable in the matter is that during the period that our mystification was heating up our friend Croismare's brain in Normandy, Diderot's brain was cooking as well" (30). Croismare was not the only person suffering in his compassion for Suzanne's misfortunes. The conspirators, by their own testimony, spent their

---

23. Auerbach, *Mimesis*, 397. Tears are pervasive in readers' responses to eighteenth-century fictions. The readers of Rousseau's *Nouvelle Héloïse* were regularly described as crying over the novel—both women and men equally, according to the *Correspondance Littéraire* (see Pomeau, intro., xxiv), thus slyly taking issue with Rousseau's assertion in his preface that *Julie* was better suited to women than to men ("convient mieux aux femmes que les livres de philosophie" [4]). In his discussion of the contemporary reception of *La nouvelle Héloïse* Darnton recalls the letters Rousseau received from readers recounting their tears and sobs in the course of their reading the novel; see *Great Cat Massacre*, 242–46. I will consider Diderot's account of his tears while reading Richardson later. For a different perspective on the tears projected here, see Caplan, *Framed Narratives*, 75. The question of Enlightenment emotion in relation to novelistic representation is discussed in Barguillet, *Le roman au XVIIIe siècle*, esp. 16.

evenings making sport of Croismare's distress. But how did Diderot, the principal creator of this entirely fabricated character, and presumably a principal participant in the amusement the plot was producing, get pulled tearfully into the pathos of Suzanne's existence—when he, better than anyone, was in a position to know that she did not exist?

The evolving practice of verisimilitude becomes crucial to our understanding of these strange reactions. Verisimilitude is not a stable, transhistorical phenomenon. It is a learned and contingent response. The formation and stabilization of such a response was a critical issue in the Enlightenment period. We need to defamiliarize our own experience of fictions to recover how strange a transaction is involved in the paradoxical combination of closeness and distance that we feel in relation to imaginary characters and events. Eighteenth-century readers did not share our expectations or our habits concerning narrative.[24]

Our "belief" in novelistic characters is a modulated and tempered one. In our responses to fiction the parties to the reading contract transact their exchanges of symbols, projections, identifications, and affects in the mode of "as if." All readers must apprentice themselves to this mode of representational language if they are to leave behind what seems to us the naive conflation of imaginary entities with real ones. In Diderot's period, however, the stability of these categories and the belief in their well-foundedness was considerably less stable. This uncertainty or lack of resolution left open ways of seeing and experiencing narratives that have been repressed in our own day.[25]

The institution and stabilization of a cultural practice inevitably shuts down some competing usage or custom; the period of such stabilization is regularly accompanied by questioning and contention. We inherit our myth of progress from the Enlightenment itself and, based upon it, we view our comfort with verisimilitude as an indispensable achievement. We may even conceive it as a congenital faculty without which we could not imagine human beings to function at all. But it is not clear that a progress paradigm, a movement from worse to better states, can serve as an adequate model for the cultural change in the evolution of reading practices in the Enlightenment and since that time.

Questions about reading, fictions, and representation were acute in the Enlightenment period. Consider Rousseau's second preface to *La nouvelle Héloïse*,

24. On the evolution of verisimilitude, see McKeon, *Origins of the English Novel*.

25. Cf. Darnton's speculation that "something happened to the way that readers responded to texts in the late eighteenth century" (*Great Cat Massacre*, 251, cited as an epigraph to this chap.).

cast as a dialogue between the novel's author-editor and its publisher. It turns around the question of whether the correspondence that composes the novel was between real or imaginary people. The issue may seem unredeemably naive to us, but in Rousseau's dialogue it is urgent. What was the basis for this uncertainty and this urgency? To begin with, there was a powerful tradition in late-seventeenth- and eighteenth-century France, starting probably with Guillerague's *Lettres d'une religieuse portugaise* (1669), of epistolary fictions being represented and accepted as real-life correspondences.[26] In turn such narratives coexisted with a parallel tradition of publishing exchanges of real letters between real individuals.[27] Frédéric Deloffre links the claims of authenticity made in Guillerague's book (as in many others in the period) with the public's distaste for or distrust of fictions.[28] This reaction made the projection of or reliance upon verisimilar but avowed fictions—as opposed to authentic narratives of real actions and events—a problematic undertaking. Such a fundamental suspicion concerning fictions is the background against which the practices of Diderot's and Rousseau's novels need to be assessed.[29]

This suspicion frames the stakes concerning the issue of narrative verisimilitude in the Enlightenment. To understand them we need to reconsider a truism that the theory of textuality in our own period has tended to obscure: verisimilitude is not the same thing as truth. In particular the performative implications and potentialities of a fictional text are distinct from those of a text whose referent is intended and accepted as real. It would be hard to conceive that a novel (or any form of language game) which openly declared its status as fiction might have attracted the Marquis de Croismare back to Paris. We might as well imagine Voltaire struggling to vindicate Calas if Calas had been a character in a novel. Only representation of the misfortune of a real person suffering authentic distress—communicated to be sure through texts, thus through means mor-

---

26. The dispute about whether these widely popular letters of a nun to the French officer who had been her lover were authentic or fictional was active through and beyond the eighteenth century. See Mylne, *Eighteenth-Century French Novel*, 26, 145; and Guilleragues, *Lettres portugaises*.

27. Mylne points out a social basis for publishing both fictive and authentic correspondences. It arose in the common eighteenth-century practice of preserving letters—both copies of ones sent and of the originals received in response—and of passing on to friends correspondences in which one had engaged. Epistolary novels could thus masquerade as real exchanges without the preservation of the correspondence seeming improbable to contemporary readers. See Mylne, *Eighteenth-Century French Novel*, 146.

28. Mylne, *Eighteenth-Century French Novel*, 145.

29. Darnton emphasizes the fact that many readers of *La nouvelle Héloïse* "believed and wanted to believe in the authenticity of the letters" (*Great Cat Massacre*, 233; see also 244–45). This phenomenon, however, reflected the general mode of response to epistolary fiction in the period.

phologically or formally indistinguishable from literary artifice—can produce that kind of pragmatic result.

What emerges as the puzzle worrying *La religieuse* is the question of how texts are related to the effects we attribute to their communicative and social functioning. But such material effects have been rendered increasingly invisible since the formalisms of the early nineteenth century. We have achieved the exquisite aesthetic pleasures that "literature" has latterly taken as its mission, but at the cost of blanking other important human affects and effects. No wonder, then, that the problems Diderot was exploring in his narratives slip through the net of many contemporary analytical paradigms. What gets missed in such constructions is worth reexamining.

CHAPTER TWO

On the Matter of Bodies

Plus, plus de confiance en celui qui peut feindre avec tant de vérité.
[No more relying on someone who can fake it so convincingly.]
       —DIDEROT, *Est-il bon? est-il méchant?* 395

Language is compliant; things are resistant. The distinction is fundamental to Diderot's reflection on the status of Suzanne Simonin's mode of existence in *La religieuse.* Language can project entities with such facility, words are so labile, that they produce effects in a mode and at a velocity that can leave us completely flummoxed. That might at first seem a heady advantage, and in the atmosphere of Postmodern textualism it has been taken to be one. But in Diderot's understanding such facility seemed a mixed and unsettling blessing. For in our sub-lunar world everything real is constituted by the kind of *limit* that it seems to be language's vocation to exceed or evade.

This difference between the registers of language and materiality haunts and fascinates Diderot in *La religieuse.* The novel's peculiar enunciatory situation injects an enigma between *realism* and *truth.* Today this distinction may seem oddly old-fashioned. Perhaps it has already dissolved in contemporary projections of an all-embracing metatheory of texts and representations. This latter conceptual complex has revealed much—particularly, a better understanding of the increasingly mystified nature of the codes by which meanings are constructed in modern social formations and cultures.[1]

1. On this problem, see Terdiman, *Discourse/Counter-Discourse,* chap. 1, esp. 101–11.

But profiting from these textualist insights has meant bracketing foundational distinctions between texts and bodies, between semiotics and materiality. So our theorizing has taken place at an increasing remove from the ground
on which it used to appear we stood and on which lives are still presumably
being lived. Under these circumstances the differential bite of the notion of
"fiction"—along with "literature" itself—has seemingly devolved into irrelevance or invisibility.[2]

Not so in the Enlightenment. Diderot's period understood and practiced
fiction differently. We need to mine and to make sense of the distinction between our own contemporary internalization of the category of fiction and
eighteenth-century constructions of it.[3] A body of thoughtful scholarship, notably in the work of Georges May and Vivienne Mylne, has traced how the
"realist illusion" we term *vraisemblance* in eighteenth-century French fiction
was disengaged from the melodramatic and fantastic surround of the traditional adventure tale and slowly organized and articulated itself.[4] But such
scholarship has typically seen eighteenth-century realism through the Enlightenment progress myth I referred to in chapter 1: as a self-validating goal toward
which literary technique was, naturally, satisfactorily and salutarily tending.

This tradition thus focused upon the "achievement" of verisimilitude as the
resolution of a writing problem contained within a quasi-autonomous literary
realm, rather than understanding it as a socialized and historically determined
practice of perception, cognition, and representation. To be sure, the rhetorical
and generic effects of Enlightenment fiction were dependent upon the formal

2. On the evolution of these conceptions, see Jameson, *Postmodernism*, 277: "Many analyses . . .
have tried to show the waning and obsolescence of categories like 'fiction' (in the sense of something
opposed to either the 'literal' or the 'factual'). But here I think a profound modification of the public
sphere needs to be theorized: the emergence of a new realm of image reality that is both fictional (narrative) and factual (even the characters in serials are grasped as real 'named' stars with external histories to read about). . . . Today, culture impacts back on reality in ways that make any independent
and, as it were, non- or extracultural form of it problematic . . . , so that finally the theorists unite
their voices in the new doxa that the 'referent' no longer exists."

3. For example, the following distinction, unexpected from our contemporary perspective:
"When an eighteenth-century novelist says that his story is 'true,' we should in many cases be
prepared to substitute the modern equivalent, 'based on fact' " (Mylne, *Eighteenth-Century French
Novel*, 28).

4. May, *Le dilemme du roman au XVIIIe siècle*; Mylne, *Eighteenth-Century French Novel*; and Barguillet, *Le roman au XVIIIe siècle*. For corresponding issues in Britain, see McKeon, *Origins*. The opening
sentence of Diderot's "Éloge de Richardson" dismissively characterizes the rhetorical and cognitive
situation of the traditional adventure tale (what Diderot terms the novel "jusqu'à ce jour"): "a confec-
tion of chimerical and frivolous events" (*DFPV* 13:192). Evidently in his view questions of verisimilitude are detached from such texts.

qualities of the texts in which they were embodied. But those effects did not arise through some self-generated logic of their own. They were responses to new cognitive and communicative demands. Novel modes of representation appear *because there are novel situations to represent.* The verisimilitude of Enlightenment "realism" needs to be conceived as a mode of writing determined by alterations in fundamental structures of social existence.

Of course, verisimilitude didn't come out of nowhere. Since the work of May and Mylne, it has been clear that two generic models underlay the style of fiction writing at issue here and fostered its emergence. The first and more prominent of these was a widespread tradition of putatively nonfictional memoir—the real or supposed autobiographical recollections of identified historical figures which flourished, frequently to a tune of gross and spicy scandal. The second was history writing.[5] But though scholarship has explained how the genealogy of genres was formally produced, it has been less sensitive to the consequences of this evolution in the consciousnesses of readers and to the inflection that such new uses of texts determined in the habits of perception and expectation which could be associated with fiction.

If we imagine the writer's task to be no more than applying appropriate pragmatic means for producing an effect whose character somehow stably preexists the representational techniques that give rise to it, we risk forgetting that the reading process is always a precarious act—particularly when paradigms of social life are changing—and that writers are involved in reading too. No less than their audience, they must apprentice themselves to unfamiliar, unassimilated habits and practices of representation; they have to learn how to construct and to negotiate the relationship between text and referential world which their writing will in turn project for other readers.

---

5. See Gallagher, *Nobody's Story*. My perspective owes a considerable debt to Gallagher's remarkable study. She argues that "the [eighteenth-century] novel can be seen in historical perspective only when the powerful novelty of its fictionality is recognized" (*Nobody's Story*, xvii n. 8). See also May, *Dilemme du roman*, 51–53 and 143; and Mylne, *Eighteenth-Century French Novel*, 20. We could understand the roman à clef so popular in the period as a hybrid special case of personal memoir and history, in the sense that it projected a narrative about identifiable individuals in a disguise *meant to be penetrated* by the reader. See Barguillet, *Le roman au XVIIIe siècle*, 18. It is a piquant artifact of the mechanisms of state repression that the two principal sorts of works clandestinely circulated in the period—politico-pornographic *libelles* and philosophical treatises—were together categorized as "philosophical books." See Darnton, *Literary Underground of the Old Regime*, 200; and Chartier, *Cultural Origins*, 78. This assimilation of pornography and politics led Diderot to a surprisingly agnostic reflection on how textual falsehood is treated by the public. In *Lettre sur le commerce de la librairie* (1763) he writes, "I will not dispute whether those dangerous books are as dangerous as people say; whether lies and sophistry are not sooner or later recognized and treated with contempt" (123).

Virtually every modern analysis of *La religieuse* has emphasized the groping and uneven realization of the text's own pretense to truth, the imperfections in the novel's creation of a seamless surface of verisimilitude.[6] Explanations have ranged from the banal ("even Diderot nods") to the over-ingenious (he introduced anachronisms and errors into his text to mimic the inconsistencies that inadvertently crop up in "factual" accounts). Scholars seem anxious about these slippages, as if the stability of their readings was undermined by their uncertainty concerning what Diderot really thought about *La religieuse*.

But what if Diderot didn't precisely know himself? What if he shared his readers' anxiety at the unsettling instability of the illusionary process he had set in motion with the initial hoaxing of Croismare? What, then, if *La religieuse* must be read not as a self-assured artistic realization but as an uncertain "essay," a writing *experiment*: the register of Diderot's own ambivalence about the techniques and limits of that fictive practice we call the realist illusion—indeed, of textual performativity in the broadest sense? Then this novel, his first serious effort in the genre,[7] represents an uncertain self-initiation into the uncanny and not-yet-stabilized world of induced belief, of what the French term *faire croire*, or what I want to call the pragmatics of texts.[8]

Perhaps that might help us understand Diderot's twenty-two-year-long history of returning to the puzzle of *La religieuse*. We will never know the facts of his intention. But what happens if we imagine that Diderot's objective in *La religieuse* was not so much to achieve as to *critique* verisimilitude as a mode of cognition—or, more accurately, to focus a critical examination on this new Enlightenment mode of relating to texts and of relating texts to materiality? What if we read *La religieuse* as an instrument for exploring the engendering of belief by pushing belief to the limit, even putting it into danger?

The distinction between *fictions* and *lies* remained troubling in Enlightenment culture. We think fictions are fine, but lies are bad. Diderot's period wondered hard about such neat segregation between them. The Croismare hoax

6. For one example, see DiPiero, *Dangerous Truths and Criminal Passions*, chap. 8. The introductions to *La religieuse* in *DFPV* catalog the flaws and inconsistencies in Diderot's realization of the illusion by which the text offers itself to readers: inappropriate or anachronistic knowledge (or lack of knowledge) on the protagonist's part relative to the portion of the tale she narrates; irreconcilable chronological elements in the story; erroneous calculations of the protagonist's age at various points in the tale; and similar apparent mistakes.

7. *Les Bijoux indiscrets* dates from 1748, twelve years before the Croismare conspiracy, and, despite some recent arguments to the contrary, might best be thought of as superior hack work.

8. On *faire croire*, see particularly Certeau, *Practice of Everyday Life*, chap. 13 ("Believing and Making People Believe").

that produced *La religieuse* manifests their almost indissoluble contamination. On the other hand, the genres that the scholars tell us modeled for fiction in the eighteenth century and out of which the cognitive capacity for "fictionality" emerged—in particular scandal memoirs and history writing—evade this problem neatly. Tied (whether delusively or not) to real places, events, and people, these modes of writing presuppose that texts and bodies *occupy a continuous world*, that both signs and referents inhabit the same veridical and potentially verifiable space. These narratives may lie, *but they lie about the real*, not about the nonexistent. They do not give themselves out as *fictions* at all. The concept has no place in the cultural contract that framed their reading.

Uncertainty over the emerging category of fictionality is detectable in reverse in the protestations of *veracity* which make up eighteenth-century novelistic prefaces. The social basis of such assertions of veridicality was the public's distaste for or distrust of *fictions*. The introductory frames of these prefaces were not just formulaic, a kind of compulsory overture to straightforward entry into a world of narrative fantasy. What still evaded unproblematic assimilation in Diderot's period was that *fictive* realm in which stories (as Catherine Gallagher's perceptive and polysemic title suggests) are *nobody's* because they are literally disembodied, because the realm in which they function is disjoined from the world of materiality.[9]

Today the *fiction-lie* distinction delimits the realm of the literary. So cultural uncertainty concerning it in the Enlightenment period seems puzzling. But it is such puzzlement that makes the Enlightenment case so compelling. When my text intends that you credit the factuality of its referent, I may either be writing truth or lying. But *fiction* is not captured within these options. Fictions only come into being when we are willing to let go a certain hold on materiality: they happen only with the *disappearance of bodies*. That is why the intense and sedimented connection of *La religieuse* to the veridical and the corporeal is so revealing.

The traditional view of the coming of verisimilitude—seeing it as a victory for new cognitive capacities—truncates the problem and turns it into a subterranean progress myth.[10] Paul Ricoeur illuminates this puzzlement over verisimili-

---

9. Gallagher, *Nobody's Story*, xvii.

10. Consider Mylne's account of what to us will seem a bizarrely undifferentiated status of "belief" in the period: "In the seventeenth and eighteenth centuries most critics made no . . . distinction [between 'imaginative' and 'literal' belief]. Belief was for them a single activity, one that admitted no differences of kind or of degree." And Mylne continues: "A system which did not allow for imagina-

tude in *Time and Narrative* by reminding us of a crucial difference between Enlightenment understanding of memory and our idea of memory today.

> [The Enlightenment] return to experience and to simple and direct language led to the creation of a new genre, defined by the proposal to establish the most exact correspondence possible between the literary work and the reality it imitates. Implicit in this project is the reduction of mimesis to imitation, in the sense of making a copy, a sense totally foreign to Aristotle's *Poetics*. It is not surprising, therefore, that neither the pseudo-autobiography nor the epistolary formula really provided any problem for their users. *Memory was not suspected of being fallacious*, whether the hero recounted something after the fact or as directly from the scene. For Locke and Hume themselves, memory was the support for causality and for personal identity. Hence to render the texture of daily life as closely as possible was taken to be an accessible and, finally, not problematic task.[11]

In the pre-Enlightenment construction outlined by Mylne and Ricoeur, "belief" is virtually inelastic. Modulating such rigidity offered new and nuanced possibilities of cognition and interpretation. The novelty of the "novel" demonstrates how exciting these innovative representational possibilities must have seemed to many of Diderot's contemporaries.[12] How could anyone in the period have been reluctant to see such a development?

But bodies matter.[13] A heady sense of liberation may arise when signs and language are released from their inflexible bonds to materiality. But there is another side to the issue that some in the Enlightenment worried was a *downside*. Once freed of material ties to referentiality, representation exhibits a positively wanton disloyalty to the truth.[14] Then *anything* can be offered for belief. *Making tales*—as the epigraph I drew from Diderot's *Jacques le fataliste* in chap-

---

tive belief had no special category for the type of work which evokes or requires imaginative belief. A story was held to be either true or, inevitably, false" (*Eighteenth-Century French Novel*, 8, 12).

11. Ricoeur, *Time and Narrative*, 2:12; emph. added.

12. Ricoeur, *Time and Narrative*, 2:12 n. 11.

13. My phrase recalls the title of Butler's *Bodies That Matter*. Daniel Brewer's intelligent discussion of Diderot's attempt to "grasp the body" is apposite here; see *Discourse of Enlightenment in Eighteenth-Century France*. Brewer argues for a close relation between Diderot's attention to corporeality and his philosophical materialism. See esp. 169–71 and 197–99. On the centrality of the body in Diderot, see also Caplan, *Framed Narratives*, esp. 46–51. Marx Wartofsky's classic essay on the philosophical foundation of Diderot's materialism remains a fundamental resource; see "Diderot and the Development of Materialist Monism," 279–329.

14. See Terdiman, *Present Past*, 291.

ter 1 put it—*becomes too damn easy*. Such untrammeled representational mobility poses a cognitive problem quite as baffling as the acquisition of fictionality is liberating. Fiction, in other words, doesn't come free—as the experience of hoaxing Croismare manifests with pertinent and somewhat disturbing clarity.

For Diderot something new needed to be accommodated in the making and the consumption of narrative. But for him it was not clear that this represented an unmixed liberation or a victory. On the contrary, as fiction slips the bonds of its connection with materiality, as the power of words diverges from the representation of a referent about which the default assumption is that it is real and verifiable, as language inflects toward the illusionistic, the phantasmatic, the hypothetical, and the counterfactual—then something discomfiting, even vaguely *unsavory*, seems to come into play. The most consequential linguistic performative of Suzanne Simonin's life, her irrevocable monastic *vow*—paradoxically uttered in an illusory space by an illusory woman—measures the distance that a pragmatics of narrative must span in the representation of materiality.

As it scans the movement between a hegemonic assumption of some material referent and an emergent practice of fictionality, *La religieuse* captures and narrates an inflection in cultural history. In its equivocal mutation from hoax to novel, from text to fiction, it probes and tracks a shift in the story reality seems intent on telling—or, looked at the other way around, in the evolution of fundamental categories of cognition, consciousness and social practice. Such things *change*. This historicity of perceptual and conceptual categories demands a new hermeneutics of reading. In the 1844 manuscripts Marx had offered a celebrated formulation holding that even our senses become theoreticians.[15] We could trope Marx's formula to say that our narrative modes are historians. They are not given forever, nor do they sit still. And, when they change, as Lacan memorably said about our relation to the signifier, such alteration in the anchors of our being changes the whole course of history.[16]

Genres lie somewhere between *capacities* and *contracts* in the relationships texts practice with their readers. They organize us and are organized in their turn. Like all institutions they are mutable and assimilable. From experience we learn how to live with them. But we don't know the right techniques in advance. Verisimilitude is not a requisite when a text gives itself out as fact (in-

15. Marx, "Economic and Philosophical Manuscripts," 308.
16. See Lacan, "Agency of the Letter in the Unconscious," in *Écrits*, 174; and Terdiman, *Present Past*, 130.

deed, the contrary may rather be the case since, as common wisdom suggests, truth may be stranger than fiction). This requires us to upset and to reconceive our assumption of an asymptotic convergence between *truth* and what *seems true*, between *le vrai* and *le vraisemblable*. Suddenly, these categories that frame our relationship to texts appear not fraternal twins, but rather antagonistic contraries.

You need verisimilitude in a world in which materiality appears to be receding, in which through the functioning of mediations of all kinds it is devolving into what seems no more than another neutral register our own period will term "textuality." What is crucial here is the increasing divergence and detachment—potentially to the point of complete disengagement which some have reached today—between the semiotic and the material realms of human activity. This is the novelty that Diderot's generation was confronting in the moment of its incipience.

Our contemporary construction of these matters seems to take on the transparency of doxa. We absolutize the capacities we have attained while forgetting the challenges that determined their creation. By dissolving contact with the roots of our own enigmas, the dehistoricization of our choices and practices makes it hard for us to see where we, and they, come from. Two points seem essential to reopen the question that the ideology of "textualism" risks shutting out. First, we didn't have to go in the direction we did. No theoretical breakthrough or scientific discovery, no incontestable logic, necessitated dissolving the enigma of referentiality which arises in the enunciatory situation of a novel like *La religieuse*. The notion of textualism is a choice theoretical culture has made to describe its operations in a certain way and to certain ends. Our construction of the world according to an encompassing and internally undifferentiated notion of representation, and the consequent recession of the forms of extra-textual designation of the material world that engaged and troubled Diderot two centuries ago, thus depend upon and react to the circumstances of our own conjuncture just as determinately as Diderot's own construction of these matters depended upon his. But there can be quite a bit of play in the reaction chosen to respond to a given nexus of determinants.

Second, there are costs to any construction we adopt of these matters. How we choose to see things determines what we risk becoming blind to. These risks and costs become patent when we measure the distance between the interrogation that Diderot was pursuing in *La religieuse* and our contemporary indifference to such questions, which today are typically relegated to the outworn registers of a pre-theoretical narratology. We need to recover Diderot's puzzlement about these matters.

> Est-ce qu'on rit, est-ce qu'on pleure à discrétion?
> [Can we laugh, can we cry, at will?]
> —DIDEROT, *Paradoxe sur le comédien*, DFVP 20:73–74

The mind-body problem haunts thinking.[17] But in contemporary theory it has taken on a radical and uncompromising form. Today we tend to conceive as a foundational principle the chasm, the incommensurability, between text and referent. But if our current absolutist construction of the problem is so self-evident, we might wonder why this insight hasn't universally determined what cultures project as the relationship between their words and their world. In particular how could Diderot have been so naive as to think that there was a connection between them worth worrying about for as long as he did in writing and rewriting *La religieuse*?

The degree of junction or disjunction between sign and referent to which we attend is never determined in advance. Rather, we construct it—to be sure, against the background of the phase-change that is always involved when we move from one realm of human activity to another, as from language world to material world. Such construction is inevitably done in relation to what we perceive our cognitive and, more broadly, our social needs to be. So, rather than puzzling over Diderot's uncharacteristic ignorance of the abyss between text and object, we might instead wonder about our own conversion of this distance to a flat incommensurability, to an absolute disjunction.

In Enlightenment and nineteenth-century Europe, clearly realism was not just an intense preoccupation; it was an imaginable objective. Realism supposes that language can capture and represent the referential world.[18] *La religieuse* stands as evidence of the conviction that sustains such a project. But as time went on, concern with this category of representation inflected powerfully. From the symbolists of the nineteenth century to Barthes, people apprenticed themselves to a different construction of the matter, learning to see it not as "realism" but as an increasingly naive and delusive "reality effect."[19] Then it

---

17. For a particularly instructive example of such haunting, consider Descartes' extravagant theory about the pineal gland in his *Principles of Philosophy* (1644).

18. Think of the relentless realism of the *Encyclopédie*, of its faith in the possibility of knowledge's and language's grasp of material reality.

19. See Barthes, "Reality Effect."

was no longer a question of achieving a felicitous and reliable match between words and their referential objects, still less of reforming the world of which those objects formed a part. Rather, in the historical sequence of cultural forms the task was to register another paradigm to which, for a while, writers and readers contracted themselves to produce the appearance—the artifice—of literary verisimilitude. In such a construction the distance between language and its referent appears beyond scale and can never be negotiated. All such separations then appear infinite.

When we conceive of language from this angle, the material world always sits out of reach.[20] But such constructions are not obligatory and are never uninflected truth. They proceed from a set of contingent, paradigmatic choices. The interest of Enlightenment fictions is that they mark a moment when those choices were still up for grabs.[21] For Diderot the cost of absolutizing or reifying—we might even say theologizing—language, however tempting it may have seemed, entailed a disabling impoverishment of language's social and political effectiveness. It meant divorcing words from the world the philosophes wanted fervently to bear upon and to change. To the theoretician of textualism the material world, the world of human consequences, can seem abstracted or irrelevant. But if you are the Marquis de Croismare in Caen waiting for a disconsolate Suzanne Simonin to step down from the Paris coach on the day appointed for her arrival, then recalling what you have learned of the intensity of her misfortunes might re-inflect this matter powerfully.

The response to such literalism seems easy today. A Modernist or Postmodernist would plausibly argue that Suzanne Simonin's story only *reinforces* the contemporary theoretical point. For (so the argument would go) Suzanne never existed to begin with, only what we might term a "Suzanne-effect." On such a view, *any* claim to referentiality is no more than a dissimulation of its own impossibility. But is this construction self-evident or unimpeachable? We could

20. On this point, see Terdiman, *Present Past*, 139.

21. The contingency of such doxic views becomes evident when we step outside the literary-critical orthodoxy that has consigned referentiality to the conceptual ash heap. Within Anglo-American philosophy, for example, theories of referentiality tend to make no assumptions about access to some metaphysical *Ding-an-sich* by the speaking or writing subject. These theories go some distance toward demonstrating how the inner structure of the referent and the structure of the world in general put *pressure* on our meanings—thereby undermining the thesis of autonomous "textuality," at least in its most rigid and uncompromising forms. See, for example, Putnam, *Mind, Language and Reality*. Putnam famously argued concerning natural-kind terms that "meaning ain't in the head" (see Callinicos, *Against Postmodernism*, 79–80). Tyler Burge takes this inquiry even farther in an "anti-textualist" direction; see "Individualism and the Mental." In Gareth Evans's theory of reference this anti-Cartesian suspicion of privileged access to thought, and coordinate unreliable access to thought's referent, is strongly argued. See Evans, *Varieties of Reference*.

hardly maintain that there can be no argument about it. The existence and the energy of divergent views graphically demonstrates the contrary.

This debate is undecidable on logical grounds. But that is the point at which *other* grounds—including frankly political and social concerns—become relevant (indeed urgent) areas of inquiry and of choice. We *choose* our models; they do not emerge ineluctably out of some revealed truth of the world. But it is important to be aware of the opportunity costs of these choices—particularly of the ones that can seem settled and self-evident today. The Enlightenment's exploration of these issues helps us to define our elections and frame their costs.

In particular *La religieuse* can help us to understand what we give up when we conceive all language use as an intra-linguistic phenomenon and thereby exclude pressure on language from the material world or language's pressure back against it. Such a choice bears upon language's social effectiveness or even projects its impotence. The image we hold and enact concerning this matter— whether of mediation between diverse realms or, alternatively, of disconnection between them—determines a consequential complex of our theoretical and pragmatic dispositions. If the world of Postmodernity seems *different* from worlds that have preceded it, this difference arises in response to an epochal mutation in our assumptions concerning the relationship of things to words, of bodies to stories.

> Thinking involves not only the flow of thoughts, but their arrest as well.
> —BENJAMIN, "Theses on the Philosophy of History," 262

With these thoughts in mind I want to return to the issue with which I began this book: theory's contingency and posteriority. Modesty before the limitations of our models constrains us to recognize a fundamental principle that determines thought's relation to its object. *Existence does not depend upon our ability to theorize it in order to occur.*[22] This relative independence of material referent from conceptual paradigm must be what drives transformation in theory to begin with. It is the shortcoming of our tools, the conviction that the ways by which we conceive the world don't manage to seize it, which drives their further development. Otherwise, why wouldn't we stick with the models we already have?

A complement of perceptual structures preexisting the moment of our encounter with the world is necessary for us to apprehend it. These structures may

22. On this point, also see Terdiman, *Present Past*, 290.

be innate or socialized, but few today would share the positivist view that the facts of the world simply self-interpret, that they are sufficient for making sense of existence. We need perceptual structures in order to see. But these need only be a kind of bootstrapping vault into perception or cognition: relatively low-level grids or models enabling our activity in apprehending the world—worked out, as we might say, more in our reptile brain than in our cortex.

"Social constructionism" has tended to homogenize such frameworks and flatten their complexity. Social construction theory blurs the diversity of constraints that bear upon the forming of models—in particular the pressure that a model's referent puts upon it. There are considerable degrees of malleability or variability possible in practices, paradigms, or perceptual structures. Even relatively basic sense mechanisms evolve over time and respond to the alteration of environmental, social, and historical factors. So, a binary, bright-line division between *instinctual* and *learned* "categories of understanding" and "forms of perception"—Kant's terms for the grids that make reality knowable—is probably not helpful.[23] The categories melt into each other. Yet there are important distinctions that can still be made. They have to do with the *kind* of perceptual or conceptual activity we undertake.

Perhaps there are multiple and diverse models for apprehending the bus careening directly at us. But their variety is probably limited. Such an interpretive situation is highly constrained. Thinking wrongly about the bus leads to the extinction of the perceptual model thus activated: DOA. A much broader range of constructions is conceivable, however, for cognitive and interpretive tasks that lie farther from instinct and closer to intellection. In the case of the latter we can increasingly recognize the underdetermination of models. If you think the bus is just an idea, the situation self-corrects—however disastrously— in an instant. But thinking that the categories of our understanding are freely formulated by a sovereign model-making intellect is not a position that reality will similarly repudiate.[24]

What we call "theory" in the diverse branches of the cultural disciplines represents a much more complex and higher-order modeling than jumping out of the way of the bus.[25] Such formations exceed the requirements and transcend the complication of everyday activity. But the crucial point is that these more

23. See Kant, *Critique of Pure Reason*, 201–66 and 290–96.

24. On these issues, see Timpanaro, *On Materialism*, 45–52. Timpanaro emphasized the exaggerations implicit in social constructionism long before most analysts were considering the matter. He writes, for example, "To maintain that, since the 'biological' is always presented to us as mediated by the 'social,' the 'biological' is nothing and the 'social' is everything, would . . . be idealist sophistry."

25. No reference is intended here to the circumstances of Roland Barthes's death.

complex constructions are less immediately constrained than are the nuts-and-bolts frameworks by which our organism adapts and accommodates to the immediate conditions—and dangers—of existence. Yet in these higher-level cases with their looser determinations there may be only a limited number of models conceivable to fit a given situation and interpretive need.[26] The limitations on this variety themselves indicate—they *model*—the constraints within which any paradigm construction is conducted. Michel Foucault put this clearly: "One cannot speak of anything at any time; it is not easy to say something new."[27] It would be irrational idealism to believe that such constraints are simply voluntarist or negligible.

No construction imposes itself incontrovertibly. But neither is there unconstrained free election of unmotivated models for organizing our understanding. The *relative* freedom of higher-order modeling is what has led to social constructionism's projection of a kind of chaotic free-for-all of paradigm making. But such an interpretation pays the price of losing track of the contrary dynamic of constraint which acts upon the construction of understanding. We can see this limitation in more fundamental perceptual and practical behavior. But it acts even upon the relatively freer higher-order cases with which theory in the cultural disciplines deals—and about which it sometimes seems that our arguments have become endless. Such underdetermination of theory needs to be thought through carefully.

This disputation may seem abstruse. But it is relevant both to Diderot's Enlightenment reflections concerning writing and language and to our own contemporary arguments concerning representation, referentiality, intention, and the production of meaning. In his fiction Diderot was seeking to understand what we might call the "limits of theory." Are there constraints upon language's ability to construct a reality *independent of constraint*? The whole millennial drama of Idealism's quarrel with Materialism—a conflict that, despite the unfashionableness of the terminology, still underlies much discussion of these matters today—links Diderot's fictional experiments with our present uncertainty concerning how far language can take us.

The key to the model we need to counterpose against Postmodern versions of textualism—and thereby decenter its doxic self-evidence—lies in conceiving language as an inseparable component of a complex of social practices. Such a complex would be situated along the continuum of everyday existence running

26. On this point, see Terdiman, "Materialist Imagination."
27. Foucault, *Archaeology of Knowledge*, 44.

from *signifying* to *acting*. These practices put emphasis upon the material *inter-connectedness* of our modalities of functioning in the world, rather than upon the problematic singularity of the linguistic phenomenon. Thus understood, the signifier, we could then say, pulls us into materiality.

We might begin the rebalancing of theoretical emphasis between *words* and *things* by resurrecting a fundamental question that Georg Simmel formulated in the title of an essay from 1908: "How Is Society Possible?" Simmel followed Vico's influential distinction between the making of nature (knowable only to God) and the making of the social world (made, and hence knowable, by us). This principle is the so-called *verum factum*. Simmel deconstructed it. Echoing Kant, he argued that, while the unity of nature may emerge only in the observing subject, the perception of *society* requires no similar outside observer. Rather, the elements of society, people—who are conscious synthesizing and acting units—directly realize this unity. And they do so in both senses of *realize*: they perceive it, and they create it.[28]

So, whatever its ontological properties may appear to be when viewed absolutely, in human practice language functions not just in the realm of some disembodied and crystalline isolation from somatic or material effects but in the world of bodies in their everyday intercourse and activity. Language is not first *contemplative* or *absolute* but *pragmatic* and *communicative*. In the daunting realm of theory meaning may disseminate ungovernably, particularly when we rack our theoretical microscope to such high magnification that all definition of our object appears unrecoverable. Nonetheless, we manage to catch our flight to the next conference about undecidability. Generally, we function capably in the social world, despite the aporias of meaning's ungovernable dissemination.

The theoretical key is to decide what register of experience we want our model to illuminate. The very question is socialized and historicized—hence, accessible to reasoned reflection and thoughtful choice. The problems that occupy us in this realm—of cognition, of linguistic adequacy to representation and communication—tend not to arise so long as organic and naturalized belief in inherited meanings remains secure. Then sentences make sense and function effectively. But when such belief falters—pertinently in the complex of developments that make up the passage to modernity of which the Enlightenment

28. See Simmel, "How Is Society Possible?" 7. On this point, see Terdiman, "On the Dialectics of Post-Dialectical Thinking," 118.

period marks a fundamental moment—then signification turns labyrinthine and refractory. Focus tends to shift from *sentences* to *words*, from pragmatics and syntax to semantics and semiotics. That is when theory begins appealing to the paradoxical stability of what in *Present Past* I termed "representational nihilism," to the notion that our meanings are constructed freely and hence cannot be referentially constrained. Then signification diffuses and risks disappearing. The cost of resisting closure through such mechanisms is considerable. So our contemporary suspicion about meaning, our familiar crisis of representation, appear as theoretical reflexes of epochal changes in the patterns of production and transmission of socially agreed sense which define modernity and project the even more intransigent formulations of the Postmodern. It might seem surprising that a crisis already two hundred years in the bottle has not yet been resolved. But its stakes have surely shifted.[29]

Today the meaning of the meaning-crisis no longer seems to translate an uncertainty about how social values and significations can be transmitted in a world turned topsy-turvy by revolutionary change. Rather, contemporary suspicion concerning meaning translates a resistance to envelopment in the meanings that, under an increasingly hegemonic and globalizing capitalism, are all too densely and all too successfully programmed and reproduced. The "single market" is not only happening in Europe. The seemingly inexorable triumph of "liberal" socioeconomic systems appears to place us all in the same economic—and discursive—space. Since the nineteenth century at least, alienation from the agencies that administer such production and reproduction has been the most notorious fact about the social fraction we term the "intelligentsia." But a complete—if undeveloped—model of the effects of such a process relating and mediating the registers of *power* and of *language* is already functioning in Diderot's Enlightenment reflections on the daunting perplexities of representation and the seductive uncertainties of fiction.

> Our age is, in especial degree, the age of criticism, and to criticism everything must submit.
> —KANT, preface to 1st ed., *Critique of Pure Reason*, trans. Smith, 9, n. a

I want to suggest how Diderot's construction of these issues might help to denaturalize and enrich our thinking about these matters. Current theories of textualism create a pressure toward discarding the category of *deception*. In the

29. On these points, see Terdiman, *Present Past*, 68–69.

postmodern dispensation *all* texts are delusive if we imagine them to refer reliably to any extratextual world. So deception becomes an empty category. The notion of "falsification" can only have traction if there is some realm of the veridical to norm it.

But *lies* always presuppose *bodies*. So for Diderot this excluded category of "deception" is at the heart of his absorption with the textual and communicative process in fiction. This is because bodies matter so much. Diderot meditates intently on deception not only as a principal theme in his narratives but as the mechanism by which a text construes its communication and intends to achieve its effect to begin with. With only the slightest dismissive bow in the direction of figures such as Barthes and de Man, *La religieuse* subverts notions of an absolute distance between text and world by venturing impenitently to deconstruct it.

The connection that replaces this chasm is, to be sure, a troubled and unstable one. But, as a *connection*, it can be worked upon and thought about. Unlike many critics today, Diderot declines to empty out the referentiality problem by dissolving referentiality itself. Rather, he *practices* it as if to refute the notion that it might simply be dispensed with. One thinks, at about the same moment across the Channel, of Dr. Johnson's even more summary refutation of an Idealism formulated by Bishop Berkeley which was no less intransigent than our contemporary theories of textualism. We need to reexamine why the Enlightenment staked so intensely upon affirming the power of texts to capture or reference materiality. To what threat were they responding?

The *political* dimension of texts and all language performances—how words get into the world—asserts itself at the heart of the question posed by Enlightenment fictions—by Diderot in particular. It emerges as a critical reflection on the part of the eighteenth-century "philosophical" party.[30] By the necessities of organized state repression, written texts had to be the form taken by Enlightenment political action. What other form could protest take? So the texts of the philosophes situated themselves in relation not only to the semiotic spectacles of monarchical and ecclesiastical ritual but to the material impositions of those forms of authority. Rousseau explained the realm of the philosophes' political action—the attempt to transform reality through writing and language—on the opening page of *Du contrat social*: "Given that I write on politics, people may ask me if I am a prince or a legislator. My answer is that I am not, and that that

---

30. On the fundamentally political aims and implications of Enlightenment texts, see (among many other important discussions) Brewer, *Discourse of Enlightenment*, 14–16, and 50. See also Darnton, *Great Cat Massacre*, 215; and Hayes, *Reading the French Enlightenment*, chap. 5, esp. 153 ff.

is why I write on politics. If I was a prince or a legislator, I would not waste my time *writing* about what should be done, I would either do it, or I would keep quiet."[31]

As eighteenth-century society transformed itself, as it grew more highly differentiated, more stratified, and more articulable into diverse demographic, professional, and hierarchical groups, there may well have been a growing sense on the part of constituted authority that the exercise of their power was becoming more complex and problematical. But the command of language over bodies that those in power could assume was still an entire revolution away from our contemporary perceptions of its disability or its arrest.

The texts of Old Regime legislation or administration provided an immediate model for the efficacy of language in the material world. Such linguistic expressions of authority were not haunted by the fear that they could not achieve performativity, determine reality, and, at the limit, control real bodies. On the contrary, Diderot clapped in Vincennes; Voltaire exiled to England; Rousseau oscillating nervously between France, England, and Geneva; Sade in the Bastille and in Charenton—these were peremptory instantiations of authority's command. In the face of such manifestations of textual pragmatics an ideology that depreciated the possibility of language to exercise its effects in the material world would have reduced Enlightenment writing to the status of mere "literature"—indeed, to the impotence familiar in our own period.

It is a well-worn commonplace in the cultural and political historiography of the period that through their deployment of language and of texts the philosophes *did* have political effectiveness. This view arose and has continued to dominate discussion of the issue on the basis of two related but separable assertions: first, the characterization of their own works by *Lumières* authors themselves, who depicted these writings as possessing precisely the pragmatic power they sought; and, second, the broadly influential perspective that stems principally from the work of Daniel Mornet, the first historian to examine the question in a disciplined manner. In a celebrated assertion Mornet claimed that "it was, in part, ideas that determined the French Revolution."[32] I want to examine these positions briefly.

31. Rousseau, *Du contrat social*, 235; emph. added; my trans.
32. Mornet, *Les origines intellectuelles de la Révolution française 1715–1787*,3. On the logic and accuracy of Mornet's seminal assertion, see Chartier, *Cultural Origins of the French Revolution*, esp. chap. 1. Chartier traces the influence of an analyst of these issues even more celebrated than Mornet: Alexis de Tocqueville, whose *L'Ancien régime et la révolution* (1856) asserted the centrality of men of letters in what he termed "the political education of a great nation" (bk. 3, chap. 1). See Chartier, *Cultural Origins*, 11–12 and 67–68.

In April 1757 the French *Parlement* declared that "all those who are proved to have composed, caused to be composed, or printed pieces tending to attack religion, to disturb minds, to attack our authority, and to trouble the order and tranquillity of our States will be punished with death."[33] Texts whose writers were placed under such an interdict could hardly be considered candidates for disconnection from the political and social world; thus construed (and thus potentially sanctioned) writing doesn't sound innocuous. On the contrary, the intense battles concerning censorship and publication in the Enlightenment period foreground the degree to which the political and social effectiveness of prose, language, *books*, was a conscious preoccupation in the period that saw the writing of *La religieuse* and Diderot's other fictional texts.

So, by virtue of their own activity, and of the activity that state and ecclesiastical authority directed against them, the philosophes were *not* likely to have been haunted by a fear that writing was condemned to some ontological divorce from the pragmatics of the political and social realm. Still less were they passively resigned to such pessimism. They must have fretted endlessly about the slowness of change which thwarted their effectiveness, but they never ceased claiming it. Thus, Diderot repeatedly made assertions such as that the philosopher was the "preceptor of mankind"; "the magistrate deals out justice; the philosopher teaches the magistrate what is just and unjust."[34]

In "What Is Enlightenment?" (written in 1784, the year of Diderot's death) Immanuel Kant made probably the most resonant statement in the period concerning the centrality of reasoned discourse—of *texts*—to material change in society: "The public use of one's reason must always be free, and it alone can bring about enlightenment among men. . . . By the public use of one's reason I understand the use which a person makes of it as a scholar before the reading public."[35] The question of the *action of texts* is likewise constant in representations by the philosophes of their own writing activity. Aside from Kant's, one of the most forceful statements on this matter can be found, with satisfying appropriateness, in the article "Philosophe" in the *Encyclopédie*: "Reason is to the

---

33. See Chartier, *Cultural Origins*, 47.

34. For the philosophes' doubts, see for example Diderot's 17 March 1769 letter to David Hume, in which the French philosopher laments to his English correspondent: "Ah, my dear philosopher! Let us weep and wail over the lot of philosophy. We preach wisdom to the deaf, and we are still far indeed from the age of reason." Diderot, *Correspondance*, 9:40. For their claims that reason (as they represented it) should determine the course of political, juridical, and social activity, see Gay, *Enlightenment*, 128.

35. In Kant, *"Foundations of the Metaphysics of Morals" and "What Is Enlightenment?"* 85.

philosopher what grace is to the Christian. Grace causes the Christian to act, reason the philosopher."[36] Alongside the familiar sly sarcasm of this Enlightenment association of religion and rationality—domesticating and simultaneously promoting the latter in the face of traditionalist social and political resistance—what is striking about this statement is its focus upon *action*.

Since the formalisms of the nineteenth century such conviction concerning *pragmatics* has increasingly been represented as puerile or deluded. A choice example of the latter dismissive attitude concerning the relationship of writing to the political sphere is Gautier's preface to his first collection of poetry, *Albertus* (1832). Gautier projected a splendid authorial isolation:

> A space of a few feet where it is a bit warmer than elsewhere is [the writer's] whole universe. The mantel of the fireplace is his heaven; the hearth is his horizon.
>
> Of the world outside he has seen only what can be seen through the window, and he has not wanted to see any more than that. He belongs to no political tendency. He only notices revolutions when bullets smash through his windows. . . .
>
> He writes in order to have a pretext for doing nothing, and does nothing under the pretext of writing.[37]

In this passage one already feels the nineteenth century's epochal antipathy to the degraded and degrading realm of the political, denoted through its most emblematic and pertinent signifier in the period: *revolution*. Gautier, born in 1811, could have had no direct recollection of the Great Revolution. But the July revolution of 1830 was bloody and dispiriting enough both to resurrect an intense cultural memory of 1830s predecessor and to motivate the intransigent withdrawal that, as the founder of *L'art pour l'art*, Gautier made into a programmatic tenet of much post-Romantic writing. When we bring the optimism about making texts work *politically* on the part of Diderot and his collaborators into confrontation with Gautier's intransigent reversal of this attitude, it becomes apparent how linked—as counter-discourse; through *denegation*—Gautier's position was to pre-Revolutionary enthusiasm about the intimacy of writing and materiality. Or, to put it differently, we might sense in this clash

36. *Encyclopédie, ou dictionnaire raisonnée des sciences, des arts et des métiers.* CD-ROM ed., s.v. "Philosophe," para. 3. There is some doubt about the authorship of this article, most frequently attributed either to Dumarsais or to Diderot. Peter Gay claims that an early form of the essay may have been circulated as early as 1730; a version was surely published in 1743. Diderot abridged it for the *Encyclopédie.* Concerning the attribution problem, see Dieckmann, *"Le Philosophe"*; and Gay, *Enlightenment*, 127.

37. Gautier, *Albertus*, 1:81. From a different angle I discussed this passage in Terdiman, *Present Past*, 159–63.

how overdetermined by the abject realities of politics in our own century Modernist and Postmodernist attitudes may be. It is as if they arise in pure apotropaism, *to ward off the danger of social activity and political hope.*

It is clear that the sort of sociopolitical effectiveness which Enlightenment philosophes projected for their writing bore principally upon political (or juridical or economic or proto-sociological) writing. Malesherbes, who served beginning in 1750 as the French government's director of the book trade (*directeur de la librairie*) and whose sympathy for the "philosophical party" is well known, discussed these writings and their social role in the inaugural speech he presented upon his election to the Académie Française in 1775. In his address Malesherbes characterized men of letters as playing the same role in the public life of France which the celebrated orators of Athens and Rome had held in the political process of classical civilizations.[38]

But a fundamental question remains about the relationship between these *political* texts, on the one hand, and, on the other, the *fictional* texts often composed simultaneously by the same writers. There is an apparent contradiction between the notion of Lumières (based upon a logic of transparent rationality and principled discursive argument) and the notion of *fiction* (inevitably mobilizing illusionistic or deceptive modes of representation). How can rationalist "philosophical" objectives be reconciled with the seductions of fable?[39]

Voltaire had addressed this issue in *L'ingénu*: "Oh, if we must have fables, at least let them be the emblem of the truth! I enjoy the fables of the philosophers [*philosophes*], I laugh at the fables of children, and I detest the fables of impostors."[40] But Voltaire's quip lacks explanatory power. Fatally, it begs its own question. For, if words can make fictions, if imaginary representations leave rationality behind, what would it mean to say that a text about something nonexistent could serve as an "emblem of truth"? Diderot's reflections on this question about the philosophes' textual practice are much richer and more challenging.

If we are to make sense both of the Enlightenment and of our own theoretical world, we need to avoid re-concealing Enlightenment insights and interroga-

---

38. Malesherbes's speech is discussed in Chartier, *Cultural Origins*, 30–32. Thomas Hobbes had already written that democracy was an aristocracy of orators. See Benrekassa, *Le langage des lumières*, 340–41.

39. See Chamayou, *L'esprit de la lettre*, 72. Of course, the division between "political" and "fictional" texts was not absolute. As all critics have recognized, *La religieuse*, however "fictive," is most immediately a powerful protestation against state-enforced ecclesiastical imprisonment.

40. Cited by Chamayou, *L'esprit de la lettre*, 72.

tions about the *political* capacity of texts and language behind the flatter paradigm of textualism. Everything may be a text, but not everything is *just* text. The entity "text" is internally differentiated and multivocal; it projects itself through complex mediations into other registers of our existence in ways that make prominent constructions of it in our period reductive in disabling ways. Some language performances invoke effects that are distinctly incommensurable with the doctrine of textuality in its Postmodern guise.

No text can determine how it will be taken up or how far it will be credited. Today when a novel asks us to believe in its veracity, it doesn't expect literal compliance. But with its address to the Marquis de Croismare, *La religieuse* did precisely that—and the conspirators worried intricately about whether they had achieved their objective. To be sure, at the end of the day it *was* only a novel, not a police report or a medical chart. It is important to remember, however, that, unlike any other of Diderot's narratives, this one was offered to its immediate audience (even if that audience beyond the conspirators themselves consisted of a single reader) not as fiction but as reportage; not in the guise of hypothesis or fantasy but in that of *witness*. The enigma of "representation"—a word by which we might designate either a text organized to produce verisimilitude or one aiming at the special form of reliance we call belief—emerges in this foundational ambiguity. That words on the page could serve such diametrical ends is the mystery I contend Diderot used *La religieuse* to think about.

So, the plot and the practice of *La religieuse* exceeded the paradigmatic limits of imaginative fiction in a critical and diagnostic way—if for no other reason than because Diderot and his co-conspirators sought through what they knew to be a fiction to produce real *corporeal* consequences. Any fictional object projects the nonexistent into that shadowy quasi-existence we allow ourselves to experience by learned suspension of disbelief.[41] Such quasi-belief, along with our equally complex and hypothetical enactment of "identification" with entities that simply don't exist, are deep in our repertoire of cognitive and affective practices. But Suzanne Simonin projects a different case. Although her mode of being parallels that of any "literary" character, it was meant by those who masterminded her genesis to be credited as *genuine*—as what, tongue slightly in cheek, we could designate as "*really* real." Creating this assuredly fictional character required a kind of fictionalizing beyond the paradigm of fictionalization, one that troped factuality in a way that we could say novels ordinarily don't.

41. See Coleridge, *Biographia Literaria*, chap. 14, 2:6.

The technical means of producing this more radical form of illusion became the objective for Diderot and his conspirators. They were not simply writing a novel; they were conjuring up a person. In doing so, they experimented with a material potential in language which we do not immediately associate with its use in storytelling. In the mode of absolute counterfeit their dissimulation was more radical than any first-order fiction can be. Except in hilarities like Woody Allen's "Kugelmass Episode," we know we will not meet Emma Bovary on the street.[42] But at a particular moment, based on credible arrangements of the kind all of us make every day, Croismare expected Suzanne Simonin to arrive in Caen on the Paris coach (see *DFPV* 11:39). By keeping Suzanne's contacts with the Marquis limited to language, rather than allowing them to fall over into the stolid and much less pliant world of materiality, the conspirators had gone to great lengths to defer this potential conversion of mediation to immediacy. But, finally, they were obliged to kill off their creation rather than be discovered to have invented her to begin with. What emerges from the piquant speech situation the conspirators had backed themselves into are the stakes involved in exposing their verbal invention to the light of corporeal presence. This strange dialectic of linguistic pliancy and material refractoriness is at the heart of the matter.[43]

In critical analyses of his texts Diderot's materialism has been a constant theme. As I argued at the beginning of this chapter, materialism imposes a *limit* that language seems able to ignore or outflank. Diderot's materialist intuition about reality's constitution by *limits* determines not only his more discursive or doctrinal philosophical positions but the most characteristic structures of his own imaginative writing. He figures the power of limits by casting many of his texts as dialogues. In the image of the contention between two subjects he conceptualizes the confrontation that is inherent in a material dialectic. In dialogue people are *bound*—in several senses of the term. Struggle, not autonomy; the clash of competing positions, not the free play of signifiers, is the way of the world when it is seen and experienced in this mode.[44]

---

42. Allen, "Kugelmass Episode," 347–60. Jonathan Culler discusses this deep fiction about fictions in "The Uses of Madame Bovary," 1–12, esp. 10–11.

43. See Terdiman, *Present Past*, 278, where I consider Freud's reflections upon the uncanny difference between semiotic and material registers of existence. Freud's characterization of the contents of consciousness is based upon what he terms the "compliance of the linguistic material" (*Psychopathology of Everyday Life*, *SE* 6:222) and contrasts directly with his description of the thought-resistant materiality of things ("Project for a Scientific Psychology," *SE* 1:334). This complex of ideas could be usefully related to Fredric Jameson's reflections on the Lacanian relation of "desire" to the "Real"—the fundamentally unrepresentable and non-narrative—in *Political Unconscious*, 184–85.

44. Foucault took a convergent—and strongly dialectical—position on this issue: "I believe one's

More broadly, constitution by *constraint* is crucial in any situation in which we imagine social action or politics to be possible. It is the mode of existence and experience in the world of bodies. Consequently, the representation of conflict foregrounds the foundational constancy of the *resistance* we encounter in any attempt to master or to change the conditions that confront us.[45] The structure of contention between subjects and the limitations that constrain their possibilities of action illuminate the discomfort with "facility" which Diderot experienced in his fictionalizing. The refractory quality of the social and political world thus provides a clue to the origins of Diderot's suspicions concerning the apparently untrammeled power of language, of narrative, and, most disturbingly, of *reason* itself.

Nothing in the material world of constraints and limits coheres with language's seemingly effortless power to evoke the nonexistent.[46] If the projection of imaginary entities is so easy to achieve in language, if it is so damn easy to make up stories, as Diderot put it in the passage from *Jacques le fataliste* which I cited as an epigraph in chapter 1, then perhaps words may simply have insufficient traction to bear upon the material world at all.

Diderot's sensitivity to the unsettling facility or compliance that he discovered was active—perhaps even irrepressible—in language and narrative becomes diagnostic here. For him this game is *too easy*—it forgets the phenomenology of daily existence's onerousness. Behind it and in Diderot's ambivalence we can sense the force of humanity's millennial experience of *difficulty*, of the brute and unforgiving materiality of the world. Things don't come as easy as language-paradigms sometimes suggest. Mules don't move as easily as words.

An unhappy subterranean conviction about materiality's refractoriness is thus at issue in Enlightenment reformism. Diderot or other reformers were not able to conceive with confidence the suspension of this immemorial difficulty.

---

point of reference should not be the great model of language and signs, but that of war and battle. The history which bears and determines us has the form of a war rather than a language: relations of power, not relations of meaning" (*Power/Knowledge*, 114).

45. This conception of the world has one of its early sources in the classical formulation by Spinoza that "to define is to negate." The theory for this structure of constitutive oppositions was developed furthest by Hegel in his notions of "limit" and "limitation" (*Grenze, Schranke*) and his analysis of "finitude" (*Endlichkeit*). Dialectic, whether in Hegel's idealist version or in Diderot's or Marx's materialist one, seeks to center opposition (contradiction, antagonism) at the heart of any description of existence. For an intelligent resume of the issues in Hegel, see Inwood, *Hegel Dictionary*, s.v. "Limit." For the relations between Diderot and Hegel, see Simon, *Mass Enlightenment*, chap. 5; for bibliography, see Simon, *Mass Enlightenment*, chap. 5 n. 10.

46. Diderot was not the only Enlightenment writer to worry this classic philosophical problem. Here is Rousseau in *Émile* (1762): "Est-ce ma faute si j'aime ce qui n'est pas?" ("Can I be blamed for loving something that does not exist?"). Cited in Howells, "Statut du romanesque," 38.

They were hopeful about change but realistic concerning it. The very terms of the problem, and the most settled and institutionalized patterns of experience, forestalled imagination of a future that could blithely shuck off the weight of things and supersede the refractory movement of time.

This contrast between the malleability of language performances that might have maintained Croismare's epistolary engagement with Suzanne Simonin's plight indefinitely, and the recalcitrant positivity of immediate experience that would have instantaneously blown her cover, marks the experimental setting in which Diderot's narrative moves. In this space we are on the edge of a proto-Popperian world, in which the potentiality for authoritative disconfirmation, for the decisive encounter with a limit, becomes the test of a representation's mode of existence, the experiment that distinguishes between the fiction and the lie.[47] For the conspirators, of course, the narrative situation was traditional—but only so long as they kept Suzanne living in language alone. In *that* world her existence remained undecidable. But she could not trade that refuge for the one Croismare was offering her in Normandy. The indeterminacy of her existence collapses on the day you wait for her to emerge from the coach she was to have taken from Paris to Caen. Then, conclusively, either she *is*, or she *isn't*.

The sign, Umberto Eco famously told us, is anything that can be used in order to lie.[48] But the relationship between the *lie* and *materiality* is crucial. Eco's construction reinserts the semiotic into the field of material and social consequentiality from which many contemporary notions tend to sever it. It contests current orthodoxies that imagine the work of language to be contained entirely within an intra-textual realm, free of the limits with which reality confronts us and divided from a world possessing the capacity to *answer* our texts. Such "answers" make meanings we can neither predict nor constrain.[49] Thus understood, Eco's notion restores an internal relief and the potentiality for difference to the flattened image of representation which such theories project.

This semiotic franchise for prevarication, the facility with which you can use

47. See Popper, *Conjectures and Refutations*.
48. Eco, *Theory of Semiotics*, 7.
49. For a striking exemplification of reality "answering" our texts, consider Michel de Certeau's analysis of such a response in his 1976 essay " Politics of Silence." Certeau projects a mode of difference producing an intense interlocution of dominant white Europeanizing power by the Indians of Latin America. In this movement on the margin, epistemology becomes bidirectional. The "others" draw us toward them. A specific experience of marginality thus begins to refigure the paradigm of social and cultural discourse. The political resonances of such a dialectic are clear. On Certeau's essay, see Terdiman, "Marginality of Michel de Certeau."

words to lie, gives language an unsettling privilege. In *La religieuse* Diderot was measuring its range and power. He did so by pushing to the limit the peculiar enunciatory situation that, over the months and years after it had first arisen as a joke in 1760, he had developed out of the conspirators' good-natured hoax of Croismare. *La religieuse* then reads as a critical experiment with the mode of unfoundable uncertainty that fictions constitute. Are there restrictions on what they can conjure up? Is there anything that reality will *not* allow them to represent? Diderot's deception suggests that, in its inherent propensity to evoke a referent whose mode of existence is inevitably *other* than its own, language may be unable *not* to project materiality and literality—even when (or perhaps especially when) its doing so has no more basis than what we could term a conscious mystification.

The themes of *La religieuse* are multiple. Momentous matters circulate within it: the reliability of promises, the opposition between duty and freedom, the complications of sex, the power of money, the sufferings we experience in injury and illness, the healing we can induce through compassion. But I've been arguing that the text deals most fundamentally with the intricate and ambiguous relations between language and bodies. There is an obvious mismatch between the weightiness of the text's preoccupations and themes and the frivolous genesis that gave rise to it in the attempt to dupe Croismare. In *La religieuse*, in an alarming disequilibrium, the weightless lability of words that conjured Suzanne and her misfortunes out of nothingness counterposes itself against the momentousness of the material and human problems with which the novel confronts us—and in particular the intensely contrasting density and materiality of the language performance, the particular form of speech around which *La religieuse* turns and which epitomizes the problem of textual pragmatics: Suzanne Simonin's vow. The vow is what got her into trouble to begin with.

The problem with words is that nothing seems able to withstand their representations. It appears that language can reference anything it wants, can conjure up anything even out of nonexistence. Such dominion, I argued, violates the constraints material existence imposes. It is as if in the world of physics friction or inertia had suddenly been suspended. Only the Almighty might be imagined to possess a power over the circumstances of our life comparable to that of language. Language thus construed seems to evade our ordinary expectation that any social force or phenomenon will be limited by the network of relationships within which it is obliged to operate and which inevitably constrain it. In the material world nothing exists alone; nothing can be absolute. The seemingly intrinsic *weight* of an object arises in and manifests a relation (we term it "gravity") with the earth itself. For bodies "abstraction" has no relevant meaning or pertinence. But with language it is as if the checks and balances of materiality suddenly evaporate.

Paul de Man once wondered if there was a limit to what tropes could get away with.[50] Diderot preceded him in this interrogation. In his postmodernist commitment to untrammeled textuality de Man responded to his own question in the negative, and asserted that there was no way to constrain language's freedom. But for Diderot material reality had not yet irretrievably lost its power to answer what texts may tender for our belief. Nonetheless, an attenuation of this capacity was perceptible to him; the problem was decidedly in the air.

This mismatch frames the enigma that fascinated and unsettled Diderot in his work on this experiment in the form of a text. But it tells us at least one thing: that rhetoric, the technology of persuasion, was intensely at issue from the start. In the business of mystification you think incessantly about stratagem; artifice is the horizon of your practice. The transaction that became *La religieuse* necessitated this focus, since its objective was to enforce a counterfactual, to hypostatize a *person*—not as an accustomed fictional "character" recognized as such by readers but in the form of someone to be taken as a breathing, suffering, authentic human being. *La religieuse* thus radicalized an interrogation that may be implicit in all narrative but which was particularly acute and anxious in the eighteenth century, concerning the ontological space to which *representation* ought to be assigned. Frothed up out of thin air, Suzanne Simonin claims for herself a unique double status: imaginative invention and biological person. Of course, part of this claim is pure deception. But compared with self-declared fictions, the text plays a higher-stakes game—not only with words but with lives.

> O peintre de la nature! c'est toi qui ne mens jamais.
> [Oh painter of nature! You are the one who never lies.]
> —DIDEROT, "Éloge de Richardson," *DFPV* 13:202

Words *do* bind bodies. Sophie Volland wrote to Diderot about how she cried when she read the end of *Clarissa*. Here is Diderot's response: "What you say about Clarissa's funeral and her testament, I felt it too. . . . Even now my eyes

50. De Man, *Allegories of Reading*, 62.

still fill with tears, I was unable to read any further; I got up and began to express my grief, speaking with her brother, her sister, her father, her mother and her uncles, and talking aloud, to the great astonishment of Damilaville who couldn't understand anything of my feelings or of my speech, and who asked me who or what was upsetting me so powerfully."[51] Here narrative has colonized corporeality, and Diderot himself takes the place of Croismare. But the paradox of this transaction has uncannily deepened. For, if Diderot is here the victim of a text-induced deception—morphologically identical to the one produced by the letters the Marquis received from his Paris friends—nonetheless the slippage in agency is obvious. As I suggested earlier, the reactions experienced by Sophie and Diderot were not unique. They parallel widely attested experience of many eighteenth-century novel readers. They cried; they wrung their hands; they exulted. Enlightenment culture was sorting out how it wanted to react to the reading of fictions. But reactions such as those Diderot and Sophie communicated to each other were still sufficiently distinctive to be worth recounting. Here the laws of genre, and all the practical experience we accumulate in living to help us sort out real from imaginary, seem to have been displaced or suspended. Then the unsettling puzzle posed by the pragmatics of narrative returns in heightened form to pose an enigma about the status of texts, language, reliance, and behavior.

It might be that Diderot writes here in figures about his emotion at Clarissa's death, that the account of his entanglement in the fiction is no more than a means to emphasize the intensity of an illusion. Of course, it is that, and we cannot know whether the scene Diderot describes for Sophie Volland might not itself be a carefully constructed performance in the mode of what, in *Paradoxe sur le comédien*, Diderot imagines an actor doing in front of an audience. But this only displaces the problem by one level. Diderot *imagines imagination* acting in this form and conceives it as inducing the kind of corporeal effects he narrates. Nor can we attribute such an effect to Enlightenment *sensibilité*. That would be to take the problem as its own solution. The question is *why* such sensitivity to the emotions narrated in fictional modes of writing became a frequent comportment in the period. Identification, the special form of textual deception in question here, is worth a further look.

Identification subverts identity. It is radically improper; indeed, it is constituted by its impropriety. However realistic, texts are not real; I *am not* the

51. 17 September 1761; Diderot, *Correspondance*, 3:306.

other. But identification swamps these rationalities. It undermines the boundaries and divisions that logic prescribes. It is the very source and heart of our experience of the deception of writing, an experience with which all readers, all social actors, are familiar—indeed, an experience without which reading would be impossible.[52] But in a world where such deceptions are not only workable but positively embraced, *how could anyone have faith in the representations made in texts?*

"Richardson" names the locus in Diderot's writing and thinking about these questions where the problem comes into clearest focus, where the writing and reading—the textual—experience reveals its complication and its uncertainty. In Diderot's view texts offer the possibility that chimeras will become material experiences. In the "Éloge de Richardson" he writes: "Oh Richardson! despite ourselves, we take on a part in your works, we join in the conversation, we agree, we criticize, we admire, we get upset, we get furious. How many times, just like what happens when you bring a child to the theater for the first time, have I not found myself crying out: *'Don't believe him, he's tricking you. . . . If you go there, you're doomed.'* "[53]

Here the somatic and affective *participation* is clear. Again, tears are its sign. This is how we must understand Diderot's weeping at the death of Clarissa Harlowe. Without hesitation or the slightest sign of false consciousness he writes, "I have heard people argue about the behavior of Richardson's characters as if they were talking about real events" (200). These are, assuredly, "illusions," as Diderot states himself. But this rationalist designation only intervenes *provisionally.* For, Diderot continues, in the face of Richardson's text, the reader *loses* the capacity to question the veridical nature of what is represented: "You will no longer be able to hold back your tears or say to yourself, *'But maybe that's not true'* " (198).

When deception attains the convergence with *perception* which Diderot designates here, the notion of "illusion" almost seems a sophistry to reassure us in the face of the unaccountable. Since *Biographia Literaria* appeared in 1817, the armature of "willing suspension of disbelief" which Coleridge posited as the fundamental element of our behavior in relation to fictions has helped us sort

52. Roland Barthes put it uncompromisingly, claiming that such identification is "the very wellspring [*le ressort même*] of literature." See Barthes, " 'Longtemps je me suis couché de bonne heure,' " *Le bruissement de la langue*, 313; " 'Longtemps je me suis couché de bonne heure,' " *Rustle of Language*, 277.

53. Ed. Jean Varloot, *DFPV* 13:193. The "Éloge de Richardson" dates from January 1762, two years after the inception of the conspiracy concerning Croismare which led to composition of *La religieuse.* I've already mentioned the text's relation to Diderot's dispute with Rousseau.

out these categories.[54] The taxonomy behind Coleridge's analysis is comforting. By contrast, Diderot's account is quite unsettling. We should take as seriously as possible his uncanny *dissolution* of the categories that nominally segregate experience into imagination and cognition. Diderot's paralogism gives us access to a strain of Enlightenment reflection concerning the enigma of the text which our own age, by construing *all* texts as delusive and equally disconnected from materiality, has tended to resolve by emptying out the difficulty altogether.

Periods of rapidly changing social norms and structures inevitably put pressure on reading. Everyone flounders somewhat. Such periods draw the roles of reader and writer closer together in a common uncertainty concerning the stability of the modes and codes that determine any language transaction. So what is for us the startling congruence between the reading experience that through *La religieuse* Diderot had sought to induce in Croismare and the one he found arising in himself reading Richardson takes root in the conditions of language and of cognitive paradigms in the later eighteenth century.

For Diderot's tears did not only arise when reading Richardson. A widely quoted passage from the preface to *La religieuse* demonstrates his vulnerability to tales. We discover him porously, delusively grieving even over a story he had *himself* created: "One day when Diderot was completely caught up in the work [of writing *La religieuse*], M. d'Alainville, one of our mutual friends, came to visit and found him engulfed in sorrow, his face streaming with tears. 'What's the matter?' d'Alainville asked him. 'What a state you're in!' 'What's the matter,' Diderot answered, 'is that I've gotten myself distraught from the story I'm making up.' "[55]

Such interpenetration of fiction and factuality baffles us because we have worked hard to segregate the strands of our response to texts. Then it is easy to see Diderot's gullibility in the image of the cognitive greenness that he evoked

54. Coleridge, *Biographia Literaria*, chap. 14, 2:6.

55. *DFPV* 11:31. Diderot added the account of this incident to Grimm's original text; see Dieckmann, "Préface-Annexe de *La religieuse*," 28. Consequently, the scholarly tradition has fretted about whether the d'Alainville incident really happened, whether we can take "literally" the preface's evidence of Diderot's reaction. But we are in a world of *representations*. What is crucial is the representation Diderot wanted to give of a *plausible* reaction to fictionality. Compare this sentence from the *Essais sur la peinture* (1765): "Un poète est un homme d'une imagination forte, qui s'attendrit, qui s'effraye lui-même des fantômes qu'il se fait" (A poet is a man of strong imagination who is moved, who is frightened, by the phantoms he himself creates); *DFPV* 14:377. Flaubert suffered in the same way as Diderot. While writing *Madame Bovary*, he described his own reaction to Louise Colet in a letter of 24 April 1852: "Les larmes me coulaient sur la figure. Je m'étais attendri moi-même en écrivant" (Tears were streaming down my face. I had upset myself in writing); *Correspondance*, 2:76.

himself in the "Éloge de Richardson" when he refers to the naïveté of a child experiencing theater for the first time and ignorant of the conventional limits of participation in a representation onstage. But the instability here does not arise in some inadequacy of personal development. It represents an unstable moment in the inflection of a whole network of cultural codes, specifically one prior to the taxonomic rationalization of the categories of fiction and fact. Fiction had emerged. But it had not yet found its settled somatic and psychological locus.

That is to say that fiction had yet to lose, to be dispossessed of, its material ability to induce belief and determine the behavior of real bodies. To put it in the language of a period still able to recall (even if at a distance) the magical world in which fictions could be *true*, that "disenchantment" (*Entzauberung*) of the modern, rationalized world of which Max Weber spoke so evocatively had yet to suspend Diderot's capacity to experience—and to feel a kind of anxious amazement at—the material power of stories.[56]

56. Concerning "disenchantment," see Weber, "Science as a Vocation," 139–41.

CHAPTER THREE

The Body and the Text

J'ai entendu avec le plus grand plaisir tout ce que votre brillant esprit vous a inspiré; mais . . . vous oubliez . . . la différence de nos deux positions: vous, vous ne travaillez que sur le papier qui souffre tout, tandis que moi, pauvre impératrice, je travaille sur la peau humaine.

[I have listened with the greatest pleasure to the inspirations that have flowed from your brilliant mind. But you forget the difference between our positions. You write on paper, which will consent to anything; whereas I, poor Empress that I am, I write on human skin.]

> —EMPRESS CATHERINE TO DIDEROT, whose ideas for a new Russian constitution she had requested, quoted in Ségur, *Mémoires*, 3:37

Il fallait partir en effet de ceci que j'avais un corps, c'est-à-dire que j'étais perpétuellement menacé.
[The first point indeed was this, that I had a body, which meant that I was perpetually vulnerable.]

> —PROUST, *Le temps retrouvé, À la recherche du temps perdu*, 4:612

What do fictions *do*? Is a text its own world? How does it connect with the realm of material consequences and practical activity in which we live outside of novels? In chapter 2 I argued that Diderot's novels could be viewed as an instrument through which he was reconnoitering these puzzles. This chapter brings these claims into closer contact with Diderot's texts themselves. Through Diderot I want to evoke a relationship with language and rationality more complex and internally conflicted than most people typically conceive this connection to have been in the Enlightenment.

In periods of uncertainty and transition, against the background of a growing misfit between customary modes of expression and their transforming referents, writers think through again the registers of consciousness, sociality, and existence. So in his novels Diderot was scrutinizing fundamental and unsettled characteristics of narrative. The evidence for such reflection needs to be found at the level of his writing practice, in the series of decisions about the individual words and sentences that explore and communicate such reflection.

Politics and *language* were the arenas in which these transformations of the world focused their implications. Abuses in the realm of politics were increasingly clear. But beyond the irrationalities of absolutist power that our Enlightenment rationalists stigmatized, a realm of quotidian practices constituting social life was also coming into view, determining limits on individual possibility through mechanisms, and with an intensity, different from those enforced by the direct exercise of royal or ecclesiastical authority.

Fictions registered these more subtle mechanisms and interacted with them. *But fictions also turned out to be at the heart of such mechanisms themselves.* Their representations could not be sectioned off from what they represented. This implication of the medium in its referent was unexpected, and it was no doubt discomfiting for the philosophes, whose political interests lay in the use of texts as levers to press against reality. But when the supposed instrument for changing the world revealed itself as the heart of the mystery it was attempting to expose and rectify, then an uncanny re-situation of the problem imposed itself.

Narratives are *not* just about narrative. Enlightenment texts aim explicitly at reform. Voltaire put it clearly: "I write in order to act."[1] So in *La religieuse*, for example, a commitment to correct appalling social and religious abuses—royally enforced incarceration for anyone having pronounced a monastic vow—frames the themes, setting, action, and narrative structure of the novel. But these textual characteristics cohere with the theoretical and conceptual preoccupations concerning language and narrative which I have been attributing to it.

The tale's engagement with the political and juridical implications of Suzanne Simonin's coerced vows, her imprisonment, her suffering, and her fate once she escapes from the convent are intensely at issue in the novel. Such offenses against rights and reason focused Diderot's reformism; he was surely accurate when he called himself "one of the most zealous partisans of freedom" in France.[2] Resonantly, *La religieuse* invokes the ideal of this freedom and stigmatizes the constraint imposed upon it by constituted power. But the novel goes on to other—I would argue deeper—insights. As *La religieuse* constructs it, freedom is not just an absence of confinement. Politics doesn't stop at the convent wall. And texts do not simply argue for reform in the juridical realm. Through the processes of representation and induced belief that they mediate,

1. Voltaire, letter to Vernes, 15 April 1767, *Correspondence and Related Documents*, ed. Theodore Besterman (Geneva: Droz, 1968–77); cited by Gordon, "On the Supposed Obsolescence of the French Enlightenment," 209.
2. Diderot, *Lettre sur le commerce de la librairie*, 16.

texts enfold the heart of the mechanism by which reality *resists* change. The world run by texts that has become familiar in our own period—not so much determined by as *living within them*—is coming into sight in these Enlightenment constructions of the social world.

La religieuse expands the field of politics beyond the theme of political and legal rights around which its narrative nominally turns and connects it with a realm of social capacities and practices—the "literary"—which was still in the process of coming into focus in Diderot's time. The novel opens up this perception because in its exercise of narrative power it perceives something about how *all* the elements and practices that determine social relationships, not simply those defined by the exactions of authority, are constituted. Here it is a question of the unexpected power of *texts*.

Modern readings of *La religieuse* have interpreted Suzanne Simonin's successive convents as figures for the prisons into which any royal subject could be clapped, for Vincennes or the Bastille, and have construed the rigidity of the ecclesiastical setting and its potentiality for violence as metonyms for Old Regime autocracy in general. But *beyond* such structures what binds individuals and limits their freedom? If we imagine eliminating these authoritarian irrationalities, it is worth asking what this substitution of *humane* structures of power for *cruel and irrational* ones contributes to resolving the problem.[3] Diderot explores the question by moving Suzanne Simonin to the Longchamp convent, where she lives under the virtuous rule of the abbesse Madame de Moni. The text thus projects a thought-experiment in enlightened rather than benighted administration. But the experiment produces an unsettling result.

Within the convent Madame de Moni presides with a sensitivity that softens the suffering of ecclesiastical incarceration and makes the abuses inherent in the structure visible by contrast. We might have thought that rectifying the evils that characterize the exercise of power would sweep away the irrationalities that perturb social existence and limit the freedom of individuals. But this does not happen. There is a significant downside to the representation of more humane social relations that in her benevolence Madame de Moni fosters in her convent and projects for Suzanne. Her words and actions are unambiguously compassionate and well intentioned. But their effect is disastrous. Suzanne acknowledges Madame de Moni's generosity and piety. But concerning the

---

3. In *Present Past* I considered this issue from the angle of post-Revolutionary reflections on the limits to freedom (92–93).

Mother Superior she writes to Croismare, "I cannot speak too highly of her, *yet her goodness was my undoing*" (117; emph. added). In this reversal we confront the enigma of textuality in the ambiguity of any person's interpretation of another's activity, of the representation someone else makes of herself for us, and in the consequences of such belief. Between these people *fiction* intervenes.

Suzanne has been manipulated—we would not be wrong to say "seduced"—by the text of Madame de Moni's kindness. Regularly in the novel other nuns offer Suzanne stories whose objective is to deceive her. Within the frame of the fiction her position thus reproduces Croismare's situation outside it. But what these mendacious stories cannot do, Madame de Moni's kindness perversely accomplishes. The sympathy through which the Mother Superior of Longchamp intends to help Suzanne nonetheless induces her to pronounce her vows and accept the veil—despite her previous unconditional resistance. Kindness thus becomes a catastrophe. Can *La religieuse* then securely stabilize a distinction between a narrative offered to deceive and one offered to sustain? If not, what does the experience of such a mismatch between intention and consequence reveal about how language is coming to be conceived and practiced in this formative period for modern consciousness?

The *sign* of these conundra in *La religieuse* is writing itself. The self-interrogating pattern that explores it is omnipresent. In *La religieuse* such literary self-reflexivity goes beyond even what we are accustomed to in Modernist texts. It has a more focused meaning—and a more disturbing one. It reflects not simply literature's self-celebratory fascination with its own conjuring power but an ambivalent reaction to the inflection that was progressively detaching narratives from real bodies and transforming *deception* into *fiction*. In *La religieuse* the framing of the literary unsettles any simple ratification of fictional power. Fiction *worries* this text as much as it enables and sustains it. Then literature in its self-absorption does not so much self-affirm through such mirroring of its own existence as it self-*questions* and self-*subverts*.

In diverse ways, some direct, some oblique, *La religieuse* identifies literature and writing as a systematic apparatus of deception. The narrative reconceives a broad texture of linguistic and social forms and practices as *political*—that is, possessing the power to determine lives and constrain their possibilities. The analysis of oppression then passes *through* the constitution of state power and the exercise of disciplinary violence to examine loci of limitation on individuals which are more mystified and more daunting. *The capacity of words and representations to order existence* then becomes a focus of interrogation and critique.

Consequently, I understand the theme of incarceration in *La religieuse* as a kind of heuristic allegory, a materialized representation of the novel's staging of a more complex and mysterious reflection of and about politics and social relations. I want to place these infrastructural issues at the center of the novel.

> On croira . . .—Tout ce qu'on voudra.
> [People will think . . . —Whatever they want.]
> —DIDEROT, *La Religieuse, DFPV* 11:153

The notion and practice of *deception* which I framed in chapter 1 is central to Diderot's reflections concerning the moment of *La religieuse* and the functioning of its culture. I argued that deception must be distinguished from fictionalizing if we are not to lose touch with the capacity for material consequence that is always deception's objective. As what we could term *"embodied* lies," deceptions disengage truth—*but not language*—from materiality. In a deception language remains intensely focused upon the willed production of material outcomes.

The problem of such consequentiality is fundamental and explicit in *La religieuse*. Consider Suzanne Simonin's analysis of the hypocrisy of convent life. With impressive psychological and sociological acuteness, she explains how the nuns and the superiors manipulate the behavior of others through language. They write or speak conscious deception: "These women take vengeance for the trouble the postulants give them, for you shouldn't suppose that they enjoy the *hypocritical* role that they play and the nonsense that they are obliged to tell you over and over again. Finally it all becomes so repetitious and boring for them, but they go through with [their deceptions] for the sake of the thousand crowns [each postulant's dowry] that their convent earns as a result. This is the fundamental aim for which they spend a lifetime lying and setting young girls up for forty or fifty years of misery" (*DFPV* 11:92).

The passage analyzes the consequences of language's detachment from inner conviction. In the text's own terms telling lies creates a hell. The analysis, however devastating, is familiar. But the congruence between the deception—the lie—stigmatized here and the one Diderot and his friends were practicing in their hoax of Croismare is more arresting. Reframed by the strange textual transaction that became *La religieuse*, hypocrisy plays the representation of the novel *itself* back into the space of bodies.[4]

To be sure the consequences for Croismare were less dramatic than the novel

---

4. Concerning hypocrisy in *La religieuse*, see Leo Spitzer's classic analysis in *Linguistics and Literary History*, 148–49. Spitzer's perspective is quite different from mine.

represents them as being for the novices in the convent. The latter consequences were heinous. The delusive representations staged for the women who are intentionally deceived by ecclesiastical authority drive them mad: "One day one of these mad women escaped from the cell where she was locked up. I saw her. . . . I have never seen anything so hideous. She was completely disheveled and nearly naked; she was dragging iron chains; her eyes were wild; she was tearing her hair; she was striking her breast with her fists; she was running and screaming; she was cursing herself and the others with the most horrible imprecations; she was looking for a window out of which to throw herself. Panic seized me, my whole body was trembling, I saw my destiny in the fate of this unhappy creature" (92–93).

Diderot's revulsion at the suffering of the mad nun which he depicts through Suzanne's eyes is clear.[5] The passage rightly takes its place in a long and passionate line of socially reformist representations. It aims at effectiveness; it wants intensely to shock and to convince; it embodies an uncompromising commitment to the pragmatics of texts. *But how to distinguish the etiology of this horrid infliction, arising in the odious hypocrisy of the convent, from the narrative delusiveness of* La religieuse *itself?* We could say that *La religieuse* risks provoking in its textual situation the very derangement it describes in its narrative. It practices precisely the lie, the mode of deception, which has led the novel's unfortunate mad nun to her dreadful fate.

The truth is *one* because it is *constrained*. You can tell nearly any lie you want—as the other sisters do with Suzanne in the attempt to manage her horror at the mad nun's plight. The breathless accumulation, the panicked superfluity of the tales the sisters tell Suzanne marks them as lies. Once language detaches itself from material anchor, from connection to inward conviction or outward reality, then constraint evaporates, and all stories become possible.[6] In that sense fictions *need* to shuck off bodies in order to unfold their capacity for invention. But the latter attainment is double-edged. The capacity for fiction doesn't come free. Acting it out, it now emerges, entails the cost of an uncanny disorientation.

We pull back from such a discovery. We would like to re-segregate narrative's

5. Diderot's sister Angélique could have been the tortured nun described. In 1748, at the age of twenty-eight, she died insane in the Ursuline convent in Langres (see *DFPV* 11:92 n. 16).

6. The situation has the same structure as the limitless transformation Freud posited concerning the contents of consciousness in the psychoanalytic paradigm, once the possibility of their mutation from the timeless registrations of the unconscious has been admitted. See Terdiman, *Present Past*, 290–92.

danger from its evident utility. We would like to distinguish diverse flavors of prevarication—"white" lies versus "black" ones.[7] But, in seeking to separate the beneficent falsehoods from the malignant ones, consciousness registers their deeper identity. In response to the rivers of lies to which she has been forced to listen, Suzanne makes her own terse pledge to hold her own language to the truth in the only way that seems dependable: *she will take no vow; she will not speak at all.* "The crazed nun haunted my mind, and I renewed my pledge that I would never take my vows" (93).

The critique of language goes still deeper. At the very center of the catalog of lies Suzanne is exposed to, we find a castigation of *literature itself* as the cause of the mad nun's dementia: "she had read pernicious books which had corrupted her mind."[8] We don't know the character of the books her sisters claim are responsible for the poor nun's insanity. Were they theologically heretical or only erotically novelistic? But what is active here is a foundational stigmatization of *pornography* as the cause of derangement. Pornography is quintessentially *embodied language.* It is always in touch with bodies.[9] To the extent that we keep the body at the center of our encounter with texts, then pornography stands as the limiting case of all writing. But the novel's reflection upon its own mode of effectiveness stabilizes nothing. The complications and the contradictions of the connection between texts and bodies pull it inside out.

Passing from the stratum of fiction through the illusion of verisimilitude, at a certain point we reach the factual and the veridical—the truth of the text's own composition. Someone wrote it, with some intention. In the case of *La religieuse* the Grimm-Diderot preface stands in for such an account. But even the preface devolves into fictionality. When does one cross the border of a fiction, and what are the consequences for textual pragmatics—and ethics—if we *don't* cross it, if we remain on the *fictional* side? Then we could reconceive the convent as the locus of an initiation into the representational uncertainty that

7. The text is conscious of this tendency and practices it in concrete situations. Thus, the pseudo-Madame Madin, who has supposedly given Suzanne asylum in Paris, writes to Croismare that he can rely absolutely upon Madin's veracity. But on the same page she reveals that she has herself lied to Suzanne concerning the seal on the Marquis's letter (43).

8. The classification of *La religieuse* itself under the category of damned and damning books only completes the complication of the contraries that a view more confident of the possibility of distinguishing verisimilitude from veracity would have sought, against the inner logic of the text itself, to insist upon.

9. See Goulemot, *Forbidden Texts.* The title of the original French edition (*Ces livres qu'on ne lit que d'une main*) foregrounds even more powerfully the characteristic of quintessential embodiment which defines pornography.

the novel itself turns into text. Deception turns out to be the way of the world—at least as the world is figured in language. And deception does not stop conveniently at the inside border of the text's own fictive frame.

Suzanne is the novelist within this novel. For her what she writes is veridical. That, we say, is *fiction*. Being a fiction, Suzanne is not lying. But what about Diderot? One frame farther from the center of the narrative, where language resutures with truth, he is deeply skeptical that the problem Suzanne's text instantiates can be solved so neatly. Verisimilitude only makes it *worse*. Thus, Diderot's anatomy of prevarication reaches beyond the partition that separates the convent from the rest of social existence. Then what circulates in the text becomes the very question of *circulation itself*: of language's intrinsic potential for detachment from the veridical and from the material circumstances in which it is utilized.

In our post-Enlightenment inheritance we may feel we have sorted out these cases. But our representations only reshuffle the deck again to pull *all* language performances into the homogenization of textualism. These two sortings do not cohere. Precisely and prophetically, this problematic preoccupies *La religieuse*. Diderot's fiction is generating its own theory about fiction and its contradictions. The novel, we might say, is deconstructing itself *avant la lettre*. Whenever human interests are involved, the link between representation and truth becomes arduous.

But with texts what else could happen? Fiction, it would seem, is colonizing the entire realm of representation. But if that is the case, the epistemology that we can rely on for stories might well induce in any reader the sort of anxiety about their credibility which Diderot seems so concerned to plumb. And, detached from their anchors to material cause, the material *effects* of narrative begin to take on a ghostly and disturbing irreality, as if a house were found floating somehow mysteriously off its foundation. Language itself seems caught in such precariousness.

Suzanne's vow is the decisive linguistic act in *La religieuse*: the performative question around which everything turns, the critical experiment for the pragmatics of narrative and language in the novel. Is her vow coerced? Is it voluntary? Or, despite the solemnity and consequentiality with which such ritual is invested, does it, rather, lie somewhere undecidably in between? What coefficient of credibility should be granted to it? And to what degree does our uncertainty about Suzanne's pronouncement reflect back on the credit we can accord to *any* speech?

In the novel law and human compassion both test their interpretive capacities upon the utterance of Suzanne's vow. From within its more soulless protocols the law decrees the maintenance of her pledge, reaffirms and reimposes it. But compassion rebels, horrified that a promise made by someone suffering this woman's jeopardy could be considered binding, still less be enforced against her by the authority of the state. Diderot's reformist commitment projects this more generous view. But behind it the novel poses an even deeper question, an enigma *no* interpretation can reliably stabilize: how could this lamentable promise have been uttered to begin with? For we cannot forget Suzanne's resolution of *silence* in response to the spectacle of the mad nun and her treatment by her sisters. Against that background how could her *own* speech so divorce itself from intention to the point of miscarrying so radically and so disastrously?

The novel is preoccupied with this paradox, and it demonstrates a deep intuition concerning it. *La religieuse* roots its understanding in the relation between bodies and texts which the novel works upon and worries about. The text construes Suzanne's vow under the sign of *fiction*—that is, as an utterance constituted by an uncanny and disorienting *disembodiment*. Here is how the novel puts it in a letter from Suzanne to Croismare:

> The supervisor of the novices and my companions entered; they took off my religious habit and I was dressed in secular clothes; you are familiar with the custom. I heard nothing of what was being said around me, I had almost been reduced to the state of an automaton, I sensed nothing of what was happening. From moment to moment little convulsions ran through me. I was told what to do; often they had to repeat because I understood nothing the first time, and I did it. . . .
>
> At that moment the bells began; I went down. There was only a small congregation; the sermon may have been good or bad, I didn't hear any of it. They determined what I did throughout this morning which was non-existent in my life, for I never knew how long it lasted; I don't know what I did nor what I said. They presumably questioned me, I presumably answered, I pronounced vows, but I have no memory of them. (123–24)

The description conveys the dissociated quality of a fugue state or a dream. But in the narrative system of *La religieuse* this is the time and the space of *fiction*, in which lived connection to the body is unhinged and broken off. Suzanne is often alienated—she uses precisely this term ("j'ai été ce qu'on appelle physiquement aliénée" [124; see also 153]) to describe her state since the profession of her vows. But nowhere else in the novel is she so radically disunited from her somatic existence, to the point that even her senses are systematically disabled.

Given the strange circumstances of her genesis, Suzanne is always an undecidable figure. Within the structure of the hoax she is an embodied, suffering unfortunate. But for the narrative that developed out of the deception she is dematerialized like any imaginary character. At the moment of the vow, however, even within the frame of the originary lie, she surrenders materiality entirely. It is as if in this ultimate instance of linguistic articulation the text's transition from *representation* to *fiction* was being diagrammatically enacted by a progressive effacement of the physical. And it is because of her eerie decorporealization in the moment of the pronouncement of her vows that the latter can take on the undecidability of any made-up utterance, detached forever from its anchor in the experience and intention of a material body. *Alienation* thus comes to be conceivable as the experiential cognate or substrate of *fictionality itself.*

> Et moi, je m'arrête, parce que je vous ai dit de ces deux personnages tout ce que j'en sais.—Et les amours de Jacques? . . . Je vois, lecteur, que cela vous fâche; eh bien, reprenez son récit où il l'a laissé, et continuez-le à votre fantaisie.
> [And for my part I'm stopping here, since I've told you everything I know about these two characters.—But what about Jacques' love affair? I can see, reader, that this aggravates you; well, take up his tale where he left off, and continue it however you like.]
>
> —DIDEROT, *Jacques le fataliste*, DFVP 23:287

When it loses its anchor in materiality, *time* volatilizes in the same way language does. Its elision is the sign of what gets repressed in fictions: real-world constraint, the irreducible refractoriness that defines the phenomenology of any process that we experience within the frame of our material existence. This displacement into the liberation of fantasy *exempts us from bodies*. The resources and the consequences of such abstraction, the pattern of such release from the duress of materiality, are fundamental elements that Enlightenment fictions were investigating.

Consider Diderot's narrative of narrative itself in *Jacques le fataliste*—the second of his great novels, begun in 1771.[10] In the French novel nothing like *Jacques* had been seen before. What I want to emphasize here is the intricacy of

10. See Undank, "New Date for *Jacques le fataliste*," 433–37.

the text's play with storytelling—its conjuring with the seemingly limitless lability of fiction and its testing of the limits of this process.

The incident at the origin of the novel was stolen from *Tristram Shandy*. But the whole artifice of *Jacques* is to diminish the importance of the originary plot, which never develops, which is in fact systematically thwarted and finally drowned by a torrent of other tales, discussions, debates, and interruptions having nothing whatever to do with the account of the protagonist's knee wound or of his fabled but never narrated love story. In *Jacques* the tale is a story of how a cascade of *other* fictions, conjured up as if effortlessly out of language itself, can displace and submerge the performance of any narrative. What emerges from such a phenomenology of the diegetic is that the limitations material reality sets in the way of action, activity, and practice are suspended when it comes to the telling of tales. *Nothing seems able to limit the creation of stories.*

Diderot's intense, seemingly involuntary, and nearly obsessive affection for narratives is pushed here to an unreasonable, excessive, scandalous pitch. Everyone in the novel has an irrepressible taste for tales. But this propensity to tell kills telling. The characters love a story so much they are unable to conclude one before beginning several others. At that point, as Diderot wryly says himself, "adieu les amours de Jacques" (goodbye to Jacques' love affair) (*Jacques*, DFVP 23:45):

Jacques—You have an uncontrollable taste for stories!

Master—It's true, they teach me and entertain me. A good storyteller is a rare person.

Jacques—And that's precisely why I don't like stories, unless I'm telling them myself.

Master—You prefer to speak badly rather than to stay silent.

Jacques—That's true. (23:171)

The struggle for the control of telling is foregrounded in this exchange. It reaches regular paroxysms throughout the text. Each such incident demonstrates something deep about the power of narrative to survive even the most concerted disruption or disturbance. But, systematically, the promise of plot continuity proves false. We will wait in vain for Jacques' amours.

This series of imaginary contentions between master and servant reads the materiality of time. It stages a fundamental dialectic: between, on the one hand, the frustration continually regenerated in suspense through which time's refractoriness is figured; and, on the other hand, the untrammeled freedom that the teller of a tale experiences in marshaling the elements of a story out of the limitless freedom of fantasy.

Diderot was well aware that the conjured form of imagination we seek in novels has been constructed in large part by our experience of them. The cognitive capacity for fictions both creates its demand upon us and provides the means—a new or renewed genre of writing—which will permit us to fulfill it. But like *La religieuse*, *Jacques le fataliste* is uncomfortable with any easy celebration of such conventions. This is why Diderot rings a series of changes on the formulas by which the novels of his period proclaimed their own veracity: "It's obvious I'm not writing a novel, since I leave out everything that a novelist would not fail to put in. Anyone who takes what I write as truth might well be more in the right than those who think of it as fiction" (23:35). The deconstructive rhetoric is artfully sly. It makes no positive assertion. Rather, it emphasizes an ambiguous and flickering hypothesis, without any conclusion. But if "belief" or verisimilitude provided a sufficient warrant for truth, the problem of fiction would neatly dissolve. Like *La religieuse*, *Jacques* stands as evidence not of its dissolution but of its arduousness and its undecidability.

Several times in my discussion I have referred to Diderot's exclamation about the ease with which we make up stories. Now it may be possible to complicate and extend understanding of it. *Jacques le fataliste* could be conceived as a textual experiment to discover whether, in the face of the apparently effortless conjuring of reality through language, there are *any* constraints upon the freedom of the maker of fictions. But, like Freud exploring the limitless transformation of the contents of consciousness, in *Jacques*, as previously in *La religieuse*, Diderot seems to discover an untrammeled *wantonness* in the capacity of fictionality to generate tales. No matter how systematically one seeks to disrupt them, they don't seem to suffer arrest. Then the puzzle becomes differentiating license from licentiousness, separating the positive gains of liberty from the more ambiguous advantages of libertinage.

So, while Diderot exults in his "fantaisie" (23:287) and his autonomy in composing the tangled fictions of *Jacques le fataliste* and in the power it gives him over the reader, whom he never ceases to provoke and to harass, in that same moment and through that same cause he uncovers the constitutive ambiguity of *any* power relationship—from the one that ties Jacques and his Master, via Hegel, to the one that ties writer and reader. This hierarchy is written into the structure of *Jacques*. Supposedly, the Master controls Jacques, his servant, but the conduct of the servant and of the story demonstrates that the contrary is true. As the Master says himself, "This rascal [Jacques] can make me do whatever he wants" (23:252).[11] A similar ambiguity or reversal links writer and reader. Diderot appears to dialogue and to negotiate with the reader at every turn in the story. But, finally, the reader turns out to be powerless in the face of fiction.

Supposedly, from fictions we gain an increase in cognitive freedom. But the configuration Diderot produces in his novel rather *subjects* readers to stories in a way that might seem threatening. In such a circumstance a nominal advantage flips over and transforms itself into something like a disability. In his conduct of the story the narrator of *Jacques* focuses upon the mechanism and the meaning of this reversal. He does so by testing whether there is *any* way of forestalling or inhibiting it. As early as the third page of the novel, Diderot begins a series of interruptions whose objective is to put verisimilitude under stress, to discover the limits of fictive illusion. But, though these interventions have the apparent purpose of submitting this illusion to a salutary and liberating *criticism*, thereby disclosing to readers their power to undo or to resist the artifice of fictionality, the result they achieve is the opposite. As readers, we remain at the mercy of an illusion that can seemingly resist *any* degree of disruption. And we find ourselves subjected to the authority of a narrative as cranky and cantankerous as the narrators we encounter, and with whom we must contend, in this tale.

This contention has attracted the attention of virtually every critic who has considered *Jacques*. Here one of the earliest examples in the novel can stand for dozens of others that punctuate and interrupt it throughout: "Jacques began the story of his love affairs. It was after lunch: the air was heavy. . . . As you can see, Reader, I'm on a roll, and it would be entirely within my power to make you wait a year, two years, three years, for the story of Jacques' love affairs, by separating him from his Master and exposing them to whatever dangers I might

---

11. Notoriously, the same reversibility is a central theme of *Le neveu de Rameau*, in the text's interrogation of the dominance of the monarch and the subservience of his subjects, progressing down a social pecking order, quintessentially including the royal fool, which turns out to invert itself before our eyes. As Rameau puts it to the philosopher: "With the greats of the world there is no better part to play than the fool. For a long time the King had his official fool, but no King has ever had an official wise man. I'm Bertin's fool and fool to many others, perhaps I'm your fool right now, or perhaps you're mine. A wise person would not have a fool; hence anyone who has a fool is not wise; if he is not wise perhaps he's a fool and, perhaps, even if he were the King himself, his fool's fool" (*DFVP* 12:138–39).

decide. What's to prevent me from marrying off the Master and then cuckolding him? Or shipping Jacques off to the Indies?" (*DFPV* 23:24–25).

Critics have offered a variety of explanations for these disruptions. One notion views the narrator's interruptions as an emblem or enactment of verisimilitude, imitating the ordinary experience of disturbance which punctuates life. Another considers that the interventions communicate Diderot's ridicule of novelistic convention.[12] In any case the form of these disruptions is clear and systematic. The tale gets going; the reader settles into absorption in the story; the fictive illusion establishes itself. Abruptly, the narrator breaks in and interrupts the flow, challenging the reader with a claim to absolute authority.

The lexicon of narratorial *power* is conspicuous here. But what stands behind its pugnacity? The discovery of this power is what led to Diderot's exultant "Qu'il est facile de faire des contes!" But a closer look suggests that the excitement conveyed by this exclamation is ambiguous. For the dialectic of telling tales which Diderot has been exploring depends not upon the narrator's triumphant conquest of sovereignty but, rather, upon the disappearance of anything that might effectively resist it. *The recession of bodies that is the enabling condition of fiction leaves narrative with nothing to stand up against it.* Then narratorial power takes on a kind of negative capability that arises in the collapse of any material constraint upon its scope, in what we might term the "metastasis" of language's mysterious and irresistible capacity to signify anything whatever.

So the narrator's proto-sadism translates a disconcerting infirmity in narrative's surround or setting. The narrator's impertinence then becomes readable as the mapping of a peculiar and disconcerting form of communicative relation, by which language is hypostatized as autonomous and turns its instrumentality back against everyone—narrator *and* interlocutor—in the perverse movement of instrumental reversal that I analyzed in chapter 1. It is as if through his derision of the reader's impotence Diderot kept trying to provoke a reaction that would finally set a limit to narrative power—and discovered that no constraint could be generated which could ever hold language to responsiveness and responsibility.

So the story line of *Jacques* goes into instant eclipse, and it never recovers. Diderot tortures his tale. But why would a writer do this? What impulse for self-destruction could explain the insistence of these interventions? An anxiety, a tension, inflect the nominally cheerful atmosphere of this novel. Beneath the

---

12. For an early expression of the first of these views, see, for example, Green, "Diderot's Fictional Worlds," 21. For the second, see Loy, *Diderot's Determined Fatalist*, 70.

bantering between author and reader, between master and servant, more profound than the complex web of the stories that begin without ever concluding, Diderot is exploring *limits*. He is attempting to discover if there are boundaries to the magical conjuration of which texts are capable and which had concerned him when he first analyzed it in Richardson. By accumulating obstacles to preservation of the fictive illusion, Diderot is measuring its power and its consequences. If fiction can triumph over these unrelenting interruptions, as over the repeated protestations of "historical accuracy" which by their very iteration eventually emphasize their falsity, over the authorial interventions whose threats to take the story in completely fantastical directions betray the already-existing fantasy that is *Jacques* to begin with—all this would demonstrate the virtual autonomy of the illusion thus challenged.

Jacques le fataliste is an experiment with the fictive illusion, a question asked about the power of texts.[13] In this novel Diderot seems to sacrifice the narrative to a contention different from the one I have traced confronting narrator and reader. This second struggle arises between the narrator's repeated protestations of the tale's veracity and his equally regular observations concerning its contingency and dependency upon will or caprice. But that conflict foregrounds the issue that I have been claiming stands at the heart of the textual operation.

The only possible guarantor of any narrative is the pressure put upon it by some material referent, some extra-diegetic reality to which it seeks to respond and in relation to which it measures its representation. Conversely, the eclipse of commitment to such referentiality leaves narrators free but also adrift. This discovery is a systematic counterpart of the one that in *La religieuse* precipitated out of the hoax of the Marquis de Croismare. Both novels are concerned to track down the lability that inheres in language and the exemption from constraint which narrative grants to anyone who deploys it. But for the political and social effectiveness of writing there are consequences of such franchise. An uncomfortable realization attends any revel celebrating the emancipation of narrative: truth recedes when texts are free.

---

13. When Robert Bresson (or his scenarist Jean Cocteau) chose episodes from *Jacques* as the basis for the plot of Bresson's "Les dames du Bois de Bologne" (1945), they directly transplanted into the film considerable portions of Diderot's dialogue. However, they systematically stripped out the frenetic torture of the narrative, which is so distinctive in the novel.

CHAPTER FOUR

Materiality, Language, and Money

> If the body had been easier to understand, nobody would have thought
> that we had a mind.   —RORTY, *Philosophy and the Mirror of Nature*, 239

Language's seeming exemption from material constraints would not be so un-settling if we didn't have our bodies to be concerned about. Without them we could blithely give ourselves over to play with the immateriality of texts. But, whatever may be our romance with such a liberation from corporeality in the contemporary period, the Enlightenment worried about bodies and about the complications of *representation* and of *politics* which arise in their irreducible consequentiality. That is why bodies are thematized so insistently—by some accounts, so scandalously—in Enlightenment texts.

I want to examine a significant emblem of such materialist concern, Diderot's *Encyclopédie* article "Jouissance" (the title enjoys the polysemy of the French word, giving the senses both of "pleasure" and of "orgasm").[1] In its celebra-tion of bodies and their physicality the article captures a powerful impulse in Enlightenment thought. Its most resonant passage may well be its representa-tion of materialism's claims on understanding and of reason's coordinate non-

1. The text has been well studied—most recently by Benrekassa, *Le Langage des Lumières*, chap. 5. See note on citations from the *Encylopédie* in the Works Cited. I cite here from "Jouissance," *DFPV* 7:575–77.

sovereignty: "When an individual meets another of the same species and of a different sex, all experience of any other want is suspended; the heart flutters; the limbs quiver; voluptuous images run through the brain; floods of humors run through the nerves, stimulate them, and end up in the seat of a new sense that manifests itself and torments us. Sight becomes distorted, delirium arises; *reason the slave of instinct limits itself to serving the latter, and nature is satisfied*"[2] (*DFPV* 7:576; emph. added).

This power of materiality to overwhelm cognition, of corporeality to submerge language, complicates any simple understanding of Enlightenment "rationality." For Diderot rationality, however capital, is rooted in organic nature and in biology, which (according to this text) it serves as if with the "cunning of reason" which Hegel would later theorize.[3] As Richard Rorty implies in the epigraph to this chapter, if only we could understand *bodies*, we might not be so obsessed with *understanding*. This perspective again urges careful attention to our contemporary hypostasis of language's domination of social existence.

"Jouissance" seeks to reassess the claims of materiality in order to foreground respect for bodies in the face of the political and theological subjections of a repressive state. But such a rebalancing in favor of the body is even more intensely at issue in *La religieuse*. Pain has the same capacity to overwhelm reason as does pleasure. So while the character of the experience at their centers is quite different in "Jouissance" and in *La religieuse*, the re-situation of rationality and of language, and the recalibration of their relationship to materiality, is revealingly parallel. But there are also complications in such a comparison.

La religieuse worries about bodies' capacities to withstand the force of representations—in effect to *survive language*. Consider Suzanne Simonin's medical and physical tribulations in the novel, from the bleedings she is described as enduring in the preface to the mortifications she is made to undergo in the *Amende honorable* to which she is condemned.[4] These afflictions are painstakingly—and painfully—described. Of course, they only concern a nonexistent

2. The homophobia (or at least compulsory heterosexuality) visible here is characteristic of Diderot's period and (along with the reflexive traces of misogyny that often marked it) form one motivation for our contemporary resistance today to the Enlightenment's claims and to its mode of understanding. Accepting the force of these criticisms, we need nonetheless to ask how much of fundamental Enlightenment insights would be undermined if these relics of intolerance were expunged. I consider Diderot's homophobia further in subsequent pages.

3. See Hegel, *Philosophy of History*, pt. 3, sec. 2 (2).

4. We could translate the term as "honorable penance." The ironic euphemism of this name for the torture Suzanne is made to undergo is another trace of Diderot's skepticism about the reliability of relationship between language and veracity.

body. But this body is intensely charismatic and projected as such, a body that (as in Croismare's imagined tears) focuses our sympathy for the suffering of real bodies. That consequence will always remain incommensurable with any purely *textual* effect.

In *La religieuse* bodies and texts interact most consequentially in *seduction*. Seduction happens when a text maneuvers for the control or compliance of a body, when it projects a false or constructed reality, believable but mendacious, intended to mislead. But that means that the theme of seduction foregrounds the enigma of *textuality itself*. Not surprisingly, seduction is a theme that *La religieuse* proclaims and presses.[5] Suzanne talks about "seduction" all the time. She describes the period of her novitiate, and particularly the contrived blandishments of her convent superiors during this time, as "a most subtle and calculated course of seduction." The pernicious function of the "mère des novices"—the nun supervising postulants—is to beguile and deceive: "She is the one who lulls you and puts you to sleep, who throws dust in your eyes and hypnotizes you." The sexualized overtones of what Suzanne characterizes as "this malignant art" are unmistakable (91). They develop thematically into the more overtly erotic passages later in the novel. But already at this relatively early point in the evolution of the imagery it is becoming difficult to distinguish between the metaphorical figure of seduction and a literal perversion or possession of Suzanne's body. *Representation* works this "malignant art": words and gestures—language—which conscript corporeality.

But the most unsettling element of the analysis of how texts commandeer materiality is not that they can be utilized deliberately for evil purposes but that they escape the agency of their own creator and work evil without anyone's intending it. Their power turns back upon us, and, because language is not masterable, we delude *even without meaning to*. Thus, as I examined in chapter 3, the virtuous Madame de Moni, whose intentions with regard to Suzanne are unquestionably benign, is nonetheless responsible for ruining her:

> I went through my novitiate without any feelings of distaste. . . . There was noth-
> ing unhappy about [this period] except a feeling inside myself that I was pro-
> ceeding step by step toward a calling for which I was not suited at all. . . . I
> would go straight to my good Mother Superior who would embrace me, would

5. Eve Kosofsky Sedgwick has provided the most careful treatment of "seduction" in relation to *La religieuse*, particularly attentive to the way the narrative draws us into the tale. My perspective here differs from hers. See "Privilege of Unknowing."

strengthen my soul, would reason powerfully with me and always ended up by saying, ". . . Come, my child, let us kneel down and pray. . . ." She would then prostrate herself and pray aloud, but with such sweetness, such eloquence, such gentleness, such exaltation and such strength that you would have said she was inspired by the spirit of God. Her thoughts, her expressions, her images went straight to your heart. At first you listened, then little by little you were carried along, *you became one with her, your soul thrilled and you shared her ecstasy. Her object was not seduction, but that is what she achieved.* (118–19; emph. added)

In its sequence of sly double entendres—recall "Jouissance"—the passage figures a classic course of debauchment through the insidious functioning of words. Such language about the power of language over bodies, so palpably responsive on the level of corporeality to the verbal enactments of Suzanne's unwitting seducer, ends up seeming disturbing.

In an extended and diagnostic form this disconcerting ambiguity reproduces itself in the celebrated homoerotic scenes in Suzanne's third convent, in Arpajon. There, in the most literal sense, the Mother Superior does indeed intend Suzanne's seduction. The scholarly tradition has generally seen this conduct as a defilement, and clearly Diderot intends his depiction to deepen his critique of the unnaturalness of cloistered existence.[6] But a closer look demonstrates some unresolved perplexities in this reading of the text.

To begin with, while the lesbian Superior of Arpajon is made to suffer extreme agony in the novel, by contrast Suzanne's sadistic Superior at Sainte-Marie is never punished.[7] In our own period we have learned that, when any pattern of sexual politics is being represented or assessed, homophobia may always be in the wings. And, despite Diderot's clear embrace of sexuality as a figure of liberation elsewhere in his work, the valence he attributes to lesbianism here is more negative than that which he attributes to a cruelty that, however grotesque, is never explicitly sexualized.[8]

But, if we examine the Superior of Arpajon closely, we can detect a veiled structure of ambiguity underlying the novel's seemingly unequivocal condem-

---

6. On the specifically situational reformist intention of the novel, see Ellrich, "Rhetoric of *La religieuse* and Eighteenth-Century Forensic Rhetoric."

7. Caplan, *Framed Narratives*, 71.

8. For Diderot's assessment of sexuality, see among many other texts the *Supplément au voyage de Bougainville*. Leo Spitzer was one of the earliest to put emphasis on the political implications of sexuality in Diderot and to analyze the meaning of the Superior of Arpajon; see his remarkable discussion (referred to earlier) in *Linguistics and Literary History*, esp. 151.

nation of her. It emerges in Suzanne's description of the Mother Superior's *sensitivity*: "In truth, that mad woman had an unbelievable sensitivity and the most intense taste for music; I have never known anyone upon whom it produced such singular effects" (223–24). After Suzanne reports the Mother Superior's conduct to her confessor and he imposes strict penitence upon her, she finds herself bewildered by his condemnation of the Superior's conduct:

> What did he find so peculiar in the harpsichord incident? Are there not people upon whom music makes the most powerful impression? I've been told myself that certain musical passages, certain modulations, completely alter my own facial expression; in such moments I was quite beside myself and I hardly knew what I was doing. Yet I don't believe I was any the less innocent for that. Why could it not have been the same with my Superior, who despite her quirks and caprices was certainly one of the most sensitive women who ever existed? She could never hear a touching story without bursting into tears. (256)

This tearful response to music and—at the end of the passage—to *narrative* complicates the Mother Superior of Arpajon. Unmistakably—if uncannily—she is transformed into something like a figure for Diderot himself. She becomes one of the primary bearers in Diderot's writing of the attribute of "sensibilité," of openness to suffering and to passion, which was one of Diderot's characteristic traits and which he regularly applauded both in his fictional and his nonfictional texts. We recall him telling Damilaville or d'Alainville of his own lachrymose paroxysms unleashed by the experience of stories.

The Mother Superior of Arpajon is not redeemed by these convergences. But they reproduce, on the level of what sexuality and erotic conduct figure in this text, the ambiguity that disturbs any simple practice of what Daniel Brewer has aptly termed "discursive politics."[9] The adequation of texts and referents, of writing and programmatic political intention, is unsettled by these moments of equivocation or involuntary signification. Here the power of language over bodies is foregrounded perhaps more forcefully than anywhere else in the novel. But the problem that *La religieuse* discovers itself instantiating and manifesting—as if against its own intentions—is the even more deeply disturbing uncertainty concerning an agent's power over language itself.

9. Brewer, *Discourse of Enlightenment*, 50.

L'argent est une richesse de fiction.
[Money is fictive wealth.]   —DIDEROT, "Argent," *Encyclopédie, DFPV* 5:470

How should we understand the problem of language and textuality about which Diderot worries in his narratives? Textuality engages us in what seems like a fruitless regress, a potentially endless series of reframings in which we seek a referential ground upon which we might distinguish the appearance of verisimilitude from the representation of truth. We live today *after* the "crisis of representation." It might seem that the path we have traveled toward skepticism concerning the possibility of capable connection between words and things could never be retraced. Yet there remains for many of us what I think is a productive nostalgia for a time when language seemed to have a more reliable relationship to materiality.

However naive such a seemingly anachronistic desire may seem in our postmodern period, it's easy to understand the impulse behind it. Despite the disdain for utility which we have inherited from nineteenth-century denunciations of middle-class ideology and practice, it would be hard to deny that language functions first of all to enable instrumental communication between real individuals in real situations. It does not seem unreasonable to suppose that *all* signifying behavior retains some connection with, and is to some degree informed by, such primal linguistic and social determination in materiality, in a world of real bodies.

So we look for bodies behind language. That is why the peculiar structure of the Croismare hoax—in which an intentionally delusive fictional narrative was devised by identifiable people to produce overt behavioral effects in another real person—seemed to offer the opening to a register of factuality that might partially extricate us from the closure of disembodied language. This, then, might permit some perspective upon the slippages of textuality which Diderot's text itself discovers in the course of its own realization—as if astonished to find itself victimized by its own attempt to victimize.

Unlike what happens in textualism today, Diderot's narratives do not dissolve or abrogate the links between language and materiality. But they *complicate* them diagnostically. Diderot bases his politics of discourse—a view, moreover, which generally reproduces Enlightenment norms—upon the notion that texts and materiality contact and mutually determine each other. It is no accident that one of the major foci of Derrida's deconstruction in *Of Grammatology* is Diderot's literary and intellectual rival, Rousseau. But Diderot's encounter with this problem can help us investigate our own perplexities concerning it.

For us a distinction between "fiction" (intended to be delusively verisimilar) and "nonfiction" (granted the capacity for reliable connection between word and referent) provides a neat sorting-out of the problem. We allow the language in poems to be about nothing, but the driving directions a Postmodern literary theorist downloads from the Web can get her to her destination without shaking her faith in language's fundamental autonomy. "Practical" texts such as the manual that came with your new printer can establish an otherwise unimaginable connection with material referentiality—or else you couldn't get on with your work. Put in a somewhat more sophisticated lexicon, "writerly" poetic and fictional texts exist in a self-referential dimension of language as it has been conceived since the Formalists, particularly Roman Jakobson and Jan Mukařovský, defined the parameters of the problem in the 1920s.[10] Poetry directs its (and attracts our) attention toward what Jakobson terms the "message" itself. Contrariwise, instruction manuals rebalance the communicative nexus and refer attention outward, toward the Jakobsonian "context."

Jakobson would have had no difficulty explaining how he could represent his own theory, or how critics such as Fredric Jameson or Jonathan Culler could explain it so cogently. He would have said that all of them direct themselves to a focus upon the practical, outwardly referential dimension of language use—to what we would call the "nonfictional" register. For Jakobson language could play the practical role or the poetic one or indeed many others, and he was able to sort out the parameters that governed what sort of language confronted us in each such paradigmatic case. In effect he was taking account of the diverse possibilities in language which Diderot was trying not so much to sort out as to *live in*. But Diderot doesn't really converge with this pragmatic discrimination between inward and outward referentiality. And his hesitation seems sensible. For, arguably, the logic of the distinctions pressed by Jakobson is entirely circular. You can write poetry if you and your reader *already know* how to mask off any irruption into the reading experience on the part of the concrete social world, of our quotidian beings and doings.

10. See Jakobson, "Linguistics and Poetics," 350–77. The structure of the distinction in question here was well captured in Jonathan Culler's discussion in *Structuralist Poetics*, esp. 56–57. Culler's account parallels Fredric Jameson's in *Prison-House of Language*, 202–3. The classic and still authoritative study of the Formalists is Erlich, *Russian Formalism*. Jakobson's influence upon Structuralism is well-known. It arose, in part, in the biographical determinations imposed by the Hitler period in Europe, which found both Jakobson and Claude Lévi-Strauss teaching in New York at the "University in Exile," as the New School for Social Research came to be known because, more than any other American institution, it received and found employment for academic refugees from Europe. Lévi-Strauss's contributions to Structuralism in Paris in the 1950s and afterward depended considerably upon his work with Jakobson in New York in the 1940s.

But Diderot would ask two questions. First, he would be concerned to know how and from where we acquire such a capacity. And, if we do acquire it, how do we know when to deploy it? For activation of this capacity assumes a knowledge that exceeds, and in an important sense overturns, the protocols of interpretation which govern the reading of a self-referential text. The act of reading, in other words, repudiates the very assumptions that made it possible. How does—how *can*—poetry know that it is *poetry*?[11]

Second, Diderot would want to know what costs we pay for such reduction or abstraction in our protocols of reading—ultimately, in our capacity for experiencing a total world. What do we lose or abandon in acquiring this new capacity? Diderot believed that the cost of resisting closure through such mechanisms was consequential. For him absolutizing or reifying language entailed a disabling limitation upon language's social effectiveness.

His way of thinking situates the problem in an area of puzzlement which challenges thinking today. Recall Jameson's critique of the orthodoxy prevalent among literary elites since the Symbolists (whose influence on the Russian and Prague Formalists needs always to be remembered and foregrounded). This orthodoxy considers the "poetic function"—in Jakobson's terms, emphasis on the message, on the utterance as a linguistic form—as having more value than any other function in language. Such preference traces its origins back to *L'art pour l'art* and to Gautier's influential contempt for utility in any form—most particularly the utility of language.[12]

Jameson's historicization of this attitude in *The Prison-House of Language* (203–4), and particularly in "The Ideology of the Text," is an important corrective.[13]

11. This paradox or *petitio principii* resembles the one that Sartre argued undermines the theory of Freud's "censor," the mind-function that determines which mental contents will remain accessible and which are to be relegated to the inaccessible unconscious. "The censor must choose [which place to send these contents] and in order to choose must be aware of so doing. . . . [But] how can we conceive of knowledge which is ignorant of itself?" *Being and Nothingness*, 52–53. I return to this issue in my final chapter.

12. I considered Gautier's Formalist formulations and motivations beginning in the 1830s earlier in chapter 2 and in Terdiman, *Present Past*, 159–63. These notions influenced writers from midcentury onward, particularly the Symbolists. I discuss the unconstrainable leakage of "auto-referentiality" in *Discourse/Counter-Discourse*, 306–21. Jameson's definition of *auto-referentiality* is helpful. He speaks of "the interpretation of a narrative in terms of language itself as some ultimate content" (*Prison-House*, 203). Although Jameson is speaking about narrative, his definition applies equally to poetic texts. But in the face of such a resolute quest for the self-containment and insulation of art language, in the mid-nineteenth century the question of genre arises with acute punctuality and disruptive force. The rise of the new genre of prose poetry subverts or worries the possibility of literary enclosure in auto-referentiality. See Terdiman, *Discourse/Counter-Discourse*, pt. 3, chaps. 6–7.

13. Jameson, *Prison-House of Language*, 203–4; "The Ideology of the Text," *Ideologies of Theory*, 1:17–71.

The analysis undercuts familiar transhistorical presumptions that the linguistic orientation valued in literary self-referentiality is privileged over the others of which language is capable. Still less can we comfortably adopt the position implied by further developments in contemporary thinking about language which transform the self-referential reduction, the choice to adopt a particular interpretive mode, into an untranscendable absolute. Then "language" becomes no more or less than Jakobson's self-referential message. But no one really believes the implications of such a theoretical narrowing. Consequently, I think one way of understanding the Derridean version of Poststructuralism would hold that the careful distinctions and modulations of linguistic registers with which Diderot was experimenting in the 1760s and afterward, and which were systematized much later in Russian and Prague Formalist theory, are collapsed in Derrida's radically absolutist projection of language.[14]

In relation to Diderot's diagnostic perplexity about the "facility" of stories, I want to ask what was happening in the *non*fictional texts he was writing at the same time he pursued his con game fictional experiment in *La religieuse*. Diderot, I argued, worried about a tendency to increasing disconnection between the concrete world and a world of growing abstraction and mystification—about a growing distance between materiality, on the one hand, and representation, on the other.

Such a tendency has clear implications for the possibilities and modalities of reform, of *politics*, in the Enlightenment period. Thus, in light of my discussion of his novels I want to examine Diderot's most resolutely instrumental texts. I construe these as analogues for the reflection on the temptations of textualism that is focused by the hoax in *La religieuse*, by the delusive construction of the suffering body of Suzanne Simonin, and by the novel's recognition of the enigmas of textual agency. So I will retriangulate my discussion of the fictional narratives by turning from the scandalous irrationalities of Old Regime monastic imprisonment to another sphere that deeply preoccupied the thinkers and reformers of the Enlightenment: the mysteries of a proto-capitalist economy and the perplexities of money.

I begin with a particularly rich text from the *Encyclopédie*. In the article there entitled "Argent" (both "silver" and "money") Diderot starts his analysis by describing the mining of silver:

---

14. Eve Tavor Bannet discusses this reformulation with particular acuteness. See *Structuralism and the Logic of Dissent*, 184 ff.

The richest and most abundant silver mines are in America, above all in the Potosí district of Peru. At first the veins of the mine in the mountains of Potosí were quite shallow. Little by little it became necessary to penetrate into the heart of the mountain to follow the veins; currently the depths are so great that it requires more than four hundred steps to reach the bottom of the mine. . . . Working the mine becomes more difficult every day; it is quite hazardous for the majority of workers on account of the vapors that emerge from the depths of the shaft, and which disperse into the air; no workers can survive such poisonous air for more than one day in a row. . . . Nearly all the workers who have toiled in the mines for a significant portion of their lives are crippled. People would be astonished if they knew how many Indians had lost their lives in this labor since these mines have been worked, and how many are still losing their lives every day. (*DFPV* 5:462–63)

The account recalls Montaigne's passionate critique of the subjections of colonialism in "On Cannibals" and "On Vehicles."[15] Like those essays, which Diderot knew well, "Argent" intends to make exploitation appear palpable and appalling. But here I want to project a connection between Diderot's article on "silver" and the larger narrative complex of *La religieuse*. The affiliation that I propose between these two texts is less a matter of conscious intertextuality than of a common preoccupation with the relationship between materiality and language, and a parallel strategy for exploring this enigma.

Given commitment to the reform of the patent abuses that each of these texts stigmatizes, it is not surprising that both foreground and focus upon the pain of human bodies—Suzanne Simonin's in the novel, the crippled and poisoned Peruvian miners in "Argent." Diderot's evocation of such corporeal suffering is intense and effective. But I want to draw attention here to the way that, in both texts, the register of the corporeal is brought into tense and problematic contact with the register of language.

Diderot refuses to isolate and abstract the bodies of the Peruvian miners or the metallic silver they bring to the surface and make available for others. These

15. From the latter essay (*Essais*, bk. 3, chap. 6), recall Montaigne's fulminating peroration concerning the early exploitation of New World people: "Who ever valued the benefits of trade and commerce at so high a price? So many towns razed to the ground, so many nations exterminated, so many millions put to the sword, and the richest and most beautiful part of the world turned upside down for the benefit of the pearl and pepper trade. Base commercial victories [*mécaniques victoires*]" (*Essays*, 279; trans. modified). The Potosí district, whose brutal silver mines Diderot was describing, is now part of Bolivia. And today the miners are still dying there. See Forero, "As Bolivian Miners Die, Boys are Left to Toil."

materialities initiate and put in motion a pattern of *circulation* which Diderot intends to trace out and pursue to loci distant from the origin of the chain of connections he is constructing. Economies are continuous. They link materialities and meanings in a way that is obscure or invisible in the case of fictional texts. The *Encyclopédie* insists upon such continuity in another of its articles, "Finances."[16] Concerning the state economy analyzed under the name of "finance," the *Encyclopédie* tells us: "Everything is connected, everything touches everything else, everything forms a whole: men and things represent each other reciprocally in every part; and nothing in any part is indifferent, since with finance, as with electricity, the least movement propagates rapidly from the person whose hand is closest to the generating globe to the one furthest from it" (CD-ROM ed., s.v. "Finances").

The imagery derives from eighteenth-century experiments with static electricity and the discovery of its seemingly magical capacity to circulate through bodies. Then the analogy between economic and electrical connection becomes particularly suggestive because it expresses the mystery by which at a distance invisible forces act upon bodies. This is the connection that Diderot is intent upon tracing in "Argent." To begin with, he does so through the polysemous title word itself. After discussing the extraction of the elemental metal, "Argent" goes on to consider what could be responsible for the mysterious transformation of *silver* into *money*: " '*Argent*' in French is the generic term for any form of the signs of wealth circulating in commerce: gold, monetized silver, notes of all kinds, etc. . . . As a metal, silver has a value like all other commodities; but it has another value as the sign of these commodities" (469).

Here a textual alchemy is happening before our eyes: elemental metal is mutating into specie, specie is volatilizing into signs. In other words, materiality is transforming itself into language. Despite the geographical and conceptual remoteness that separates the different parts of the circulation system of which they form the origin, the suffering bodies of the Peruvian miners and the products of their excruciating labor are indissolubly linked to the creation of meanings *in France*.

The link between bodies and representation in "Argent" parallels the one I have been analyzing in the case of Diderot's fictional narratives. Each starts with corporeality and ends with semiotics. Each then evokes a diagnostically

16. By Charles Étienne Pesselier, an official in the Fermes Générales, the French national taxation administration. See Lough, *"Encyclopédie,"* 50. See note on citations from the *Encyclopédie* in the Works Cited.

puzzling experience of transformation—one whose mechanism is not the less obscure for all its quotidian familiarity. But the analogy I am pressing between the economic and the literary circuits may help us understand the latter. For the objectification of economic existence makes it easier to seize the links in *that* system than is the case of the truly mysterious networks of exchange, circulation, reference, and meaning which circulate in the secret convent world of *La religieuse* or, more broadly, in the literary mutations that transform a hoax into a narrative and bodies into fiction.

The mines of Peru are situated at the material, *embodied* origin of a circuit that reaches increasingly far from the mountains of Potosí. From metal to money and beyond, the connection is continuous, unbroken. Then the traces of the labor performed by these miners and the horrifying dangers to which these bodies are exposed in procuring what will progressively transform itself into specie dissolve and eventually become invisible. That is the heart of the enigma. In "Argent" Diderot figures it in the structure and images of his account itself, by the progressively increasing depth of the mine he described by the descent into it, by the growing difficulty of the extraction, and even by the progressively hazardous vapors that emerge from the bottom of the shaft. The image of the mine and its increasingly mysterious and mystifying product then stands both as an instantiation of and as a paradigm for hermeneusis. Textualism here enacts and simultaneously reflects upon its own transformative and interpretive activity.

Simultaneously, it signals another mode of mutation, from the excruciating temporality of the miners' labor to the increasingly timeless time of the circulation of increasingly impalpable value—the *fictions of wealth* Diderot speaks of in the passage I cited as the epigraph to this section. This conversion of diachronicity to instantaneity is particularly disturbing for analysis. For specie is not the end point of the circuit that begins in the silver mine. In the eighteenth century the heart of preoccupation about the economy was an even more baffling transmutation of value from its material avatar in metal (or for the Physiocrats in land) to progressively more enigmatic and ethereal appearances in banknotes and, above all, in *credit*.

Diderot's period still remembered well the collapse of John Law's credit system, which nearly bankrupted France in October 1720. Law had sought to convert the French economy from reliance upon specie to radically expanded forms of credit. The *Encyclopédie*—in the article titled "Système (*finance*)," attributed to the chevalier de Jaucourt—gives a striking account of the disaster: "[Law's plan was to] introduce paper money and banknotes in the French kingdom to circulate and represent specie. It was an edifice built by a clever architect, but one whose foundations had been designed for only three stories. However a powerful conspiracy formed against the architect and had sufficient power [*crédit*] to induce the government to build the edifice up seven stories high, such that the foundation could not support the extra weight and it collapsed, the edifice being destroyed from top to bottom."[17]

We are far from the silver mines of Peru. The attempt to represent Law's chimerical system seems to drive analysis itself away from literality and toward a sequence of increasingly baroque images that might capture the inherent mysteriousness of intangible representations of value—and particularly their baffling capacity to evaporate instantaneously. The Encyclopedists, and Diderot in particular, were familiar with Montesquieu's representation of Law's system and its collapse in *Les lettres persanes*. It occurs in *Lettre* 142, in the celebrated "Fragment d'un ancien mythologiste."[18] In this text Law is figured as the son of Eolus, who had taught him how to capture the wind in a goatskin. Accompanied by the god of chance, Law traveled the world selling his merchandise. When he got to Bétique (France), he addressed the populace: "People of Bétique, you think you are rich because you have gold and silver. Your misapprehension fills me with pity. Believe me, leave the country of vile metals and enter the *Empire of Imagination*. I promise you riches that will astonish you" (307–8; emph. added).

Law persuades the French to abandon their gold and precious stones. In exchange, in the form of bills of exchange and paper money (*écriteaux*), he promises them *imagination* as wealth. These phantasmagoric representations supersede materialities (308). The results parallel the outcome of most such seductions. A satire of the process from this period is direct, if vulgar:

17. *Encyclopédie*, CD-ROM ed., s.v. "Système (*finance*)." An extended discussion of Law's system and of Montesquieu's opposition to it can be found in Kavanagh, *Enlightenment and the Shadows of Chance*, chap. 3. Fernand Braudel gives a powerful evocation of these developments on the economic and socio-ideological levels in *Identity of France*, vol. 2: *People and Production*, chap. 15.

18. Montesquieu, *Lettres persanes*, 307–10. In *L'Esprit des lois* (bk. 19, chap. 27) Montesquieu provided a more serious analysis of how society might understand and marshal the new resource of credit. For him the key was tying any credit (state debt) to the material—if mobile—goods of society. Clearly, the further one gets from materiality, the more one moves toward abstraction, then the greater the danger: bullion is better than demand notes; demand notes (whose value can be converted to specie at will) are better than bonds (whose value is convertible only at the term of the bond), and so on.

Un écu est un écu
Un billet de banque un billet de banque
Un écu est un écu
Un billet de banque un torche-cul.[19]

[A gold crown is a gold crown
A bank note is a bank note
A gold crown is a gold crown
A bank note is a bum wipe.]

The mechanism of the promise that Law's system offered is homologous with *any* imaginative blandishment. Diderot had argued in "Argent" that monetized silver is no more than "fictive wealth" (*DFPV* 5:470). How much more delusive is the impalpable conceit of credit.[20] In any case, in Montesquieu's account Law's currency bubble evaporates like the wind—or like any figment of "imagination"—and the French populace is left bankrupt (*Lettres persanes*, 310). The result is that the stable commonsense distinction between fiction and nonfiction and between narrative and political economy turns labyrinthine. And a conflation of narrative *vraisemblance* and financial credit begins to emerge as a serious worry in a socioeconomy and a culture increasingly given over to mediations, abstractions, and the impalpable exchanges of imaginative—or *imaginary*—products.

But whatever its mysteries and its dangers, the new institution of credit was being introduced and was producing its paradoxically combined benefits and ravages all across Europe. The mechanism by which such transmogrifications and traumas might be understood preoccupied political economists and

19. Cited by Braudel, *Identity of France*, 2:617.
20. The Encyclopedists were not all of one mind concerning the relation of imagination to economic value. Diderot's skepticism concerning specie in "Argent" seems to have been the most radical position. By contrast, the chevalier de Jaucourt, author of the article "Monnaie," repeatedly refutes the thesis that the value of specie is imaginary, a mistaken idea that he attributes to Locke (see *Encyclopédie*, CD-ROM ed., s.v. "Monnaie"). Jaucourt's view is resolutely realist: "What constitutes the real value of a piece of money is the number of grains of fine gold or fine silver that it contains." Du Four, author of the article "Emprunt (*finances*)," makes much of the violent inflation that resulted from Law's system and attributes it to a displacement of materiality by imagination: "imagination takes over, and people give in without prudence to dangerous effects." These discussions communicate a need to base value upon concrete materiality, hence a strong suspicion of "fictionalizing" carriers of value—whether it be monetized silver for Diderot or paper instruments for Jaucourt and Du Four. This uneasiness relates to Diderot's discomfort concerning the status of *literary* fictions detached from concrete situations and people.

intellectuals concerned with public affairs through the eighteenth century and beyond. The puzzle of materiality's mutation into signs parallels Diderot's preoccupation in his narratives concerning the recession of bodies and the consequent lability of language and representation. The suspicion in the economic realm which was so patent in the Enlightenment period concerning credit here sensitizes us to a correlative skepticism concerning fictions in the literary one—also governed by the credit, the belief, that the new category of verisimilitude was mobilizing in favor of representations whose relationship to factuality was no less bewildering than was paper money's to specie.[21]

Property, transfer, exchange, alienation, turn out to form a lexicon for the enigmas about economic value on the one hand, about representation and reference on the other, which Diderot and his colleagues were puzzling about and seeking to think through in this period. Once a seemingly indissoluble relationship between a sign and its material carrier—between money and precious metal; between words and the corporeal person they reference—was interrupted through the introduction of paper financial instruments in the economy and of fiction in narrative, then along with these new semiotic associations, new ideologies, new ways of understanding and of processing social life, became required. By no means were these innovations obvious or trivial, for they bore upon the solidity of categories of consciousness—notably, our relations to otherness and to time—which are among the most fundamental registers of existence.[22]

Materiality is the name we give to the quality that stabilizes reality by constraining volatility and mutability in the objects of our experience. Suspend materiality, and you get a frenetic transience. Anything—unremitting slippage, even chaos—becomes possible. For what would inhibit it? Where in Idealism could you root or derive a dynamic reasserting the familiar resistance of the world to being *anything whatever* or to becoming that *anything* instantly? But in these new forms of semiotic association linking the puzzles of finance and fiction, materiality seems to have been superseded. Then our relations to social existence and to time are fundamentally transformed.

Enlightenment theorists were conscious of such epochal transformations in their world. They had no difficulty seeing that something new in the socio-

---

21. The analogy between *language* and *money* is explicit in Diderot's *Salon de 1767*: "nous en avons usé avec les mots, comme avec les pièces de monnaie" (we have come to use words in in the same way we do coins); *DFPV* 16:218.

22. My analysis here of the relationship between money and literature seeks to extend those I offered in *Discourse/Counter-Discourse* (114); and in *Present Past* (131–32).

economy challenged understanding and that a form of property theretofore unknown had arisen. J.G.A. Pocock has examined eighteenth-century reflections on these developments.[23] With the rise of government credit in the creation and institutionalization of a novel concept and a new budgetary category, the national debt, many things in spheres seemingly distant from finance were altered just as consequentially as the mechanisms of state finance themselves.[24] Pocock's analysis of what he elsewhere terms this "momentous intellectual event" is revealing:

> The National Debt was a device permitting English society to maintain and expand its government, army and trade by mortgaging its revenues in the future. This was sufficient to make it the paradigm of a society now living to an increasing degree by speculation and by credit: that is to say, by men's expectations of one another's capacity for future action and performance. . . . Far more than the practice of trade and profit, even at their most speculative, the growth of public credit obliged capitalist society to develop as an ideology something society had never possessed before, the image of a secular and historical future. . . . But in what was belief in such a future to be rooted? Not in experience, since there is no way of experiencing a future; not in reason, since reason based on the perception of nature cannot well predict the exercise of capacities that have not yet been developed; not in Christian faith, since the most apocalyptic of prophecies is not concerned to reveal the future state of the market. *There remained imagination, fantasy or passion.*

And again:

> Government is therefore maintained by the investor's imagination concerning a moment which will never exist in reality. The ability of merchant and landowner to raise the loans and mortgages they need is similarly dependent upon the investor's imagination. Property—the material foundation of both personality and government—has ceased to be real and has become *not merely mobile but imaginary.*[25]

23. See *Virtue, Commerce, and History*, esp. "Modes of Political and Historical Time in Early Eighteenth-Century England" (91–102); and "The Mobility of Property and the Rise of Eighteenth-Century Sociology" (103–23). Pocock's investigation focuses on England more directly than France, but developments in France paralleled those across the Channel, though with a certain time lag, given the greater conservatism attributable to French centralization and to the character of the French monarchy. Nonetheless, there is considerable commonality in analyses on both sides.

24. See in the *Encyclopédie* the article "Emprunt," to which I have already referred. There Du Four is uncompromising in his hostility to state debt: "Recourse to such an expedient is an evil for the state" (598). The painful memory of Law's system flickers at the edge of this monitory judgment.

25. Pocock, *Virtue, Commerce, and History*, 108, 98, 112, emph. added.

Thus, passing through the seemingly dessicated heart of eighteenth-century socioeconomy, we find ourselves pulled back to the problem of fictions.

> [In language,] as in political economy, we are dealing with the notion of *value*. In both cases, we have a *system of equivalence between things belonging to different orders*. In one case, work and wages; in the other, signified and signifier.   —SAUSSURE, *Cours de linguistique générale*, 115; *Course in General Linguistics*, 80; trans. modified

> Pourtant, il est, cet or. . . .
> [Nonetheless, it *exists*, that gold. . . .]   —MALLARMÉ, "Faits Divers," 1577

The collapse of Law's system in 1720 precipitated an extended reflection on the peculiar ontology, sociology, and psychology of money—in particular concerning the strange mutation, from *material* to *immaterial*, of which it appears capable, indeed which appears fundamental to its functioning. I've tried to suggest how closely these nominally economic transformations track the cultural enigma that in this book I have identified as the *body-story* doublet—the mysterious cohabitation, in our experience and in our understanding, of the seemingly incommensurable realities of corporeal beings and of the language by which we refer to them.

Diderot's *Encyclopédie* article "Argent" ("Silver") found a notional successor in Mallarmé's prose poem "Or" ("Gold"), written more than a century later following the cataclysmic *krach* in 1889 of the Compagnie Universelle du Canal Inter-Océanique (the French Panama Canal Company). Just as was the case with the collapse of Law's system in the eighteenth century, this bankruptcy ravaged the French economy and set off a long process of anxious reflection.[26] Had anything changed between 1720 and 1889? I want to suggest how we might see Mallarmé's text in a line of development which runs from Enlightenment reflections on the body-story puzzle to our own contemporary perspective on equivalent issues.

Ferdinand de Lesseps, celebrated for his success in building the canal at Suez, set out to construct one in Panama. The company he founded to execute the

---

26. Understanding the confusion and upset in the aftermath of the 1889 *krach* would need to take into account a contrary model of heightened self-congratulatory nationalism fostered by that year's centennial of the Great Revolution, the Exposition Universelle, and the opening of the Eiffel Tower. The sense of incongruity must have been acute.

project sold shares to thousands of French people—one of the first firms in France to achieve the marketing of its securities to small investors. The Compagnie Universelle had the backing of high government officials and important financiers. Its bankruptcy in 1889 caused a scandal that destroyed the reputations of many prominent figures and ruined many of the company's middle-class investors.

Economists can tell us important things about the ongoing development, between 1720 and 1889, of notions such as *credit* and *value, money circulation* and *exchange*, notions that the Encyclopedists were already finding so fundamental and so mysterious. But when we pass from the intense materialism of Diderot's "Argent" to Mallarmé's deliquescent prose poem "Or," the literary refractions of these catastrophic financio-social events prove as revealing as the strictly economic facts.[27] In turn the successive inflections of the mysteries of money-taken-as-sign mark three positions in the process that has brought us to our theoretical culture of dissemination and simulacrum today. Diderot and Mallarmé mark points on a developmental curve that leads to the propositions of Poststructuralism.

"Or" reflects, and reflects on, what I have been viewing as the modal *mismatch* between signs and referents, the incommensurability between language and materiality. The text captures the spirit of this enigma. I've conceived contemporary Poststructuralism as overdetermined by efforts to reduce or obviate this mismatch. I've argued that this rationalization has been accomplished by dismissing or disabling one of its terms. We can see in Mallarmé's text the evolution of the process in which Diderot was already engaged.

"Argent" signifies through its narrative. The mutation of the article's referent (from "metallic silver" to more and more abstract and mystifying forms of "money") is what Diderot recounts. This process gives its shape to the article's diegesis and its significance to the text's own referent. Silver is fundamental in Enlightenment France not because it *is* money but because it *becomes* money. Diderot defines *argent* by telling its story.

Mallarmé's text differs from Diderot's in consequential ways.[28] But the contrast between narrative and lyric is the most pertinent distinction. The dif-

27. "Or" was published in a first version in 1893: entitled "Faits Divers," 1577–79. The final version of the text, "Or," appears on 398–99. I read the final version in the light of its predecessor, which more clearly identifies topical referents that the final version renders so obscure as to become nearly unrecognizable.

28. I am not suggesting that Mallarmé was familiar with Diderot's *Encyclopédie* article. The intertextualities I discuss are much more likely to be conceptual than genealogical.

ference between "Argent" and "Or" lies in the recession of narrative and the coordinate progression of the mode of literary representation which *does not progress*—or, at least, which seeks to de-emphasize the sensation of change or transformation in favor of something more like atemporal stasis.

Time can always be figured either as progression or as state. But in the modern period the representation of temporality or process regularly transforms itself into the timeless time of stasis. We're still working through the questions raised in Joseph Frank's seminal essay on "spatial form."[29] Such a metamorphosis into stasis or spatiality veils or suppresses the density and distension of time. The obvious way of understanding it is as a variety of reaction-formation, an antidote both to the finitude of our existence—what the Greeks figured as Atropos snipping our string—and to the acceleration of time itself which so defines and threatens us. Against the dead end of mortality or the anxiety of speed-up, we take refuge in synchrony; we grind time to a halt. The *image* then becomes a powerful resource to be counterposed against the stresses of modernity.

"Or" deals with three declining referents: *gold, sunset,* and *reputation.* With a logic of images it constructs a paralogistic figure in which the text's concerns circulate and mysteriously morph one into another. The facts of the Panama scandal seem straightforward ("Here are the facts," Mallarmé wrote in the first version of "Faits-Divers" [1578]). An inconceivable mass of money evaporated and dematerialized in the crash of the Compagnie Universelle. In a familiar Mallarméan mode the image of sunset evokes the disappearance of the gold but *differently.* And de Lesseps's reputation—a national and international hero after Suez, a convicted criminal after Panama—undergoes a similar devolution and dematerialization following the judgment of the court that tried him and the other officers of the company.[30] From these metaphors and mutations Mallarmé constructs a reflection on materiality and language, on economy and literature, which recirculates issues already urgent in Enlightenment reflection upon the eerily insubstantial foundations of seemingly concrete realities like money.

"Or" is thus filled with images of fall, decline, and descent. They are not structured sequentially or causally but atemporally, paratactically, as associative or figural analogues. "Or" conjures its effects out of these multiple and

---

29. See Frank, "Spatial Form in Modern Literature," 3–62. See also Frank, *Idea of Spatial Form.*
30. De Lesseps was sentenced to five years in prison but never served his term. On appeal his conviction was reversed.

seemingly incommensurable drops and dives—solar, financial, personal. But the collapse of diegesis into stasis here needs to be added to the falls that define the representation.

How can we understand money's eerie impalpability, its strange decorporealization? After all, as "Argent" had traced, money starts out seeming so . . . *material*. Silver ingots, gold bars: we can feel their uncommon density in our hands. But then this heft seems to deliquesce, as it did with the collapse of Law's system or of the Compagnie Universelle. "Pourtant, il est, cet or . . ." ("Still, it *exists*, that gold . . ."). Where did it go? It is as if after it disappears we cannot believe it had ever been real: "millions by the hundred or even more leave me, concerning their existence, incredulous" (1577). Thus, the fundamental mediation of *credit* reenters and enriches the seemingly antinomic structure that makes materiality (money) and aesthetics (the sunset) appear at first incommensurable. It founds their connection just at the moment when its vulnerability appears most evident.

The *combinatoire* of the text's falling movements, first sketched by Mallarmé in "Faits-Divers" then decanted into the text of "Or," could be conceived as follows. In its substance and in its effects the fall of the Compagnie Universelle—of money—is solidly and stolidly *material* and contemptible on just those familiar grounds. "If a Bank crashes, [the result is] vague, mediocre, colorless." Counterposed against this pallid fall, the spectacular evening descent of the sun is imaged as an effect not of material gravity but of impalpable, ephemeral, spellbinding color, conceived under the gossamer aspect of the ideal—thus (automatically for Mallarmé) of the aesthetic, of *poetry*: "Toward the fantasmagorical setting of the sun, when only clouds collapse, a liquefaction of riches creeps, gleams at the horizon." This antinomy separates "economy" ("[whose] sums equate spiritually to nothing") from "poetry": "The gift occurs in the writer to accumulate radiant clarity with the words that he offers like Truth and Beauty") (398–99). This is Mallarmé's familiar rewriting of the repulsion between practical life and art which dominated nineteenth-century Formalism beginning with *L'Art pour l'art*.

But a paradox arises. So far the text, as so often in Mallarmé, has represented what seems an absolute opposition, a zero sum, indivisibly valorizing one term, depreciating the other without appeal. We could translate this familiar appraisal into: politics and economics lack worth; beauty alone is valuable. But against this background something unexpected seems to be happening. The collapse of de Lesseps's *reputation*, the third center of the text's imagery, begins paradoxically to seem the richest of the three linked figures of fall in the text.[31] It is a psycho-semiotic reflex of materiality which reaches into the realm of the immaterial and impalpable. We could conceive it as the personal analogue of financial *credit* standing (as it has since Enlightenment elucubrations about its mystery) as an intermediate term between the two seemingly incommensurable others. Its presence reveals the complications that are elided in Mallarmé's counterposition of these contraries and in his vehement proselytizing for aesthetics over economics. It functions—like all "third terms" that upset a binary opposition—to project the possibility of mediation between entities previously conceived or experienced as incommensurable and unconnectable. Then the resonance of the term *Divers* in the title of the text's original version (and in the overall rubric in which these prose poems eventually appeared) transmutes from a word carrying the sense of *division* into a more modulated suggestion of mutual *implication, engagement,* even a mysterious *inter-determination.*

By virtue of its rootedness in the untidy materiality of social life, this text cannot comfortably sustain Mallarmé's habitual ascent to the aesthetic empyrean. It is, after all, about *falls.* The final version, "Or," takes its place in the larger rubric of "Grands faits divers" in the prose poems of *Divagations* and *Variations sur un sujet.* The most characteristic of Mallarmé's aesthetic dogmas is his influential apotheosis of the literary. We find it, for example, in this sentence from "La musique et les lettres": "Yes, let Literature exist and alone, to the exception of everything else" (646). But against this admitted "exaggeration," in "Or" something like a self-deconstruction of Mallarmé's absolute polarity or hierarchy seems to happen like a return of the repressed.

I want to conclude this excursus into the fin de siècle by recalling a moment in "Faits-divers" and its reflex in "Or." In this moment the impossibility of isolating the polar terms of the economico-social circuit overwhelms the figure of antipathy through which Mallarmé usually seeks to represent them. Here are the two passages in question. I cite them in reverse chronological order for reasons that will become clear:

["Or"] Fumée le milliard, hors le temps d'y faire main basse: ou, le manque d'éblouissement voire d'intérêt accuse qu'élire un dieu n'est pas pour le confiner à l'ombre des coffres en fer et des poches. (398)

---

31. This is more clearly readable in the text's first version. In the final text of "Or" this concern with the mediatory term recedes.

[The billion up in smoke, faster than the time (needed) to grasp it: or else, the absence of fascination or even of interest reveals that selection of a god is not enough to confine it to the obscurities of iron vaults or pockets.]

["Faits-divers"] Toutefois ne pas perdre de vue que la fonction de la Justice est une fiction, cela par le fait seul qu'elle *ne rend pas l'argent*. (1578; emph. added)

[Nonetheless do not lose sight of the fact that the function of Justice is a fiction, by the simple fact that *it doesn't give back the money*.]

Two things—unaccustomed in Mallarmé's habitual rhetoric—assert themselves here. The first is the inappropriateness, indeed the impossibility, of resolving the conflict of materialities, signs, images, and values with which social existence confronts us simply by occulting the circuit or network—economic *and* semiotic—in which they find their meanings. The divinity that society has elected uncannily escapes from the restricted realm of its nominal existence. Like the fiction that Diderot and his friends organized for Croismare, it radiates beyond intention and returns to subject *us* despite our expectations of control.

The second point is a striking reassertion of materiality's claims and a coordinate skepticism concerning fictions. We can see these in the text's common-sense remark that apportioning the guilt of the officers of the Compagnie Universelle entirely misses the issue for the people who have been defrauded and ruined by the company's evaporation. Classification, taxonomy, aren't enough; *economy* must still be served. Thus materiality isn't some voluntaristic interpretation of reality which we accept or decline depending upon the caprices of desire. *Materiality puts pressure on thought*. It has consequence. It bites back.

We may not quite be able to conceptualize how this occurs, but we do not fail to experience it. As I asserted at the outset of this book, existence doesn't require our theory in order to happen. In that sense Mallarmé's familiar venture to resolve the contradictions of modernity by jettisoning the contaminations and complications that freight it down in the socio-practico-political realm—anticipating our own contemporary apotheosis of textuality and our theologization of language—here runs up against the limits of its own attempt. These realities are never reducible to pure aesthetics or pure language, as even their most intently aestheticized or absolutized representations inevitably disclose.

Now I want to return to the passage from Saussure's *Cours de linguistique générale* which I placed as an epigraph to this section. Saussure's brilliant disengagement of semiosis and his clarifying taxonomy of the sign have underlain and inspired much subsequent theorization of language and textuality. What has been less attended to in Saussure—what has too often been entirely jettisoned in consideration of his work—is his constant insistence on the *material* foundations of signification. Recall his celebrated image of the sign as a sheet of paper whose indivisible recto and verso represent the material sound of language on one side (the signifier), the thought content (the signified) on the other. Saussure writes, "It is impossible in a language to isolate sound from thought or thought from sound."[32] Let us therefore not isolate them. In Saussure's representation the sign begins as a material artifact and never loses this connection with a world that is less labile, less volatile, than the seemingly instantaneous caracoles of thought. In that sense the frictionless movements of dissemination suppress an important register of Saussure's insight.

To be sure, Saussure placed most of his explanatory emphasis on the conceptual side of the sign. Tactically, he was resisting the positivist and empiricist cast of linguistics in his period. But, as with Freud, whose seminal work was simultaneous and bears powerful parallels to Saussure's, the constitutive *relation* between the realities and registers which their respective theories sought to illuminate always remained fundamental. My Saussurian epigraph emblematizes the irreducibility of such conjunctions. The "system of equivalence" upon which he insists (between work and wages; between signifier and signified) is what in a different lexicon we would call a "mediation" between diverse realms of existence. That is what permits the mysterious but constitutive "phase-change" that I have been referring to in my discussion.

But one of the most striking things about Saussure's argument is what he doesn't speak of—the mediation *between* the two terms of the dual relationships he analogizes: the world of the social and the economic on the one hand; the world of language on the other. This awkward pairing of body and story is the relation at issue in "Or." Mallarmé also seeks to hold its terms at a hermetic distance from each other but finds them refractory to such convenient segregation. They will not remain disjoined.

Once we entertain the idea of mediation, as Saussure does in the passage in question here, and as Mallarmé discovers when would-be contraries like those on which his text turns appear to have forged mysterious but inescapable connections, then transversals begin to assert themselves between the aspects, modalities, and representations of our world and our experience. Relationships

32. Saussure, *Cours*, 157.

proliferate; connections between what might have seemed incommensurable registers start to engage. We are closer than we might have thought to Diderot's reflections on these issues and their mysterious connections, to his insistence on holding language, referentiality, and materiality in the same conceptual field and maintaining—despite the difficulty of doing so—critical attention to their intertwined and inter-determining complication.

> Je défie qu'on explique rien sans le corps.
> [I defy us to explain anything absent the body.]
> —DIDEROT, "Éléments de Physiologie," *DFPV* 17:334

Yet another register of the mediatory relationship between materiality and language whose complications the Enlightenment worried about so persistently might help us to renew our own sometimes arrested conceptualization of them. In the relationship that mysteriously ties the seemingly disjunct worlds of socioeconomy and literature, things are *gendered*. Pocock makes the claim for the former realm:

> In the eighteenth-century debate over the new relations of polity to economy, production and exchange are regularly equated with the new ascendancy of the passions and the female principle. They are given a new role in history, which is to refine the passions; but there is a danger that they may render societies effeminate—a term whose recurrence ought not to be neglected.
>
> A contrast in these terms between "patriot" and "man of commerce," between "virtue" and "politeness" or "refinement," emerges during the first half of the eighteenth century, with Montesquieu as . . . an authoritative exponent.[33]

In the literary sphere the feminization of narrative was less a matter of metaphorical association than of genre, dramatis personae, tonal preoccupation, and theme. Men of letters were finding themselves impelled to imagine and to represent *women's* thoughts and perspectives. Of all the acts of fictionalizing, this cross-dressing may well be the most consequential. For it willfully trav-

---

33. Pocock, *Virtue, Commerce, and History*, 114. On the gendering of these categories, see also 117–18. Pocock refers particularly to *Esprit des Lois*, bk. 4, chap. 8. Following Pocock, the question of such gendering has recently been discussed by Mulcaire, "Public Credit," 1029–42. The relations of women to eighteenth-century fiction have been widely studied. See, among many others, Armstrong, *Desire and Domestic Fiction*; Cook, *Epistolary Bodies*; Favret, *Romantic Correspondence*; Gallagher, *Nobody's Story*; and Miller, *French Dressing*. Already in Molière the extravagant imagination characteristic of novel writing was associated with *women's* consciousness. See Howells, "Statut du romanesque," 24.

esties, it programmatically alienates, one of the cardinal properties of identity. Its impropriety, then, might stand as the diagnostic sign of *fiction*.

"Je suis une femme, peut-être un peu coquette, que sais-je? mais c'est natu-rellement et sans artifice [I am a woman, perhaps a bit coquettish, who can say?—but naturally, not as a result of artifice]" (288). These are the concluding words of Diderot's nun and of *La religieuse* itself. They point to a perplexity that exceeds what the critical tradition has attended to. What did it mean for Di-derot to *write as a woman?*[34]

We can imagine him composing this astonishing final sentence in a mode way beyond mere "coquetry"—a mode of antic, indeed extravagant, antiphra-sis. The hoax of Croismare began with the desire to explore the capacities of language to *mis*-represent, as a critical experiment with mendaciousness. So it should not surprise us to see the novel conclude with a particularly choice and bald-faced lie. But the protestation against "artifice" which Diderot chose to end with is nonetheless exquisite. Writing fiction always involves an act of chutzpah. But here we have its self-reflexive quintessentialization, a gratuitous lie about lying itself—mendaciousness squared.

Nothing in the narrative can respond to this misrepresentation. Indeed, the enigma of textuality is that texts can *never* reliably or authoritatively guarantee their own veracity. Verisimilitude, then, comes to stand in as a kind of next-best possibility, like our crediting paper money as a substitute for specie. In both spheres the advantages of such innovative representations are clear. But we must not bury or misrecognize their simultaneous ambiguity. I have been track-ing the downside that, despite them and the liberatory play they authorized, I believe preoccupied Diderot in his fictions. This relay of increasing abstractions along the chain of signifiers makes it simplest to accept the flattening of all truth-claims into nothing more than neutral enactments of textuality itself, as some have determined to do in our own period.

But Diderot was skeptical and troubled by such a capitulation to the un-groundable non-referentiality of texts. For him, if representation was not an-swerable to materiality, then indispensable foundations of politics and reform simply evaporated. For all the energy he put, over many decades, into promot-ing the transformation of his society—the elimination of irrationalities and the establishment of rights—he was uncomfortable with the telescoping of time

---

34. A piquant convergence ties Diderot's gender travesty to a case closer to our own time. Here is Derrida: "I want to write like a woman" ("La question du style," 228).

and truth which fictional representation necessarily entails. Something within his projection of the world required accrediting the resistance of materiality and the refractoriness of time which it carries with it. This is a fundamental implication of his unremitting commitment to materialist doctrine.

Materialism is no panacea. Two millennia of one of the most fundamental contentions in the history of philosophy—between diverse materialisms and whatever form of idealism we counterpose against them, demonstrate that no knock-down argument exists that could unanswerably enforce materialism's claims. But we could understand Diderot's materialism as much simpler and more straightforward than abstract philosophical doctrine. He projects materialism as an antidote to logomachy: as a constraint against the facility with which human beings manipulate language and *make up stories*—against what in contemporary terms looks very much like the free play of signifiers. And he does so because such unimpeded compliance, such free play in language, gives us no traction against the refractory elements in our social, political, even biological existence. Whatever paradigm we use to model our experience, we need to capture and to communicate the fundamental *feel* in lived reality of such resistant elements.

We want the changes in the world that we imagine; indeed, we want them soon. But the collapse of temporality into instantaneity which we have become familiar with in fictions places such reforms not nearer to hand but more distant, as the gap between language and the material world comes to seem unbridgeable. Imagination thus bears within itself an irreducible and inherent capacity for deception about its own functioning and utility. How to make sense of this equivocation in the fundamental faculty with which we conceive of change and project the future?

Today we are so immersed in the construction of these issues which has developed out of the Enlightenment's engagement with them that we can hardly think that there ever were alternatives. But if imagination has been found insufficient, we might deploy its resources to reimagine it itself. This is what I have argued that Diderot, preoccupied in programmatic ways with the efficacy of language in the alteration of the world, was seeking to explore in his narratives. It remains to consider whether it is possible to trace a relationship between these Enlightenment speculations and the contemporary construction of these matters which has become Postmodern orthodoxy.

Part II / The Conflict of Theories

CHAPTER FIVE

The Enlightenment Discovers Postmodernism

Nothing . . . may seem more unbounded than the thought of man, which not only escapes all human power and authority, but is not even restrained within the limits of nature and reality. . . . Thought can in an instant transport us to the most distant regions of the universe, or even beyond the universe. —HUME, *An Enquiry concerning Human Understanding*, sec. 2, 65

Freedom in thought has only *pure thought* as its truth, a truth lacking the fullness of life. Hence freedom in thought . . . is only the Notion of freedom, not the living reality of freedom itself.
—G.W.F. HEGEL, *Phenomenology of Spirit*, 122

Toute action de l'esprit est aisée si elle n'est pas soumise au réel.
[The activities of our mind are effortless so long as they are not obliged to answer to the real.]
—PROUST, *Sodome et Gomorrhe II, À la recherche du temps perdu*, 3:51

In the last century there were philosophers who argued that nothing exists but ideas. In our century there are people who write as if there were nothing but texts. —RORTY, *Consequences of Pragmatism*, 139

Our story so far: in the Enlightenment stories were changing. They played with shucking off bodies, but the game ended in a labyrinth. The truth-status of narrative, the pragmatics of language, the density and the self-evidence of materiality, all began to seem more and more problematic. These fundamental registers of human beings' comprehension of the world appeared to be readjusting, seemed to be trying to reframe their character, their capacities, and their relationship in order to accommodate some powerful new determinants.

The principal determinants were two. First, the reformist intentions of the philosophes could only be realized through practices of language. Other modalities of public activity and political action were blocked by the same absolutist strictures that Enlightenment thinkers were programmatically stigmatizing and seeking to destabilize. So a newer puzzlement inherent in words' capacity for material agency was counterposed against language's own internal perplexities, compounding the enigma. Second, European society's growing urbanization, internal differentiation, and socioeconomic complexity were requiring signs to learn and to play extended roles in order to accommodate unprecedented augmentations and complications in economic and information exchange. The increasing impalpability of fundamental social, cultural, and economic entities opened many questions.

These changes defamiliarized the accustomed scope and character of linguistic and semiotic practices. Language began to seem strange not only in its ability to take on these augmented tasks but particularly in its capacity to stand in for materiality while at the same time traducing materiality's most constitutive quality, the constraining and refractory *weight* of things. Despite (and because of) their impalpability, diverse forms of language—particularly narrative and commercial fictions—began increasingly to substitute for matter. The phase-change such substitution entailed seemed uncanny; such practices thwarted comprehension. This is the background against which I have sought to place Diderot's interrogation of the displacement of bodies by language. And I have been suggesting that these inflections and interrogations can help illuminate theoretical choices and quarrels today.

To pursue his narrative and conceptual reflection, Diderot composed a series of conspicuously odd stories. They explored language's and materiality's exchanges and metamorphoses. Over several decades Diderot revised and ruminated on his tales and the questions they raised and tested them against other modes of his writing. The tales he fashioned seemed to enact a gleeful effacement of the real, but one that unsettled him. The pull of these stories in the direction of corporeality's dematerialization is a dynamic we're familiar with today. Its horizon is the enticing fantasy that with language you can do whatever you want—that language is *what is*. Yet, despite this challenge arising in his own writing experience and practice, Diderot maintained allegiance to a materialism that sought to centralize in the seeming impalpability of discourse the foundational characteristics of human corporeality and vulnerability.

In our own period, over the past few decades several waves of reflection have centered upon the character and functioning of language: on its capacity for truth and, conversely, on its propensity for fabrication. These reflections have naturalized an elegant—but, I will argue, a problematic—resolution of Diderot's perplexity concerning the veridicality and the lability of words. This resolution developed in several phases. In the 1960s Structuralism shifted the concerns of cultural theory to the realm of signs and *their* relationships. The semiotic by no means excludes materiality—on the contrary, Saussure took pains to assert its irreducibility.[1] Yet in the work of Lévi-Strauss, Greimas, Lacan, Barthes, and others, Structuralist practice focused elsewhere than upon extra-linguistic referentiality and upon the extra-semiotic entities that referentiality designates.

Partly, no doubt, this was because the realm of material objects, time, and contingency forms a messy register for analysis.[2] It isn't hard to see how the encumbrances of the everyday world, the refractoriness of material existence, the vulnerability of our bodies, resist being captured in the elegant arrays cognized in Structuralist *combinatoires*.

Perhaps after World War II—I'm speculating now—it was an apotropaic reaction against the catastrophic experience of corporeal vulnerability itself which propelled the postwar inclination to bracket bodies.[3] But whatever the motivation, the effect of Structuralist practice was to privilege the impalpable, mutable, fungible, and abstracting character of *language*. This asserted itself over against what increasingly was made to seem language's misprized *other*—which was then cast as the primary obstacle to critical analysis, the true enemy of a Structuralist "science of the text."[4] Thus receded the bulky and balky realm of "use-values," "referents," Kantian "things-in-themselves," and Humean "objects of sense perception." Structuralism wanted no truck with such unwieldy realities, which (like the stone palaces that refused incorporation into Mallarmé's poems) simply don't *fit*.[5] So Structuralism's own structure progressively exiled these awkward relics of an apparently outworn metaphysical realism.

Then, near the conclusion of the 1960s, a reaction to or an inflection within

1. See Saussure, *Course in General Linguistics*, 66, 111.

2. Viggo Brøndal thus stigmatized time itself as the "great impediment to any rationality." See Timpanaro, *On Materialism*, 159.

3. The principal figures to whom these new waves of thinking appealed for their inspiration—Saussure and Nietzsche—of course preceded the war by many decades. What is significant is the rediscovery and wide deployment of their ideas after nearly a century of relative critical neglect. Bodies have been on the critical agenda—as Terry Eagleton dryly put it, "more bodies in literary criticism than on the fields of Waterloo" (*Illusions of Postmodernism*, 17). On this hypertrophy of studies of "body-liness" as a reaction against the tendency of much contemporary criticism to drown bodies in Idealism, see also Ellmann, *Hunger Artists*.

4. On seductive postulations of a "science of the text," see Culler, *Structuralist Poetic*, chap. 11.

5. For "use-values" (or "values in use"), see Smith, *Inquiry into the Nature and Causes of the Wealth of Nations*, 34; as well as Marx, *Capital*, vol. 1, chap. 1, esp. 125–28. On Mallarmé's unmanageable material "palaces," see my introduction. The reference is to Mallarmé, *Oeuvres complètes*, 366.

Structuralism began to lay down its markers. The figures we associate with this new phase are too varied in their assumptions and analytical practices to permit rounding them up in a coherent "school." But they are tied by powerful resemblances in core assumptions and conceptual practices. The meaning of *Postmodern* has probably been the most vexed question in critical reflection over the past decade or two. Coordinately, the relation of Postmodernism to its cousin Poststructuralism spills continuing quantities of ink. The qualities that characterize Postmodernity flicker in and out of critical focus, depending upon what writer, artist, architect, or theorist we consider or consult.

I want my categories here to be flexible and indicative—not definitions but designations and evocations. Yet we need ways of talking about Postmodernity if we are to make sense of our own experience and of the determinations that bear upon it. At times I conflate *Poststructuralism* and *Postmodernism* while recognizing that for some practical usages they must be distinguished.[6] I want to understand *Postmodernism* as the reflex within the interpretive disciplines of developments whose characteristics I specify in what follows.

Taxonomy haunts us—in large part owing to the "natural science envy" that the human sciences or cultural disciplines have inherited from nineteenth-century Positivism. Careers depend upon the classificatory system one adheres to. We dream of unambiguous, "objective" distinctions to sort out the protean phenomena that confront us. A lot of our job depends upon making and deploying them. But the desire to achieve bright-line separation between the categories into which we distribute social facts has some disadvantageous consequences. It can push us in two equally unfortunate directions. Either we are tempted to hypostatize cultural entities as if they were palpable beings—thereby blinding ourselves to the variable, multifarious, and overdetermined character of such phenomena. Or else we are unstrung by our inability to frame and unambiguously identify the objects we examine—and at the limit, anxious to avoid being convicted of the crime of "reification," we prefer (in a nominalism that has become familiar today) to treat them as if they simply didn't exist.[7]

---

6. For example, virtually no one calls Frank Gehry's architecture "Poststructuralist."

7. This latter pattern reproduces one that the eminent psephologist Daniel Yankelovich once hilariously stigmatized as "McNamara's Fallacy" (his reference was to the U.S. secretary of defense during the Vietnam period): "The first step is to measure whatever can be easily measured. This is okay as far as it goes. The second step is to disregard that which can't be measured or give it an arbitrary quantitative value. This is artificial and misleading. The third step is to presume that what can't be measured really isn't very important. This is blindness. The fourth step is to say that what can't be easily measured really doesn't exist. This is suicide" (qtd. by Smith, *Supermoney*, 286).

Taxonomic literal-mindedness cannot take us far toward understanding social phenomena.[8] No more than the complex we term "Postmodernism," most empirical processes in what Max Weber termed the "disciplines concerned with human action" do not fall into neat patterns definable by the presence of the "objectifiable" factors and variables that we would expect, for example, in geometry or in physics. The most thoughtful account of the sort of taxonomic practice that is appropriate for cultural and social phenomena is probably Weber's, in his speculations on what he named the "ideal type."[9] For Weber representing sociocultural entities depends upon construction—that is, upon generalization and abstraction from particular sets of facts. Hence such definitional tools are heuristic and pragmatic, not apodictic. They always involve interpretive judgment.

There is always a reduction involved whenever, based upon particular cases, we seek to articulate general characteristics or concepts. Methodologically speaking, there is nothing guilty or inappropriate about such abstraction or reduction, so long as the heuristic purpose of the exercise is not forgotten and no slippage occurs toward representation of the objects of our descriptions as if they were "real" in the commonsense way we take *trees* and *tables* to be real. Of course, there is a sense in which Postmodernism doesn't "exist." As Terry Eagleton observed, you can't see the "id" either.[10] But even when they start out with none, social phenomena have the uncanny characteristic of generating their own reality.[11]

Even with such caveats and qualifications, I need to provide some delimita-

8. On this point, see Terdiman, *Present Past*, 65–67.

9. See Weber, *Economy and Society*, 1:18–22. Here is Weber's account of what we might think of as the ideal type of "ideal types" themselves: "The same historical phenomenon may be in one aspect feudal, in another patrimonial, in another bureaucratic, and in still another charismatic. In order to give a precise meaning to these terms, it is necessary for the sociologist to formulate pure ideal types of the corresponding forms of action which in each case involve the highest possible degree of logical integration. . . . But precisely because this is true, it is probably seldom if ever that a real phenomenon can be found which corresponds exactly to one of these ideally constructed pure types" (1:20).

10. Eagleton, *Illusions of Postmodernism*, 9.

11. As I mentioned in chapter 2, in 1908 Weber's contemporary Georg Simmel addressed this paradox in "How Is Society Possible?" Simmel observed that, while the unity of nature emerges in the observing subject exclusively, perception of society or action in society requires no similar independent observer. Rather, the elements of society—people, conscious, concept-generating, synthesizing units—realize this unity through the notions by which they understand it. They do so in both senses of *realize*: they *perceive* it, and they *create* it. The categories they employ for understanding their experience then end up defining and determining that experience. In that sense Pirandello's *Così è, se vi pare* describes not some lawless relativistic fantasy but the social-constructivist epistemology of all social entities. See "How Is Society Possible?" 7.

tion of my field of inquiry. The most influential taxonomy of the traits associated with the Postmodern complex was articulated by Fredric Jameson
in his 1984 essay "Postmodernism or the Cultural Logic of Late Capitalism."
These are the principal characteristics Jameson associated with the object of his
examination:

- depthlessness
- waning of affect
- fragmentation of the subject
- prevalence of pastiche
- collapse of the referent
- replacement of temporality by spatiality.[12]

Jameson concludes, "We are left with that pure and random play of signifiers
that we call postmodernism."[13]

It is easy to see how these characteristics derive from the same cultural dynamic—language displacing bodies, signs edging out materiality—which was
already fascinating and perplexing Diderot in the Enlightenment period and
which he was worrying about in his narrative experiments. Of course, the force
and breadth of the determinations that produce these contemporary effects has
grown since the eighteenth century, where I began tracing its story (moreover
there is nothing absolute about the starting point I chose). What is significant
is the sense of a pattern of development, even across and through powerful
perturbations and historical differences, which makes the increasing assumption of language's primacy the condition of possibility of Postmodernism's self-
understanding.[14]

12. The essay was originally published in *New Left Review*, no. 146 (July–August 1984), 59–92. Reprinted as chap. 1 of Jameson, *Postmodernism*, 1–54. In the latter volume the tableau of characteristics
will be found on 6.

13. Jameson, *Postmodernism*, 95–96. The turning-moment imagined here by Jameson is not so
different from the one Derrida himself projected "when language invaded the universal problematic, the moment when, in the absence of a center or origin, *everything became discourse*" ("Structure,
Sign, and Play in the Discourse of the Human Sciences," (1967), in *Writing and Difference*, 280; emph.
Added). Jameson motivates this turning historically; Derrida, still perhaps under the influence of
his teacher Foucault's notion of *epistemes* and ruptures, casts it as an unmotivated event. Paul de Man
was perhaps the most intransigent proponent of a totalized languaging of the world. Cf. "To the
extent that all language is conceptual, it always already speaks about language and not about
things. . . . If all language is about language, then the paradigmatic linguistic model is that of an
entity that confronts itself" (de Man, *Allegories of Reading*, 152).

14. In suggesting this convergence or this interlocution between the Enlightenment and Postmodernism, I might appear to be ignoring Jameson's insights concerning the historicization of the

We may command materiality to dance, but everyone's experience confirms—and often painfully reaffirms—that it regularly declines to do so. Nonetheless, these Modern or Postmodern symptoms treat materiality as if it could be handled, as if it could be processed and manipulated, like text. Consequently, they turn away from the network of constraints and framings imposed by factors in experience not nearly so labile nor malleable as the elements of language by which they can be represented and expressed. These they then bleach out of consciousness.

Poststructuralism is what happens when the world has been languaged wall to wall. For my purposes here the distinctive element in a number of the thinkers associated with Postmodernism—Derrida, Lyotard, and de Man, to begin with—is their commitment to a radical conception of the relationship between language, on the one hand, and, on the other, the entities that most quotidian subjects think of as "real." It might seem hard to ignore such universal intuitions, but this conception effectively scrubs out commonsense connection with what is not conceived as language or as subject to its sway. Moreover, Poststructuralism goes beyond Structuralist practice by making a strong and central *theoretical* claim in favor of this exclusion. The consequences of this position, the logic that sustains it, and the pressures that tell against it are at the heart of my further discussion.

So the aspect of Poststructuralist conceptualization upon which I focus is its effacement or denial of a language-referent relationship. The emblem of such a view is Derrida's resonant—and intransigent—dictum concerning the vacuity of the *"hors-texte."*[15] To designate this attitude toward language I have quietly

---

Postmodern, despite the fact that from the beginning Jameson's work has informed and shaped my own. It might seem completely to miss Jameson's historicizing point for me to suggest contact across the centuries between Diderot's period and our own. Yet we can look at my linkage in a different light. What Diderot was discovering about language in the later part of the eighteenth century is a characteristic of its social and cultural functioning that has not evolved into something truly *different* across more than two hundred years of intervening history. Nothing paralleling the technological innovations that have transformed the socioeconomy has happened to transform language or texts. Once language began in the Enlightenment period to be conceivable as a detached and abstracting instrument, with all the lability and fungibility that such a formation can demonstrate, then the trick is turned. The condition of possibility of Postmodern understanding of language is the invention and propagation of a notion of language's use, of its place in the repertoire of our practices and assumptions about the world, which was already present and under exploration in Diderot's narrative experiments and in Enlightenment reflections more generally. That foundation for contemporary experiences and practices still underlies and enables the manifestations of the Postmodern in the world of words.

15. *"Il n'y a pas de hors-texte."* See *Of Grammatology*, 158. Over against revisionist views of Derrida's principle that have tended to soften or underestimate its claims, Derrida goes on in the same passage

adopted Richard Rorty's term *textualism*.[16] "Textualism" holds that there is no referent cognizable for human beings. There is only language, and language goes "all the way down." In its very radicality the notion brings into critical focus the fundamental problem with which I argued Diderot was preoccupied in his fictions: *what happens when language disengages from bodies*.[17]

To situate the stakes in this foundational question, let me offer a summary tableau of the possible positions that might be held concerning language's connection with the non-linguistic. We can distinguish three cardinal alternatives. The first of these sees the connection between language and referent as *unproblematic*. On this view words refer capably and reliably to what they name. Typically, such a relation is theologically guaranteed. Over many centuries European culture was dominated by this position. We find it in medieval epic in the eleventh century and in Descartes in the seventeenth.[18] We find it as well in more or less naive literary realism, in philosophical positivism, and in most people's quotidian interactions. It represents a neat solution to the problem of referentiality: the problem quietly disappears. But in developed or developing societies in the West since the Enlightenment, with the increasing perfusion of culture by attitudes associated with rationalism and the sciences, and with an

---

to assert a total "absence of the referent." Whatever "meaning" may be in Derrida's conception today, at the time of *Grammatology* he *meant* about referentiality what his intransigent assertion stated was the case.

16. See Rorty, "Nineteenth-Century Idealism and Twentieth-Century Textualism." Rorty names Harold Bloom, Geoffrey Hartmann, J. Hillis Miller, Paul de Man, Jacques Derrida, Michel Foucault, Hayden White, and Paul Rabinow as "textualists" (139). I do not agree with all the details of Rorty's analysis. But it succinctly identifies the distinctive element in the morphology of such views of language.

17. The notion of "textuality," akin to "textualism" in the sense I'm considering here, is rooted in the work of the Tel Quel group (particularly Barthes, Derrida, Sollers, Goux, and Kristeva). See the article "Text" in Oswald Ducrot and Tzvetan Todorov, *Encyclopedic Dictionary of the Sciences of Language*, 356–61. Peter Dews traces the history of theories of linguistic absolutism in *Logics of Disintegration*, chap. 1. Dews argues that the theses of classical German hermeneutics, particularly Schleiermacher's concerning the primacy of language, are essential precursors of the Derridean position (see esp. 11). On many aspects of textuality and textualism, see Mowitt, *Text*.

18. In the case of many Christian texts belief in language's adequacy is simply untroubled—the problem doesn't even come up. I will return to this happy obviation of the problem in chapter 7. However, the case of Descartes' belief in the veridicality of our concepts and of their relation to the external world is more complicated. In Descartes God's still-reliable epistemological guarantee is mediated by conceptual knowledge. Descartes does not assume such adequation or posit it as an axiom but, rather (in the *Meditations on the First Philosophy*, first and second "Meditations"), he attempts experimentally to falsify it entirely. Then the third "Meditation" demolishes in their turn the doubts he has raised and founds Cartesian certainty in the adequation of language to its referent.

ever-growing density of signs and semiotic exchanges, this position has become unavailable for most theorists.

The second position in my tripartite tableau of models for conceptualizing referentiality sees relation between language and the extra-linguistic as *impossible*. From within this second view the notion of the "extra-linguistic" empties out and disappears; no link is possible with what simply doesn't exist. Such a resolution-by-truncation is symmetrical with the first position I sketched. From within neither of these views can one conceive that there is a problem to begin with. This second position is that of radical Idealism or—more pertinent for contemporary debates—of Rorty's textualism. It is the conception many would associate with the Nietzsche of "Truth and Lies in a Nonmoral Sense"[19] and—most pertinent here—with Derrida's assertion of the vacuity of the extra-textual. It provides the "elegant resolution" of the language/referent conundrum to which I referred at the opening of this chapter. But it does so at the cost of eradicating an entire term of the relationship.

Later I will consider the advantages and the shortcomings of such a reduction. But we can already see how such a position generates, as if by the logic of an internal necessity, the reification—or the deification—of "simulation" and the "simulacrum" that have been so influential in Postmodernity. With the negation of referentiality, and with it the disappearance of any basis for claiming contact with a nonexistent originary entity, everything that this second, textualist, position can cognize must (and does) demonstrate the foundationlessness of language itself—belonging to no one, used indiscriminately by everyone, and always partaking of the status of the inauthentic or the fake through the very fact of its constant yoking to a medium of rootless reproduction.[20]

But not everyone agrees, even among the highest of High Modernists. Despite his general orientation toward Idealism, Proust deconstructed such positions in a hilarious Dr.-Johnsonian moment in *Du côté de chez Swann*.[21] Proust's narrator and his refractory beloved Gilberte Swann are playing in the Champs-Elysées gardens. Real contact with her seems to him an unattainable dream; for him Gilberte is the referent with whom cognizable—still less corporeal—relation is inconceivable. Yet whatever we think we know about the uncertain-

19. Nietzsche, "On the Truth and Lies in a Nonmoral Sense," 79–97. Carlo Ginzburg discusses aspects of this doctrine in *History, Rhetoric, and Proof*, esp. 14–15.
20. See, for example, Baudrillard, *Simulations*, 12, 48, 53, 143, 146.
21. On Proust's generally uncritical Idealist adherence, see Terdiman, *Present Past*, 169.

ties of referentiality, such conceptual conviction evaporates in the face of our need to credit and to rely upon it: "[Gilberte] handed me the ball; and, like the idealist philosopher whose body takes account of the external world in the reality of which his intellect declines to believe, the same self which had made me greet her before I had identified her now urged me to grasp the ball that she held out to me."[22] Thus, the apparent stability of this second position in my tableau—achieved by obliterating the troublesome referential term of the dialectic and with it the very notion of a dialectic to begin with—collapses before the seemingly magical banalities of quotidian existence.

My third paradigmatic position sees the language/referent relationship as possible *but problematic*. This (as Proust's comic parable suggests) is a messier solution. Despite this, it has been prominent since Kant, and it has had numerous varieties. All of them join in declining the twin simplifications that define the other, more monothetic challengers in my array. Every version of this third position is obliged to hover unstably between its two competitors. Each is tempted by and drawn toward them. It would be much neater if the problematic relationship between language and materiality, the puzzling phase-change that such a passage requires, could simply be elided or obviated. But the work of such a model is to resist or forestall the slippage that would attract it to either of these extremes and thereby shut down the tension between these twin reductionist solutions. Hegel is the emblem of this third position of possible ways of thinking about the world and the world of words. And the dialectic, with its instrumentality of mediations and determinations, is the mode by which the tension between the two more extreme positions that bracket this final one in my array is maintained and practiced.[23]

This third model is where I want to situate Diderot's challenge to textualism. His (admittedly parachronic) critique is pertinent for the contemporary period because he clearly experienced and understood the attraction of the textualist alternative—he already knew you could make words dance if you wanted to. But despite the seductions of such semiotic conjuring, Diderot found cogent

22. *Swann's Way*, in *In Search of Lost Time*, 1:571; trans. modified.
23. Thinking about how meaning is generated in Flaubert, Jonathan Culler seizes an important aspect of the difficult but foundational maintenance of paradigmatic *tension* between two unelidable terms. "Matter," he writes, "becomes the 'opposite' of the story, its 'other' " (*Flaubert*, 108). On the grounds of such a perception Flaubert cannot be fully assimilated to the textualist model, however great his own temptations may have been to leave materiality behind, however great temptations in our own period—including Culler's in his Flaubert book—may be to assimilate him to the Poststructuralist paradigm as its privileged predecessor.

means and motivation for resisting it. In his thought-experiment with Suzanne Simonin and the Marquis de Croismare—and more broadly throughout his narratives, dialogues, and "mystifications"—his exploration of and work upon the category of "storytelling" scrutinizes the conceptual and pragmatic possibilities of eliding the referent—of forgetting about bodies and their attendant attributes of materiality, vulnerability, and resistance to abstraction and fungibility. In *Encyclopédie* texts such as "Argent" he follows and foregrounds the process of the referent's deliquescence and final disappearance. But throughout he displays not only the gains but also the coordinate *costs* of such elision. Diderot's exploration of this enigma is the paradigm for the Enlightenment wrangle with Postmodernism.

In recent decades the Enlightenment has had bad press. It appears to have been *superseded*. Thus, in *Dialectic of Enlightenment* Horkheimer and Adorno reconceived the Enlightenment as a precondition for Hitlerism. Nietzsche's and Bataille's critiques of its notion of "reason" have re-echoed more recently in Foucault, Lyotard, Derrida, and numerous others. Feminists and critical race theorists have stigmatized the blindness of Enlightenment liberationist projects to the categories of gender and color.[24] Many, particularly Postmodernist theorists, have ridiculed *Lumières* commitment to indefensible notions such as *progress* and *teleology*. Positions that invoke elements of Enlightenment models are frequently treated with derision; arguments that appear convergent with the apparently outworn theses of eighteenth-century rationalism or Hegelian dialectic seem to push against a nearly universal reaction of disdain.[25]

I acknowledge this contemporary frame of the issues I seek to address in *Body and Story*. But contestation of these recent near-hegemonic critiques of the na-

24. Karen Offen makes a strong case, however, for the position that Enlightenment inattention to the situation of women has been considerably overstated: "A return to the sources demonstrates unequivocally that the European Enlightenment is far richer in content and scope on gender issues, indeed far more explicitly 'feminist' in its claims and aspirations than has been generally acknowledged" ("Reclaiming the European Enlightenment for Feminism," 99).

25. Concerning the overdetermined hostility between Postmodernism and the Enlightenment, see Gordon, *Postmodernism and the Enlightenment*. Gordon puts the antagonism directly: "The bias [of Postmodern thinkers against the Enlightenment] is acute because 'Enlightenment' is to postmodernism what 'Old Regime' was to the French Revolution. The Enlightenment, that is to say, symbolizes the modern that postmodernism revolts against" (intro., 1). In the same volume Arthur Goldhammer puts it even more succinctly in his essay: "Distaste for the Enlightenment is the pathognomonic sign of the postmodern" ("Man in the Mirror," 31). Goldhammer details the bases offered by major Postmodern thinkers (Derrida, Rorty, Baudrillard, Foucault, de Man) for their suspicion concerning Enlightenment conceptions.

ïveté, credulousness, or downright dangerousness of Enlightenment positions is becoming more vigorous. Upon examination the views of the philosophes turn out to be more subtle and insightful than they have been portrayed over the past few decades. Thus, representations of supposedly unsophisticated *Lumières* beliefs in reason, teleology, and progress need to be significantly reconceived. Diderot's faith in "reason" was hardly univocal or uninflected, as my discussion of "Jouissance" in chapter 4 suggested. His philosophical dialogues question and destabilize it. Similarly, Voltaire's description of the collapse of buildings in the Lisbon earthquake ("The foundations disintegrated"), like most of the critiques of Leibnizianism in *Candide*, must surely be taken to refer to the destabilization not only of masonry but of rationalist epistemology.[26] Likewise, when critics stigmatize the "teleology" of Enlightenment thinking, they are likely referring to Hegel but not necessarily to any of the French philosophes we associate with the *Lumières*. Nonetheless, these latter get swept into the round-up of the guiltily gullible. Simpleminded Enlightenment commitment to "progress" is similarly contestable. It is perhaps truest of Condorcet, but it is distinctly questionable in Rousseau (whose second discourse rather traces the *degeneration* of humankind) and in Montesquieu.[27] And it would be particularly hard to think of Diderot's *Supplément au voyage de Bougainville* as a celebration of the progress or potential of European ideas and practices.

So a reductionism pervades recent unfriendly responses to Enlightenment thinking. Yet such views are generally credited today. Thus, I need to situate my argument in relation to the key unsavory theses that the "philosophical party" in Europe is supposed to have catapulted into the discourses of the West. To begin with, simpleminded or unidirectional notions of progress, versions of teleology or of ever-growing and mechanical adequation to some apodictic truth, are not pertinent to my argument—particularly to its focus upon the functioning of language and of texts. In the spirit of the most insightful positions articulated in the Enlightenment itself—say, Diderot's sophisticated sense of the *complication* of crediting apodictic truth—let me exemplify my sense of the intricacy of the problem by returning to my tripartite tableau of possible models of the language-referent relationship. On internal grounds, none of the three models I identified could be judged to be "better" than the other two. All three address the problem of how words get (or don't get) into the world. All

26. See Gordon, "On the Supposed Obsolescence of the French Enlightenment," 214.
27. Gordon, "On the Supposed Obsolescence of the French Enlightenment," 204.

have good claims, all have had committed adherents—some over a protracted period. None deploys a knock-down argument against its competitors—for no such argument exists.

The reasons that could adjudicate between these positions are not situated on the plane of their own claims but on levels invisible to them which seek to cognize the *consequences* of holding each view—its coherence with other fundamental epistemological propositions, its situational appropriateness, and the like. To be sure, there has been a historical progression of these solutions. Each is associated with and has been influential in a different period. This *progression*, however, is not reasonably conceived of as *progress*. Indeed, I will argue the contrary position shortly. Thus, I seek to disengage myself from critiques of the teleological character of eighteenth-century rationalism which have been familiar in recent accounts of the Enlightenment.

Second, I want to join the feminist and antiracist critiques of Enlightenment concepts of liberation because of their tendency to forget the liberation of those who were not European males. Enlightenment thinkers generally failed to prolong their critiques of culture- and conjuncture-bound inequalities to the point of detecting and stigmatizing *those* discriminatory presuppositions. Some Enlightenment writers shared them explicitly (others, Diderot in particular, began a reappraisal of some of their tenets, without, however, carrying it through to a principled universalization of *égalité*). While progress may not be the general form of human history, in *this* aspect it surely feels that our groping but ever more egalitarian position today, in most of the developed West at least, makes the deficiencies of Enlightenment emancipatory views evident and salutarily supersedes them.[28]

28. We can see such deficiency, for example, in the racist note Hume added to his 1742 essay "Of National Characters" in *Essays, Moral and Political*. In *Observations on the Feeling of the Beautiful and Sublime* (1764) Kant approvingly cited Hume's views on blacks and added racist commentaries concerning Japanese, Indians, and other supposedly inferior groups. For example: "The Negroes of Africa have by nature no feeling that rises above the trifling"; see "Of National Characteristics, So Far as They Depend upon the Distinct Feeling of the Beautiful and Sublime," 110. One codicil, however, is necessary. In addition to the numerous slave revolts that challenged the slave system in the circum-Caribbean world, by all accounts attacks on the institution of slavery by Enlightenment thinkers were a powerful precondition of abolitionist movements. Diderot's *Supplément au voyage de Bougainville* powerfully condemns slavery, along with colonialism and ideologies of European superiority. The *Encyclopédie* article "Esclavage" ("Slavery") by Jaucourt is uncompromising concerning the heinousness of the institution: "In the period of the century that followed the abolition of slavery in Europe, the Christian powers, having made conquests in countries where it seemed it would be profitable to have slaves, permitted buying and selling them, and forgot the principles of nature and of Christianity which make all men equal" (*Encyclopédie*, s.v. "Esclavage"). The article continues by

Third, I want to reconsider the notion of *reason* itself. At least since Hork-heimer and Adorno, if not since Romanticism, reason has seemed suspect. In *Dialectic of Enlightenment* it is construed not as a precondition for liberation but as a means toward higher forms of interpersonal and social control. It is viewed as a discriminatory tool for those in positions of superiority to use against their gender, race, and class subalterns. Finally, it is guiltily *Western*: white and Euro-centric. Many multiculturalists have expressed their distrust concerning the imposition of such a mode of thinking upon societies and groups supposed to utilize less hierarchizing, less instrumental, and potentially less destructive modes for conceptualizing the world. These critiques have considerably dimin-ished the prestige and perhaps the effectiveness of the category of reason to which the Enlightenment referred hope for the amelioration of human lives.

On the cardinal question of reason, and despite critiques such as those I men-tioned, my view remains indebted to Enlightenment paradigms. In the face of reflexive condemnation of the naïveté, dogmatism, finalism, sexism, racism, chauvinism, and embedded irrationalism characteristic of the Enlightenment—elements whose detection and stigmatization, as I suggested, have been a cardi-nal feature of the "theory renaissance" in France and beyond since the 1960s—I believe that even the most unsympathetic denunciations today of these En-lightenment "errors" are rooted in tenets of reason and judgment framed in the Enlightenment period itself.[29]

It seems to me that the values that the European Enlightenment advocated and propagated—particularly, belief in individual and collective reason, and commitment to the irreducible worth of every person—remain the only prac-tically available and widely held paradigm for political emancipation and social development upon which human beings might rely in the face of increasing claims of cultural and political exceptionalism—not to speak of continuing gross injustice and murderous violence.[30] There can be little doubt that Enlight-enment reason was limited by a relatively unthought normalization of French and European social and cultural assumptions. Like all of us, the philosophes

calling the institution of slavery a crime and claims that it has destroyed the Americas. Enlighten-ment writing had powerful effects on abolitionists in the United States. See Fanuzzi, *Abolition's Public Sphere*.

29. That is the heart of Jürgen Habermas's heterodox defense of the philosophes' project (see *Philosophical Discourse of Modernity*).

30. See, for example, Amartya Sen's authoritative refutation of the thesis that the cultural and political specificity of so-called Asian values justifies suppression or limitation of "Western" versions of democracy in China, Singapore, India, Pakistan, and elsewhere. See *Human Rights and Asian Values*.

were bounded by their conjuncture. What nonetheless remains inspiring two centuries after their period is how resonant and productive their conceptions have proven, far beyond the time and the place in which they were originally articulated or to which they originally referred.

Many people see Jacques Derrida as an antagonist of *Lumières* metaphysics and claims to stable reason.[31] In chapter 1 I considered what some might have thought a surprising (if hesitant) recurrence of and appeal to Enlightenment values by Derrida himself. In these passages, I argued, the limitlessness of language's dissemination and figurality ran up against what feels almost like a physical *arrest* on Derrida's part before the consequentiality of human bodies. My discussion drew from the dedication of *Specters of Marx* (1993) and from a 1997 address by Derrida in which he evoked the suffering imposed upon the Polish people and nation during the twentieth century. But there are numerous places in his texts, in the last decade or so particularly, where similar evocations of affliction movingly occur. In such passages the supposedly irreducible figurality of language suddenly begins to appear suspect, even *inhumane*.

In passages such as the ones I quoted in chapter 1, Derrida takes on the sound of Enlightenment humanism—and perhaps of some skepticism concerning his own theory of figurality. And, perhaps just as unexpectedly, he names the misprized Enlightenment as inspiration for his own practice of critical deconstruction.[32] The sort of self-reflexive interrogation such passages demonstrate is quintessentially in the spirit of Enlightenment ideas and ideals. Habermas's theoretical conflict with Derrida is well known, and Habermas's position has been frequently criticized.[33] But in the wake of this surprising if oblique return to the *Lumières* by Derrida, usually thought of as one of the Enlightenment's most emblematic skeptics, I want to recall and to press Habermas's heterodox—perhaps even scandalous—dictum: "There is no cure for the wounds of Enlightenment other than the radicalized Enlightenment itself."[34] So far, it seems to me, no better physic than Enlightenment ideas has yet appeared for

31. See Hoy, "Splitting the Difference," 230–51, esp. 242–43. Derrida's attitude toward the Enlightenment is a recurring theme in the essays in Gordon, *Postmodernism and the Enlightenment*.

32. "This concern for critical independence belongs to the *Lumières*, to the *Enlightenment*, to the *Aufklärung*, to the *Illuminismo*, to the *Oswiencenie* of our time" (Derrida, "Discours," 124).

33. See Norris, *What's Wrong with Postmodernism?* Bernstein, "Allegory of Modernity/Postmodernity," 204–29; and the essay by Hoy in Madison, *Working through Derrida*, 230–51.

34. Habermas, *Autonomy and Solidarity*, 158. Habermas is principally reacting here to the fundamental critique of the *Aufklärung* prosecuted by his Frankfurt School predecessors, Max Horkheimer and Theodor Adorno. See *Dialectic of Enlightenment*.

the social irrationalities and afflictions that arose in the wake of the twin revolutions at the end of the Enlightenment century and which all over the world have
only become more heinous in our own.

So we expose Enlightenment reason to critique. It is not a false paradox or a
verbal trick to say that in doing so we remain faithful to the protocols of reason which we put under examination. The Enlightenment urged us to question everything. That liberating but potentially cannibalistic notion of self-
reflexivity is already visible in Descartes' decomposition of his own ideas in
Meditations on the First Philosophy.[35] But its locus classicus and its resonant emblem is Kant's notion of *Kritik*, first systematized in the *Critique of Pure Reason*
(1781 and 1787) and put most influentially into circulation in *Was Ist Aufklärung?* (*What Is Enlightenment?*) in 1784. Kant's resonant *Sapere aude!*—"dare to
know"; or, as we might expand the dictum, "have the courage to use your own
reason!"—is the emblem of this critical attitude.[36]

But why should *knowing* require *daring* if it did not entail overcoming threats
and resistances of diverse sorts, up to and including the arduousness of self-
reflexivity that puts *one's own* fundamental theses under challenge? So what in
Kant's maxim might have first appeared an *ethical* imperative turns out, rather,
to be a new *epistemology*. This is what makes Diderot's dialogues—*Rameau's
Nephew* in particular—so stirring. In *Rameau* the disputation really questions
the questioner. We could think of the dialogue as an embodiment of the unsettling but indispensable process of self-reflexivity, broken out now into its con-
stituent and constitutively contradictory moments. To be sure, the character we
call "The Philosopher" in the dialogue (the one identified as "Moi") is not
precisely Diderot. But Moi stands for an unrestricted *self*-interrogation because
his own position of mastery is contested through the most operational form of
dissent—by ideas, fully as compelling as his own, which his interlocutor counterposes, often brilliantly, against him.

If we understand the social practice of thinking as involving an ongoing
process and network of thinkers in a matrix of mutual interlocution, then the
self-correction of thought, the self-repair of concepts through such a practice of
challenge and self-challenge, becomes the register of Kant's "daring." Such a

35. See n. 18.
36. Kant, "What Is Enlightenment?" The notions of "daring" and of "challenge" are also central
to Diderot's title article "Encyclopédie" in the *Encyclopédie*. Kant's celebrated Latin phrase is quoted
from Horace, *Epistles*, ed. Roland Mayer (Cambridge: Cambridge University Press, 1994), bk. 1,
chap. 2, 40.

process defines the vocation of intellectuals since the period when the category itself began to take shape in the notion of "men of letters" in Diderot's period. To some degree the Enlightenment can be accused of the blindnesses and transgressions that *Dialectics of Enlightenment* and other critiques have attributed to it. But the criticism itself reinforces the more fundamental impulse within Enlightenment reason which *solicits* such a dialectical challenge. To find remedies for the outrages, excesses, and distortions that confront us, we rely still upon the protocols and values that Enlightenment writers formulated.

CHAPTER SIX

The Epistemology of Difference

. . . aussi transitoire que les mots.
[. . . as ephemeral as words.]
                —DIDEROT, *Pensées sur l'interprétation de la nature, DFPV* 9:94

"Liberation" is a historical and not a mental act.
                —MARX AND ENGELS, *The German Ideology*, 44

La philosophie a toujours tenu à cela: penser son autre.
[Philosophy has always insisted upon this: thinking its other.]
                —DERRIDA, "Tympan," *Marges de la philosophie*, i;
                                                    Margins of Philosophy, ii

La résistance des autres reste la condition de son propre progrès.
[The resistance of others remains the precondition of our own development.]   —CERTEAU, *L'étranger, ou l'union dans la différence*, 217

Our questions are about *us*. Why else would we ask them, and how else could
we make sense of the answers? The reason to go back to the distant period of the
Lumières is that, despite mystification and denegation, the Euro-American Enlightenment remains a foundational part of who we conceive ourselves to be
and how we think. The problems that preoccupied Enlightenment thinkers—
the rights of human beings; the legitimacy of power; the constitution of government; the organization of fundamental institutions and social practices; the
necessity and productivity of public discourse on social questions—remain fundamental issues today. To be sure, some of these conundra have been with
human beings for millennia. But in a remarkable proportion of the cases we
worry about today, our framing of the issues reproduces the Enlightenment's
conception of them. We can no more eliminate the Enlightenment's influence
upon us than Flaubert was able by an unremitting malediction of his class to

extirpate the reality of his guilty implication in the bourgeoisie.[1] Our interlocution with the Enlightenment continues whether we like it or not.

With regard to the issues of language and materiality which my book has been considering—particularly representation, referentiality, and the pragmatics of texts—Diderot's perplexities still puzzle us today and still converse with our puzzlement. His exemplary and diagnostic experiments with narrative grew out of his period's increasingly unsettled connection between the semiotic and the material registers of experience. Such uncertainties arose within a socioeconomy characterized by growing segmentation, stratification, and differentiation—consequently, one increasingly dependent upon the mediation of signs and language for circulation across the borders, separations, and differences that eighteenth-century society was constructing for itself. But, in our different present today, what does Diderot's Enlightenment analysis of the costs and gains of fictive illusion tell us about *our* relation to language and meaning, to bodies and materiality?

Today our conjuring with words has become denser, more ubiquitous, and more sophisticated. But arguably the processes and practices that sustain it are not different in kind from the ones Diderot was exploring. What has changed is Diderot's acute (if unresolved) sense of the *downside* to language's mobility and to its seeming sovereignty. The notion that the Enlightenment could help us understand contemporary perplexities seems counterintuitive on significant grounds. For, even beyond its repudiation of the Enlightenment, Postmodernity exhibits an intense and concerted suspicion about the past and our connection to it. Elsewhere I've termed this attitude "chronological chauvinism," the projection of contemporaneity as unique, as incommensurable with any other time.[2] Such a vision of our relation to history rewrites change as *difference* and development as *discontinuity*. This sounds and functions like a strategy to conceive the present as nonpareil—or, more cynically, to sell "then" short and market "now," to hype today's symbolic capital and maximize the profits to be made upon it. But despite such "presentist" puffery, are things now as different from the past as they are sometimes made to seem?[3]

---

1. On Flaubert's formative loathing of the bourgeoisie and the insistent return of this abhorrent repressed, see Sartre, *Family Idiot*.

2. On "chronological chauvinism" and its misrecognitions, see Terdiman, "Afterword: Reading the News," 353.

3. The "discontinuity" evoked here is a characteristic figure of Postmodernity's self-conception. In

The liberation of language and textuality has become the emblem of Postmodernity. I want to argue that their archetype and model is an untrammeled and ludic fictionality of the sort Diderot was projecting in his narratives—the sense that with words you are free and can do whatever you like; the sense, even, that language has the capacity to be so free that it can escape our own control and turn our encounter with it from game to agon. But, however heady this promise may have seemed to Diderot, however intriguing the reversal of agency which appeared potential in the medium itself, Diderot didn't swallow whole the detachment of language from other orders of our activity. His tales explore what happens to narrative in the face of meaning's seeming potential for uncontainable lability, but, simultaneously, they test the material boundaries that frame the fictional, just as they constrain *all* human beings and doings.[4]

I don't want to pose an Enlightenment vision of language and the world as a contrary axiomatic to the one that Postmodernism has articulated. The relationship between Enlightenment thought and Postmodernism is assuredly complicated. But it is not a relationship of negation or antinomy. The word *modulation* more closely captures the mode of interlocution or inter-determination which ties these two frames to each other. Here, too, what in my concluding chapter I propose to discuss as "skeptical truth" suggests a mode of relation between nominal antagonists which can complicate and enrich their confrontation.

To construe Derrida as rejecting Enlightenment notions of rationality, referentiality, and determination would be to replicate the exclusionary move that from the earliest period of his work he has himself consistently repudiated (e.g., in *Speech and Phenomena* [1967]): the establishment of a binary opposition (in Gayatri Spivak's words) by means of an "ethico-political decision" that estab-

the face of it we might do well to recall Albert O. Hirschman's understated but fundamental dictum: "The new arose out of the old to a greater extent than has generally been appreciated" (*Passions and the Interests*, 4).

4. Diderot's uncertainties concerning fictionality are put into fascinating relief through the ludic speculations of another writer to whom one might argue he is linked through their common Postmodern sense of playing with language, Jorge Luis Borges: Borges's "Tlön, Uqbar, Orbis Tertius" projects the takeover of the formerly "real" world by fiction. In this new dominion the chief heresy is faith in verifiable objectivity of the real, punished as the crime of "materialism." See Borges, *Ficciones*, 67–81. We can tell a plausible story that links the playful Enlightenment self-awareness of *Jacques le fataliste* with Postmodern celebrations of the autonomy of language. Such an account has recently been offered by André Brink; see *Novel*.

lishes "centralized norms by means of strategic exclusions."[5] Such oppositions falsify the ontology of most social realities, which are not antinomically counterposed to each other in Manichaean binarity so much as they are interdetermined and interdetermining. On the other hand, neither is it the case that Enlightenment thinking rejects the insights of "textualism." Enlightenment models of language and reality are pertinent here *because they are so close* to Postmodernism.

So my aim is not to issue a grant of priority or authority to Enlightenment as over against Postmodern modes of thinking and theorizing—whether about language, narrative, theory, representation, logic, or anything else. On the contrary, my argument concerns Diderot's prefigurement and even his proto-deconstruction of Postmodernism—that is to say, his anticipatory restoration of what Postmodernism has tended to suppress or disable in order to constitute its "textualist" construction of the world. I want thereby to resurrect the possibility of *relation*, and therefore of *negotiation*, between these modes of thinking. They are much more closely tied together than has generally been suggested, particularly in the wake of the anathemata that have been directed by Postmodernists against what they have in effect characterized as irredeemably benighted Enlightenment thinking.

This more supple form of relation—neither reproduction nor repudiation—then joins with powerful "skeptical" tendencies in each of the modes of thinking under discussion: Diderot's brilliant dialogism that destabilizes any settled truths; Derrida's equally forceful deconstructive reconsideration of the blockages and closures by which binarism restricts understanding. These modes open the path to new ways of thinking about human beings and doings and to a more supple form of conceiving our relation to theory. The point is to de-absolutize *everything*, to read back into these modes of thinking themselves, and to the interaction possible between them, their own insights concerning the nonexclusivity and non-apriorism of thought. Then as we seek ways of understanding, it becomes possible to talk about methodological choices. But at the same time this epistemological, ethical, and pragmatic complex becomes the angle from which we can put some pressure on Postmodern textualism.

Textualism is a possible stance. But it's too simple. There's no point trying to prove that textualism is "false." It *isn't* false. But for certain purposes, in certain

5. See Spivak, "Il faut s'y prendre en s'en prenant à elles," 506. The passage is discussed by Nancy Fraser in " French Derrideans," 53–54.

environments, textualism feels wrong. It leads analysis in a direction that is arguably inopportune, perhaps—given the ubiquitous dangers to human bodies all over the world; the magnitude of the destitution that confronts them today; the urgency of reforming the political, economic, social, and medical conditions in which more than half of the world's population are living—even irresponsible. It posits a fundamental modality for understanding our heteronomous existence and the manifold forms of our interactions in a world of rich diversity. But that modality is itself single-voiced.

The problem at the heart of textualist theory is its compression of the relationship we conceive between language and its other. In such a dispensation, this *other* fades away. And this is happening just when we would want the other's difference to be vivid and demanding. The leveling by linguistic absolutism or textualism means that diversity tends to be rewritten, resorbed, and eventually marginalized or erased.

This claim would be contested by deconstructionists. They would express astonishment at its obtuseness; they would point to the foundational ubiquity of differences that are projected in Derrida's notions of "dissemination" and "différance."[6] And it is true that Derrida's concept of dissemination does center upon and proliferate differences: no signifier can ever be thought of as stable; each calls up another along an unending chain of semiotic connections. But *these* are probably not the differences we need most urgently to foreground in the construction of the world that faces us. Dissemination pulls everything back into language, and that is where its monologism arises. It routinizes difference to the point where the Heraclitean non-self-identity that it projects loses any differential bite. Oddly, *language itself* has no other. So it can't be different from anything. The result is that alterity, materiality, the constraints of non-linguistic existence whose resistances can hardly be modeled from within a language paradigm—all these shrink toward nonexistence. This is an unhappy outcome for a mode of thought and analysis which seeks comprehension of a reality whose fundamental characteristic, whose constitutive complication, is its multifariousness, the richness of its difference. The problem is not that a textualist model can't represent these things. It is that, in order to do so, it rows awkwardly against its own tendency.

This is what Foucault was criticizing in 1971 in his stinging assessment of his

---

6. On "dissemination," see Derrida, *La dissémination*. On *différance*, see Derrida, "Différance," 3–29; English trans.: "Différance," trans. Alan Bass, 3–27.

former student Derrida's textualism. Foucault was responding—nine years after the fact—to Derrida's critical analysis of Foucault's *Histoire de la folie*, in a lecture Derrida presented at the Sorbonne on 4 March 1963.[7] In his time-delay response Foucault contrasted the openness to alterity of his own theory of "discourses" with a corresponding impoverishment in Derrida's notion of the "text" and the "trace." He criticized a series of paradigmatic limitations in Derrida's system, limitations that he characterized as: "the reduction of discursive practices to textual traces; the elision of the events produced therein and the retention only of marks for a reading; the invention of voices behind texts to avoid having to analyse the modes of implication of the subject in discourses; the assigning of the originary as said and unsaid in the text to avoid reinserting discursive practices in the field of transformations where they are carried out."[8]

Foucault went on to paraphrase Derrida's celebrated *il n'y a pas de hors-texte* in order to draw out what he conceived as its negative implications. He wrote that the dictum "gives the teacher's [the analyst's] voice that unlimited sovereignty which allows it to repeat the text indefinitely" (602). The force of this somewhat cryptic critique lies in its focus upon the way in which the textualist position surreptitiously asserts too simple and too absolute control over what it finds confronting it. Through simple iteration, Foucault claims, it pulls the *difference* of the objects of its analysis back toward reabsorption. Textualism reduces to the anodyne neutrality of repetition the challenge of others' heteronomy.

The problem isn't that textualism is reductive. Theories are *always* reductive. Your map has to be smaller than the territory. The trick is to capture what you most need to make available in your theory even as, in order to achieve usable scale, your paradigm washes out most of what constitutes your referent.[9] On the grounds of what we need to model, textualism is often the *wrong* reduction. As Foucault contended, it impoverishes what theory can see and say. But the crucial point is that this impoverishment occurs at the heart of what in our present conjuncture needs today to be explained and opened up to understanding in our globalizing and multifarious world of differences.

7. See Derrida, "Cogito et histoire de la folie," *L'écriture et la différance*, 51–97; "Cogito and the History of Madness," in *Writing and Difference*.

8. Foucault, "Mon corps, ce papier, ce feu," 602 (hereafter cited in the text); "My Body, This Paper, This Fire," 27; trans. modified. The foregrounding of "body" in Foucault's title is worth noting. Foucault meant his essay as a "response" to Derrida's. When he published it in 1972, nine years after Derrida's lecture, Foucault sent Derrida a copy. It bore a sardonic inscription: "Sorry to have answered you so late." See Eribon, *Michel Foucault*, 119–21.

9. For a qualified defense of "reductionism," see Terdiman, *Present Past*, 22.

That's just the disquiet or the mismatch Diderot was already worrying about when, in his antic mode in *Jacques le fataliste*, he began to coquette with something like pure textualism. That's what it meant for him to say, in a perplexed and premonitory combination of exhilaration and apprehension, that it was "so damn easy to make up stories." Conjuring with words proved not to be some special and thorny trick; it was disarmingly effortless. Producing language exempt from contact with or limitation by bodies, materiality, or determination turned out, unsettlingly, to be a piece of cake.

This uncanny propensity of language to project *anything* and seem *everything* is the principal source of Postmodernism's power.[10] But this power is rooted in a fundamental paradox. In every aspect but their own metacritical groundwork, Postmodernist and Poststructuralist modes of analysis are anti-absolutist and anti-essentialist. They refuse the isolation or absolutization of any element that enters their field of vision. *Everything is linked*: that is the very meaning of dissemination. But their own foundation resists this insight.

The founding impulse of Postmodern thinking is the radicalism of its attempt to *free itself from roots*. But this liberation contravenes the originary impulse of always insisting upon *links*. Indeed, the link Poststructuralists most rigorously refuse is material determination—just what resists recoding in language's volatility. This perverse refractoriness of what exceeds language cannot be well captured in a Postmodern paradigm. It is just the link whose energy and often importunate intensity Diderot's thought sought to comprehend and to credit.

So Postmodernism's founding exclusion cuts it off from *determination*. Thus its radicalism is fissured. It strives to escape counter-discursivity. That is, it seeks to evade any determination that would covertly ventriloquize it or pre-script its own characteristic mode of encountering the objects of its analysis.[11] In particular it tries to evade the relationship of simple *negation* of other discourses. It projects not binding but freeing. Above all, it wants to free *itself*. But Postmodernism's project nonetheless looks something like a neurotic or overdetermined reaction to constituted discourse. The Enlightenment lurks over its horizon to challenge the transparency of its self-constitution. Its emancipation is thus paradoxically constrained. To frame my perception along the lines of an

10. This portion of my discussion returns to issues I considered in Terdiman, "On the Dialectics of Post-Dialectical Thinking."

11. See Terdiman, *Discourse/Counter-Discourse.*

earlier and celebrated call to revolutionary liberation, this brilliant latter-day example of the same impulse—Postmodernism—still needs to make one more effort to be free.[12]

Since early Modernism, literature has been (and remains for many today) the realm of freedom in a world of often grim and dispiriting necessity.[13] Why should we begrudge literature this role? Some have been tempted to do so—one thinks poignantly of Sartre in the period following World War II, facing along with so many others the necessity of making sense of what the war had brought and brought to light.[14] In what might seem to us his mode of Calvinist moralism, Sartre insisted upon a literature that would fight against evil and struggle for justice at a time when, no doubt exhausted by the war, so many were hopeful that they could simply delight in the pleasures of the text.[15] And, if we make the vertiginous move two centuries back to Diderot, we can see, with a kind of Rabelaisian intensity, an early-modern example of the intoxication that texts

---

12. For this earlier adjuration, see Sade, *La philosophie dans le boudoir*, fifth dialogue. "Yet one more effort, French people, if you would become republicans" (*Philosophy in the Bedroom*, in Sade, *Three Complete Novels*, 296, trans. modified.

13. Probably the most influential account of this separation derives from Max Weber (though many who invoke it hardly know its origin). He was already identifying as modernism's enabling—or disabling—condition the increasing differentiation and division of labor since the advent of capitalism. Callinicos's account is cogent: "This process of differentiation involves the institutionalization of a specific kind of action, what Weber calls purposive-rational (*zweckrational*), or instrumentally rational action, which is oriented to selecting the most effective means to achieving some pregiven goal. The rationalization of social life consists for Weber in the increasing regulation of conduct by instrumental rationality rather than by traditional norms and values, a process which is accompanied by the . . . ever more widespread use of the methods of post-Galilean science to determine the most efficacious course of action available to individuals in pursuit of their goals. [. . .] Weber did not, of course, regard the process of modernization thus characterized with much enthusiasm, both because of the subjective nature of *Zweckrationalität*, which could offer no objective criteria for selecting the goals of action . . . , and because the outcome of its institutionalization seemed to be the imprisonment of humanity in the 'iron cage' of bureaucratic structures"(*Against Postmodernism*, 33–34). Then, as Habermas puts it, what occurs is a "colonization of the lifeworld" by such rationalization (*Theory of Communicative Action*, 2:304).

14. Sartre, *What Is Literature?* The theoreticians of textualism in effect thought that through deeper understanding of the capabilities of language they could undermine or transcend the injunction framed in Sartre's responsibility for *engagement*. Sartre's ideas and practices had presided over the period of their own formation. One could reasonably argue that their reactions were not motivated alone by logic but by politics. And that, in the intergenerational mode familiar to us, they were covertly determined by what they sought to subvert. There are not a dozen new alternatives that we could generate out of this controversy. The fundamental structure of our choices about language, texts, and action in the world remains today essentially what in the eighteenth century Diderot saw them as being.

15. Barthes, *Le plaisir du texte; Pleasure of the Text.*

could induce, that writers could produce in their practice upon them—in a mode of joyfully sly and devious manipulation in *La religieuse*, in a mode of uproarious *jouissance* in *Jacques le fataliste*.

There is no reason to deny to the realm of texts the joys and aesthetic epiphanies that can be generated by and experienced in them. We might feel that the compensatory need for such joys is framed precisely by that against which it so intimately reacts—the degraded world of the economic and the political, of dismal science and social misery, of Flaubert's *bourgeois* and Mallarmé's newspaper, of the dispiriting realities of the quotidian. That would leave us with a powerful paradigm through which these gloomy realities, for which the aesthetic serves as compensation, are represented in the purified realm of art in the very denial of their representability. Modernism lives in this barely disguised hypostasis of one of the registers of life, the realm of language and text. But, as the most quotidian experience with discourse tells us, the absence of something in a text can carry two quite disparate meanings. The first proceeds from an uninflected unconcern with the referent not referenced. The second, on the other hand, inscribes what is denied with the intensity of evasion or denegation.

Texts won't tell you what they mean or where they come from. Interpretation is always indispensable. We can't absolutely know the motives that determined the aesthetic purifications of Modernism or their intricate tropings in the Postmodern. We tell the most plausible story that we can. Yet the mistreated and damaged bodies that keep fetching up in the story I have been telling about Diderot and about contemporary theory—for example, Suzanne Simonin's torture in the *amende honorable* in *La religieuse*; or the euphemistic knee wound in *Jacques*, itself imported from another text brimming with bodies; or, closer to us, the hecatombs of 1939–45 or of the Korean or Indochina or Algerian or Iraq wars—make it hard to insulate a purely textual referentiality from two centuries' worth of mutilated human beings, of *corpses*, which in Modernity form a kind of subterranean or mystified referent for the literary. Stories are about *bodies*, however diaphanous these material realities become in the register of language with its vertiginous and liberating lability. Stories are about bodies and, like the dead bodies that come to the surface of the Thames in *Our Mutual Friend*, these signs of materiality will never allow the denial of materiality entirely to satisfy our desire for pleasure or our need for knowledge of what is the case.

We can understand why people denounce Postmodernism as Idealist. Its resistance to cognizing and responding to developments in the "material" world is a consequence of its fundamental strategy of declining determination. Postmodernism cannot countenance determination because it knows that determination acts in a world that can only be considered "textual" if we extend the category of the textual to the point of forsaking useful distinction. *Material* is the outside that frames and enables *textual*. It designates a realm different from the conceptual because, whatever we think about it, this realm retains independence from language, *from what we think*.

We can agree that our concepts construct the world for us. But that doesn't entail accepting such construction as voluntaristic or arbitrary. From that perspective Postmodern and Poststructuralist modes seem hermetic, absorbed in their own paradigms, allowing too little of the *outside* and the *other* to infiltrate and disturb their development. Textualism then practices an epistemological endogamy and suffers an empirical underdevelopment. This is a condition parallel to the one concerning the "simulacrum" identified by Guy Debord in contemporary society, when "the image becomes the final form of commodity reification."[16]

The objection I've just formulated against Poststructuralism may seem too simple. In particular it is insensitive to Poststructuralism's own skeptical and anti-foundationalist impulses. We could ourselves deconstruct the opposition between the ideal and the material realms upon which it rests. Yet this skeptical retake exerts a helpful pressure upon the wall-to-wall leveling—the textualist— tendency in Poststructuralism's thinking. It helps to discern the character of the quite definite and restrictive notions about what forms of relation are legitimate in Poststructuralism's conceptual discourse—and about what forms of relation are unacceptable.

Let's say we claimed that Poststructuralists were responding to developments "in society." From within their own paradigm that proposition would appear a fundamental metalepsis. The textualist compressions of Postmodernism make it hard to cognize what such a separation—*this* influencing *that*—could mean. That is why, for example, in the opening paragraphs of *La communauté désoeuvrée* Jean-Luc Nancy writes that history hardly exists anymore, and con-

---

16. Debord, *Society of the Spectacle*; qtd. by Jameson, *Postmodernism*, 18. Jameson there frames this reframing of the locus of experience and of meaning this way: "The culture of the simulacrum comes to life in a society where exchange value has been generalized to the point at which the very memory of use value is effaced."

fidently evokes its exhaustion. Jean-François Lyotard had already coined the slogan: no metadiscourses, no *grands récits*.[17] Postmodern logics of the differend (Lyotard), of dissemination (Derrida), of transgression (Bataille, Foucault), or of ecstasy (Barthes) have a common trait: they refuse to countenance the sort of metanarrative which, we once naively said, could "bring people together" or "make sense of history." So much for the possibility of actualizing the humanist values of the Enlightenment!

When Poststructuralists look closely at it, history has no single or stable sense. Thus, in a notion such as Lyotard's "link"—*enchaînement*—elements of discourse are conceived as cohering only in terms of the most attenuated form of connection, a kind of zero-degree logic of succession. *Post hoc* but never *propter hoc*. On this reading, if there can't be a level *up* or *down*, then history is flattened into a narrative of radical parataxis. We haven't seen such a form since the medieval epic, in its transcendent theocratic faith, consigned discourses of causality and determination to the exile of irrelevance. In Poststructuralist diegesis we unexpectedly find ourselves reliving the logic of the *Song of Roland*.

But not exactly. In the eleventh-century *Roland* meaning was guaranteed by cultural assumption of the doctrine of the Logos according to which signs point unerringly to their divine referents.[18] So no force of causality or of teleology had to be or really *could* be represented within narrative; all determination flowed from the ineffable world beyond the text and unceasingly referred it back to such transcendence. This was a world of *parole pleine*—what we might term "materialized language"—to which we can claim no access today. Quoting Thales, Jean-Luc Nancy speaks in *La communauté désoeuvrée* of a similarly enlarged semiosis in Greek society: *panta pléré théon*, "all things full of the gods." And with perhaps a tiny trace of nostalgia Nancy identifies this "uninterrupted world of presences" as responsible for what he terms the greatness (*grandeur*) of the Greeks (124).

Contemporary Postmodern construction of these issues projects, instead, a

17. And, as for these latter, we might not need them anyway, since (excuse the paradox) it might appear that all of the diversities and differences that have defined our millennial and global conflicts are converging in a ubiquitous and harmonious Euro-American paradigm that—if the name had not already been taken—we might have called the "final solution." See *La Communauté désoeuvrée*, 11 (hereafter cited in the text); *Inoperative Community*, 12; and Lyotard, *La condition postmoderne*, 7 (hereafter cited in the text); *Postmodern Condition*, xxiv.

18. This is another example of the first mode of resolution for the language/referent problem that my elementary array in chapter 5 sought to sort out. The medieval epic's belief system and its narrative syntax (or "paratax") are strikingly analyzed by Eugene Vance; see *Reading the "Song of Roland."*

world in which signs point to nothing at all or only to themselves. Yet, unexpectedly, the effect is parallel: in the medieval case meaning referred unambiguously to an inaccessible realm by virtue of its absolute transcendence; in the contemporary one there is no longer a division, bridgeable or not, between sign and significance, since—absent metadiscourse and the extra-semiotic realm—there is no stable significance to begin with. In terms of our old ambitions about history, meaning has become irrelevant, and we are left not with history but with chronicle—with the Lyotardian link. Not *sense*, just *sequence*.

Consequently, in connection with the problem of the *social* which still flickers on the horizon of Postmodernism, in a poignant reappropriation of Bataille, Nancy evokes Lyotard's paradigm of an unending, untotalizable succession. It's obvious why the social is a problem: if metadiscourses are inherently delusive or totalitarian, then we can hardly appeal to them for constructing a different form of community. In response, following Bataille, Nancy tells us, "Nous ne pouvons qu'aller plus loin" (68 and 102). "We can only go further." This Beckettian apothegm we must take as the Postmodernist version of an answer to Lenin's "What is to be done?" The answer is: just go on. But what makes this sentence poignant is Nancy's exact *repetition* of it at the conclusion—indeed, his repetition of it *is* the conclusion—of *La communauté désoeuvrée*. The trope is revealing.

Such repetition subverts any dynamic of temporal flow, of political project, of conceptual *process*, which we might have felt at work in the text. We can only go further. But by repeating the sentence that makes the claim—to use my terminology in *Discourse/Counter-Discourse*, by "re/citing" it—the text self-subverts. It denies and seems to mock its own injunction. It doesn't "go further"; rather, it marches in place. Its hortatory tone ("We can only . . .") appears to project us somewhere, but toward what project are we projected—especially when a suspicion about *projects* is the issue? Further (*plus loin*) than *what*? This reappropriative, citational move transforms the time-sensitive and desire-determined dialectic of social activity into a logic, into tautology or circularity. We go, but our going doesn't *go* anywhere. Even here finalism is prohibited. So, at the conclusion of Nancy's text, appropriating the Bataille quotation about "going" is a way of enforcing stasis. It bleaches out time. This is the cost we pay for expunging final causes or any form of purposive activity.

In the history of the twentieth century's unprecedented social catastrophes, one can see the outcome of totalitarian system-fanaticism. And ethically I think we must support impulses that react against it. But not all reactions, however well intended, are effective. It is possible to attack the wrong target. Postmodernists such as Nancy and Lyotard stigmatize a *form* of discourse characterized by purposiveness. They reflect the historical experience of Europe and much of the rest of the world that such purposiveness can become fanaticism and that the effort to build a better society can, rather, determine massacres. But is *teleology* the villain here?

In particular how can we distinguish formally between Lyotard's repudiation of *grands récits* and the *grands récits* he repudiates? Not on the grounds of "purposiveness" or "teleology"—these are present in both. It's not the *form* of the performative which is crucial here, but rather its *content*. But the meaning and bearing of content isn't cognizable on the flattened plane of a language-world that rejects overarching structures of value. These are what that world rejects to clear the ground for liberation. The tactic, however, seems delusive. You can't separate the sociopolitical or theoretical or even the aesthetic programs you want to keep from the ones you want to expunge without . . . *a program*.

Assessing the content of a narrative is an effect of metanarratives. It implies a broad and fine-grained knowledge of just the history and social knowledge whose exhaustion or extinction (as I recalled earlier) Jean-Luc Nancy proclaimed in *La communauté désoeuvrée*—again on the grounds that "history" can only be written in the sway of some inadmissible organizing principle. So, theoretically and formally, it may not be easy to distinguish the terrifying results of totalitarian metadiscourses from the more local ones that animate our everyday purposiveness. Which goal-animated *récit* should we eschew? Can we know in advance which one will produce another Khmer Rouge or Taliban and which the livable freedoms of liberal democracy? It seems almost as if the Lyotardian formulation of these matters in *The Postmodern Condition* sought, in a very textualist spirit, to expunge a terrifying social calamity by proscribing *a form of language*.

But that may not be the lever we need to save human lives. We know the difference between proto-totalitarian and proto-communitarian programs not by their *being programs* but by their *having content*. We measure this content against an account of values that themselves project a *grand récit*. This account is a metanarrative that we have inherited from the Enlightenment. It is this structure of values which gives force to our conceptions of egalitarianism, of liberation, and of common humanity to begin with.

Then why has Postmodernism given up (or given up on) history? The answer is that history is a *constraint*. Any metadiscourse speaks us. It turns us into its tools. In a world characterized by increasing programmation and penetration of discourses, any prior scripting, any form of transcendent control, feels like a servitude, what Pierre Bourdieu would have called an exercise of "symbolic violence."[19] The middle-class ideal of liberty which in the period since the Enlightenment and the French Revolution has animated much of the social project in the West is still alive in contemporary theory. As was the case with Hegel, freedom, liberation, are still its teleology. The eighteenth-century revolutionaries sought to be free of feudal exactions. Today we want to be free of metanarratives. But we need to ask whether the project of purging the conceptual realm of its epistemological and ontological servitudes isn't a defense, a screen, the cultural or conceptual equivalent of a neurotic substitution, for more intractable social complications.

There are other, less cerebral servitudes, other forms of exaction, which fetter us. But contesting *them* involves modes of action less cerebral and textual. The issue isn't whether textualist paradigms can cognize such action (for you're always free to see as a text everything you can perceive or imagine). The issue is whether such a paradigm is well suited to the task of liberation. Hegel suggests the stakes and the limitations in the passage from the *Phenomenology* which I quoted as an epigraph to chapter 5: "Freedom in thought has only *pure thought* as its truth, a truth lacking the fullness of life. Hence freedom in thought . . . is only the Notion of freedom, not the living reality of freedom itself."[20] Textualism doesn't capture the elusive but alluring *otherness* that is the referent of Hegel's resonant "fullness of life." This perception on the part of an Enlightenment culture perfectly familiar with the attractions of a world conceived as language—that you give up profoundly consequential freedoms in order to achieve *that* one—is the heart of Diderot's fraternal challenge to textualism and to Postmodernity.

Let me pursue these connections and divergences in a consideration of the following passage: " 'Despite everything you've said,' the reader will object, 'we have still learned nothing about that woman's unpleasantness; but since you've already delayed the story for such a long time already, allow me, Mr. Author, to hold you up a moment more to tell you how annoying it is that, despite your youth . . . , your memory was already so defective as to leave you unable to recall the name of a woman you knew perfectly well.' 'Indeed it is annoying, Mr.

19. See Bourdieu, *Outline of a Theory of Practice*, 191.
20. Hegel, *Phenomenology of Spirit*, 122.

Reader. . . . ' 'Well, did Madame d'Arpajon finally introduce you to the Prince?' 'No, but kindly shut up and let me return to my story.' "

This quarrelsome tonality is familiar to readers of *Jacques le fataliste*. The passage seems a fine instantiation of the way Diderot chaffs his reader and seeks to reassert narrative control of the story.[21] But what is going on within this text is not just kidding around. Why should narrative control be contested to begin with? How can it be? Obviously, it's the writer who writes; no one else can utter anything without the author's sanction. So this agon might appear bogus. But it is consequential nonetheless. The contention depicted here incorporates and simultaneously spoofs the mode of "presence" of the hidden interlocutor in any narrative transaction. It registers and it complicates the connection that brings two people "together"—as we somewhat delusively say—in the transmission and reception of a text, at the moment of the latter's metamorphosis from private mental event to objectifiable social action. It foregrounds what we customarily forget or suppress: that when interlocutors encounter each other in such commonplace transactions, their connection is *problematic*. Reading might seem to depend upon a nominal harmony between reader and writer. But our passage suggests that at best this is an insecure presumption. It insists that when we talk, others are listening—*and they have language too*. What the passage really points to is the problem of others' difference.

Increasingly since the Enlightenment, the developed West has been a culture of words and texts intended to be read by others. Our passage foresees a more developed, *interactive* form of reading, the technology for which is only now appearing. What happens in this little text is what really happens all the time in daily life, but generally without being represented in texts at all. As this passage indicates, *others are a problem*. But, typically, texts don't integrate this difficulty into their diegesis. They write the other *out*. Here, on the other hand, what Bakhtin called "dialogism"—the simultaneous presence in a text of multiple subjectivities and languages—gets internalized, pulled into the text itself, in a consequential "baring of the device."[22]

The conditions of possibility for the writer-reader contention and the need for a mode of imagining their interlocution have been present for a long time.

---

21. See William B. Warner's conclusion ("The Freedom of Readers") to *Licensing Entertainment*, for a useful perspective on the issue in question here.

22. On "baring the device," see Tomashevsky, "Thematics," 94. On "dialogism," see Bakhtin, *Dialogic Imagination*, esp. 259–422; and "Glossary," 426–27. Julia Kristeva renamed Bakhtin's dialogism as "intertextuality." See Kristeva, "Mémoire," 39–54.

As the undermining of all other forms of authority proceeded in the Enlightenment, how could *authorial* authority have remained exempt? So a conflict of relatively independent subjectivities emerges in the modern reading process as elsewhere in wider political and social exchanges. Ordinarily, we imagine the reaction of dissatisfied readers as limited to chucking a book that displeases them into the circular file. What else could they do? They would seem silenced by the technology of text.

But the possibilities of readerly dissonance or even antagonism are more extensive than simple commercial repudiation. They vote with more than their feet. They have voices, even if most times we can't directly hear them. The representation of such a voice in the passage above is critical because it depicts what *exceeds* the subjectivity of an author-actor who (since nineteenth century formalisms at least) has regularly been imagined as sovereign. Such sovereignty is a paradoxical and contradictory aspect of theories of textuality, even though such theories would deny this. They would point to the aspects of the theory itself which undermine our "control" of language. With *some* justification. But Foucault's critique of Derrida's textualism pulls our interpretation of deconstruction back in the direction from which it sought to distance itself, toward the silencing of the very others to whom it claims to want to give voice.

People have standpoints—not just writers but everyone. And everyone reads. Just as others' standpoints inherently challenge our own, so the reading process is not an oasis of concord but a field of tension. In the language I have been using in this book, readers are one register of "materiality"—of the elements of a world that resists the thought of any individual subject, the project of any agent. In the reading process these extrinsic irritations defying authorial control of the transaction have implications for the way we conceive the relationship between subjectivity—language—and that which most of us think of as beyond the immediate control of words. They foreground alterity as that which *is not assimilable to my language.*

Following a reflex familiar in Postmodernity, we could dismiss or redescribe the represented struggle and the entire problem. Everything can always be recontained into "text." Then we would claim that the "reader" projected in and by this little narrative is no less a "fiction" than anything else within it—hence no less under authorial control than any other element in the telling. Consequently, the little skirmish in our passage would be no more than a camouflaged form of self-dealing.

Yet I don't believe this is true. Readers are not *just* textual effects. The reason for this consequential difference is that others' objections aren't in the same register as the questions I raise myself. One would need to forget or repress what we know about the world and our activity within it to think that readers could be conceived as if they were nothing but fictions I spin out in the way that Diderot's Jacques and his Master are. The point of the notion of "referentiality"—a concept more or less exiled after Saussure made it part of the semiotic triad along with signifiers and signifieds—is that what language refers to is *not* part of language, not possessed by it or by those who use it.

But how can you conceptualize resistance to control from within a paradigm based upon the behavior not of *things* but *words*? The problem with textualism is that it is difficult for paradigms based upon it to project and represent the *limitations* on our control which characterize the perverse resistance of what I have been terming "materiality." That's the world that houses the readers who pipe up with unwelcome cavils and complaints. We may not cherish wrangling with them. But they are the ones who tell us there's *something else*. Textualism tends to dry up such difference. Before returning to the spat between narrator and reader in the passage I've cited, I would like to consider further how we might think about this sort of unanticipatable and unrecontainable diversity.

Others surpass us. How can we conceive them? Only as the irreplaceable. Michel de Certeau put this luminously in *The Writing of History*: "I could not know how [or: it would not be possible] to substitute [my] text for what only *another* voice could reveal about the place from which I am writing."[23] It's this "what we 'could not know'" which discloses the indispensable existence of otherness. Thereby, Certeau's sentence measures the limitation of textualist paradigms. And it frames the epistemological stakes that for any subject arise in others' irreducible difference from us.

Texts, on the other hand, have the potentiality to seduce us into a vision of the world coterminous with them. The pertinent problem arises when we realize that there is a downside to such seduction and begin to cognize its consequences. This is why the tangled ambiguities of "seduction" recorded and played out in Suzanne Simonin's delusive narrative in *La religieuse* are so diagnostic and instructive. The Enlightenment was not only about the positive side of "reason" but about revealing and elucidating the power and the mechanism of reason's *other*. But this irreducible otherness is best conceived along the lines

---

23. Certeau, *Writing of History*, 212; trans. modified. The French original is even more striking: "Je ne saurais substituer un texte à ce que seule une voix *autre* peut révéler du lieu d'où j'écris" (*L'Écriture de l'histoire*, 218).

of a vision of materiality as the unanticipatable and illimitable unpredictability of difference.

It might appear that my vision of textualism promotes a straw argument concerning the imagination of alterity. The claim would be that I conceive of the text in terms limited to *one* individual's subjectivity, whereas textualism construes the entire world as text. Then my strictures concerning Postmodern conceptions of a totalized textualization of the world could only be justified if there were but one transcendental author composing such utterances. We don't believe that some supernatural being writes the lines everyone is given to perceive or to pronounce. Rather, we conceive of a super-individual entity variously named "language" or "ideology" or "reason" or "desire" (and so on) whom we can project as the agents or "locutors" of textualism.

This is a viable view. The model it projects works. My argument is that it doesn't work very well just where we need it to: in the articulation of how difference is possible and how to apprehend, process, and respond to it—how to experience the quiddity of its divergence. The reduction or leveling irreducible in textualism understands difference as that which can be inscribed (as it were) upon the writing pad of the world—maybe on a different page from ours but readable by us.[24] But in such a construction it's the refractory *difference* of difference which fades away. So partly the attraction of what I'm calling "materiality" lies in capturing the arduousness and challenge of what diverges so much from what *we* might have imagined or uttered—a response to a problem; a model for conceiving of the world; a representation of that orchard over there—that the difference hardly appears scalar or negotiable any longer. *Our* words may take a lot of effort, but they are unproblematic compared to *others'* words.

Dialogue is the prototypical modality for figuring this difference. But dialogue is itself internally diverse. Take the classical case in philosophy. In many of Plato's dialogues the text brings a knower into contact with someone who doesn't know but who will soon learn through the process of the text. Euthyphro starts out with false ideas about Justice and Piety. But he ends up having learned better from Socrates. Now he comprehends the inadequacy of his prior beliefs. By the process of dialogic *elenchus* he is brought to the skeptical point where Socrates himself already stands.

This is a model of difference, but it is truncated. However arduous it may be to modify somebody's thinking and bring it into convergence with our own, it

---

24. My allusion is to Freud's "Note upon the 'Mystic Writing Pad.'"

is a different kettle of fish to confront a perspective irreducible to ours and able to sustain itself quite as well as we think we sustain our own. That's *alterity*. And that is what Diderot sought to capture in his very un-Platonic dialogues. The principal characteristic in Diderot's dialogues is the equipoise sustained between two represented positions—say, between the Philosopher and Rameau in *Rameau's Nephew*. The work of this form then is not convergence or reconciliation. Rather, by showing us what we could never ourselves have conceived, the productivity of the form is to stretch our notion of what can be thought and must be credited.

Then Rameau's nephew fetches up in Hegel.[25] Let me seek to clarify the pertinence of this connection by considering the theory of difference—what he called "heterology"—developed by Michel de Certeau.[26] Following Certeau, I want to ask about the epistemological opportunities and consequences of difference. This should better explain what is at issue in the writer-reader skirmish that I have been appealing to as the emblem of this portion of my discussion—and in any interlocution, dialogue, or dialectic more generally.

Understanding difference needs to integrate the role of the problematic border that separates us from others. That border, and the resistance to passage which it signifies, is what creates the conditions of possibility for *any* understanding. Certeau's insights are important because his focus on the ubiquity and productivity of difference urges us beyond any easy normalization of diversity toward reflection upon the material conditions that produce and sustain the heteronomy of the world—and upon those that, in their turn, this diversity determines.

An operational explanation of difference flows from Certeau's analysis. Difference is signified by a content that can pass from one locutor to another only

25. It is well known that Hegel had read Diderot (particularly *Le neveu de Rameau*, no doubt in Schiller's German translation, which was the form in which the work was originally published). In the *Phenomenology of Spirit* Diderot's work appears several times as inspiration or example. See the translation of the *Phenomenology* by A. V. Miller, 298, 317–20, and 332. Beyond these specific references, the social content and dialectical tension of *Rameau's Nephew* may well have influenced Hegel's conception of the celebrated "Lord-Bondsman" (or "Master-Slave") dialectic (*Phenomenology*, sec. 176–98). On the textual connections between Diderot and Hegel, see Hulbert, "Diderot in the Text of Hegel," 267–91; and, for a penetrating analysis of the philosophical relationship, Simon, *Mass Enlightenment*, chap. 5. On 15 April 1869 Marx wrote to Engels about the presence and importance of Diderot's dialogue in Hegel's thought. See Marx and Engels, *Selected Letters*, 139.

26. Here, from a somewhat different angle, I am revisiting issues I discussed in Terdiman, "Marginality of Michel de Certeau." More detail and documentation will be found in that essay.

through a significant *resistance*—one that we cannot reduce in a simple trans-coding or control by a straightforward performative command. Difference results from a determined obstruction of one locutor's ability to join the text that another produces. It is a matter of impeded or stressful communication. Perhaps this suggests why textuality can't exactly capture it.

The etymology of *communication*—related to English *common* and German *gemein*—carries the root notion of "exchanging with." But difference is what is *not* common, *not* unproblematically exchangeable, or not exchangeable at all. It pulls in the other direction from language. For this is not just a matter of "translation" from one linguistic tongue to another. It is, rather, a matter of that "phase-change" that I talked about in earlier chapters. It is an alteration not in medium but in ontological mode. The image would not be that of trying to understand a text you couldn't read (as if it were in a language you didn't know, for those can always be deciphered). It would be like trying to put the stone of Mallarmé's palace into the body of your text.

How these impediments and resistances occur is at the heart of Certeau's analysis. They lead us from linguistics to the less malleable domains of political economy and history. For example, we can see how Certeau understands certain socially determined blockages in *The Capture of Speech* or in "The Politics of Silence: The Long March of the Indians." The economy of discourses seeks to frame this problem, establishing the vectors of domination and subordination which make the possibility of access to *communicable* expression socially and materially differential. Some inhibitions of the capacity to participate in locution, to speak and be understood, are enforced by what Althusser termed the overt "repressive apparatuses" of the state. Speak, and they shoot you. However heinous, that's clear. But the more theoretically daunting involve those other, ubiquitous apparatuses that stealthily regulate social existence (Althusser's "ideological" ones).[27] One doesn't easily pass over the border of difference any more than we can cross sensitive political frontiers without anxiety and danger. The point is not only that it is difficult to understand the differences inherent in others' speech, text, and standpoint. The point is that it is hard even to be aware that their experience, their standpoint, their *text*, stand over against our own. And hardest of all is to ventriloquize for difference—to say in *their* voice what *they* would say, given that they are not *us*.

In his solicitation and citation of *different* voices Certeau anticipated the

27. See Althusser, "Ideology and Ideological State Apparatuses."

concerns of Postmodern anthropologists from James Clifford and George Marcus to Johannes Fabian. Across the borders that divide individuals or cultures, epistemology becomes *bidirectional*. Those whom we call "the others" draw us toward them and make meanings we can neither predict nor constrain. So the movement is two-phased: we are attracted by another's meaning, but simultaneously obtaining access to it is challenging. Both of these vectors of force are consequential, and the effacement of either traduces the arduousness and the interest of the paradigm—and of the experience of difference it seeks to model.

"The resistance of others is the condition of our own development [*progrès*]."[28] This resonant formulation of Certeau's which I placed as an epigraph to this chapter projects a productive model of social practice and understanding. Leaving aside liberal guilt and thinking only of the methodological moves this insight suggests, we could say that Certeau's conception of communication with those others foregrounds the stressful production of "knowledge" through difference. Such knowledge must arise in bidirectional and *mutual* exchange.

The process of transfer isn't unproblematic; indeed, it might almost seem at first incomprehensible how in situations of significant difference meaning can pass over at all. But without such passage across difference we are condemned to a life constrained by the limits of our own experience and imagination. An individual might be brilliantly original, but the world of heteronomous difference is far richer in surprises, challenges, and unanticipatable realizations than any one of us could ever be on our own.

Gayatri Spivak's question about whether the subaltern can speak thereby receives a practical and emphatic answer: all of us must *insist* that she do so. Nor on our part is this just a matter of generosity or noblesse oblige. Even in dominance not only they but *we* are victimized by our franchise to speak about those who are not free to answer or upstage the answer that we put into their mouths. In situations of unequal power our own discourse can only be enabled to the extent that it enables the discourse of those who are nominally its object.

While every difference remains different, our mode of awareness and openness to the claims of what diverges from us can be deepened through the insights of Certeau's heterology. The horizon of his model is a convergence between *difference* and *critique*; indeed, these become alternative modes for the same set of epistemological potentials and interpersonal realities. Their union-in-difference constitutes both an epistemological resource and a political im-

28. Certeau, *L'étranger*, 217; my trans.

perative in a world that tends to regard itself as increasingly massified, centralized, and univocal or monothetic.

Against such projections heterology insists that no single formulation or conceptualization can ever be adequate to the complications of contemporary lives—complications that arise not only on account of empirical profusion or plethora, of the multiplicity and scattering of facts, but from an authentic and multivalent diversity of interests which can never be subsumed, never be reduced, to a single utterance or interest. Heterology then becomes a fundamental intellectual discipline for a multifarious world, allowing us to relate structures of difference across the whole range of social and cultural (but also temporal, geographic, and even theological) differences. The horizon of this vision of the world is the same aspiration toward public reason and democratic process which animates Enlightenment reflection about sociality and politics.

An ethics thus underlies the heterological project: uncompromising commitment to an egalitarianism for which the old (now sadly suspect) name was *humanism*. From the Enlightenment we inherited the possibility of a belief in the irreducible value of every human life and of all human experience. It guides the need we have for a model that could help us understand how difference exists, functions, and could be understood. But what would be the epistemological consequences of taking heterology seriously? What happens to our knowledge when we attempt to ascertain and to relate to the knowledge of the other? Heterology projects an epistemological advantage onto difference itself. How to understand such a privilege of diversity?

There are several ways in which the epistemological value of difference could be argued. The first derives directly from the humanist ethic to which I just referred. It posits an a priori advantage to diversity analogous to the biological advantages of species differentiation—a salutary richness in the primary material of existence. According to this view, held by most cultural pluralists, it is better if many sites and sources, *multiple options*, prevail in any aspect of human existence.

A distinct but related vantage would follow from shifting the emphasis to the proto-critical potentiality of difference, manifested as a multiplicity of perspectives decentering the authority and undermining the self-evidence of any single dominant position. Heterology deterritorializes hegemony. It posits the indispensable founding condition for ideological critique. Such a position helps to explain why skepticism isn't just a blasé liberal relativism. We could see how difference puts pressure on orthodoxy in the image of Montaigne's "Cannibals" or Montesquieu's "Persians," posed (in accordance with their authors' sly assumptions of naïveté) to marvel over the bizarre and incomprehensible practices of the French.

On this second view, if they are to remain vital, discourses must be critically regenerated by exposure to difference. But there are limitations, not only advantages, in the heterological processing by which such regeneration can occur. We need to look more closely at the incompleteness inherent in my first formulation of heterology. Its limitation emerges when we notice how within this first view the *power* differential in such situations of difference has been overlooked or ignored. Paralleling (and often outflanking) such positional or practical engagements between *our* position and *theirs* is the verticality that frames them, inscribing the material superiority of the one and the corresponding subordination of the other. My second construction of heterology then seeks to restore the reality of hierarchy.

Any practical, ideological, or conceptual system has a repertoire of elements that are licit and admissible within it. On the other hand, elements extrinsic to it, heteronomous factors, initially can seem incomprehensible or meaningless. But the process of understanding doesn't stop there. Theoretically, anything *really* meaningless would simply drop out of a given social or imaginative transaction, and disappear. But in experience almost nothing falls into this category of absolute and unbridgeable difference. In social existence borders may be difficult to cross, but they are never airtight. What cannot be immediately accommodated or integrated into the system appears, rather, to pose a challenge or a threat. Both working on the system and being worked upon it in its turn, its processing continues until some sort of negotiation, violent or peaceful, brings about the possibility of connection, relation, even assimilation.

Difference thus injects a perturbing (and potentially transforming) impulse into the system. It propels systems out of logic and into history. Through its challenge it initiates a process. Thus, heteronomy is not only a register of difference but a determinant of *change*. Consequently, this second formulation of the privilege of difference does not simply celebrate diversity in the way that a zoo might value increasing the number of species in its collection. It draws attention to difference's *system-altering* potentiality.

But beyond these two conceptions stands a third—and much stronger—form of difference's claim to epistemological privilege. Although the methodological roots of this final avatar have been established for nearly two centuries, its

influence on contemporary models of alterity has not been sufficiently integrated into the way we think about the question. This is why I believe we need to
reexamine the relationship between Certeau's heterology and Hegel's account
of dialectic. In a period as reflexively anti-Hegelian as ours, proposing such a
convergence risks seeming a provocation. Indeed, a plausible way of defining
Postmodernism might be to see it as an attempt to *purge* Hegel from methodology and representation. I believe, however, that our blindness to Hegel's presence in contemporary models is itself an effect of ideological repulsion.[29]

Certeau had studied Hegel (particularly the *Phenomenology*) around 1954, as
part of his Jesuit training. Later he spoke of the extraordinary influence of this
reading of Hegel upon his intellectual and political development.[30] There are
few explicit references to Hegel in Certeau's writing. But a deep atmospheric
and conceptual filiation links his heterological project to Hegel, particularly to
the famous account of the dialectic in the *Phenomenology*.

So, while the first of my models for understanding the epistemological status
of alterity celebrates diversity as abstractly desirable, and the second re-registers
the existence of the power differential that the first had ignored, Certeau's
heterology projects and practices a third, and more penetrating, construction
of difference's privilege. This third model recapitulates a fundamental move in
Hegel and recasts in an intriguing way one that is present in Foucault. Since
Foucault, many analysts have internalized the power differentials inherent in
social or cultural difference. What distinguishes the third position concerning
the privilege of difference is a startling *inversion* of these differentials.

The image of such a reversal arises in Hegel's analysis of consciousness and
recognition in the *Phenomenology*.[31] The essence of Hegel's assertion in the
"Lordship and Bondage" section of the *Phenomenology* is this: while common
sense attributes a relative impotence to the subordinate individual in any rela-

29. This repulsion is partly of the intergenerational kind that Harold Bloom has termed the
"anxiety of influence." In France the material basis for this anxiety (or, at least, this influence) was
particularly strong. Beginning in the 1930s, the so-called Hegel revival involved important French
figures. Between 1934 and 1938 Bataille and Lacan, Queneau and Merleau-Ponty, were members of
Alexandre Kojève's seminars at the École Pratique des Hautes Études. See Roth in the appendix to
Knowing and History. On the general phenomenon of Hegel's influence upon French thought since
the 1930s, see Butler, *Subjects of Desire*.

30. See Giard, "Biobibliographie," 248. Some of this material is based on personal communication
with Certeau during the period of his appointment at the University of California, San Diego (1978–
84). Giard has provided the most thoughtful reflections on Hegel's importance for Certeau; see "Mystique et politique," 27–36. Speaking of Hegel's "decisive role" in Certeau's intellectual development,
she refers to the "structuring presence" of Hegel's thought in Certeau's work.

31. Hegel, *Phenomenology of Spirit*, particularly pt. B, sec. 4-A.

tionship defined by a power differential, in the practice of social life an epistemological *advantage* constitutively (if counterintuitively) *complements* this sociopolitical inferiority. Conversely, the position of nominal superiority occupied by the dominant person in a social relationship paradoxically entails an intrinsic handicap. These unexpected determinations of any structure characterized by a social differential *invert* the disadvantage of disadvantage and make consciousness of social existence from a position of difference an indispensable feature of our potential for understanding the world.

We need to look more closely at how Hegel reconceives the link between individuals and redefines their relationship within the *Phenomenology*'s dialectic of consciousness and recognition. What happens is a surprising reversal. This is the innovation at the heart of Hegelian dialectic and the one most directly relevant to the problem of language's relation to materiality. A clear hierarchy would seem to determine the positions of the Lord and the Bondsman. But Hegel projects overturning this hierarchy through the differential possibility of knowledge.[32]

In Hegel's allegory the Lord achieves control over the Bondsman through acceptance of the risk of death. Whatever we might think of Hegel's myth about the origin of such authority in allegorical combat, its structure corresponds to everyday experience of power relations and domination. We internalize such structures almost before we have the language to describe them, and we live them every moment of our lives. The verticality of such domination is hard to fit into a textualist paradigm.

The existence and power of structures of domination is the point that, following Foucault, many understandings of difference reach. But I want to bring Hegel's notion of epistemological reversal into contact with Certeau's representations of subordinated individuals and groups and of their potentiality for producing knowledge. In Hegel, as the dialectic proceeds, the Bondsman's subservience unexpectedly flips over to reveal itself as the determining condition of a privilege of understanding. The Bondsman—the inferior—turns out to have a capacity for vision which propels him into a position of epistemological advantage. For Hegel this potentiality is determined by the structure that dictates the Bondsman's experience of subordination. It stems from the *work* which his social inferiority imposes upon him. Inferiority, then, paradoxically becomes the condition of possibility for insight.

---

32. On the reversal in Hegel's Master-Slave dialectic, see Jameson, "Transformations of the Image in Postmodernity," 104.

In part 6 of the *Phenomenology*, on "Self-Alienated Spirit," Hegel offers a concrete example of this sort of unexpected reversal. He draws it from *Rameau's Nephew*. Hegel conceives Rameau's apparent ignominy as enabling his perception of fundamental truths concerning society and human existence: "The shamelessness which gives utterance to this deception"—that is, the content of what *Geist* says about itself—"is just for that reason the greatest truth. This kind of talk is [Rameau's] madness" (*Phenomenology*, 317). It articulates a perspective that for Hegel is the opposite of mad.

The energy that drives this inversion, destabilizing the hierarchy that initially arises in the Lord's dominance, emerges from the unassimilably *different* position occupied by "inferior" figures like the Bondsman and Rameau: "Through this rediscovery of himself by himself, the bondsman realizes that it is precisely in his work in which he seemed to have only an alienated existence that he acquires a mind of his own" (*Phenomenology*, 118–19; trans. modified). The Bondsman then turns out to be in fuller contact than the Lord with the world and its oppositions.[33] He knows what, from his superior position, the Lord *can't* know. This is the significance of a form of difference which cannot be smoothly transcoded into sameness or immediately absorbed by it. The metaphor that could represent this sort of exchange is closer to the mediated complications of *metabolism* than it is to the flattened communication of textuality.[34]

The paradigm for these diverse but converging reconceptualizations of difference and disadvantage is the notion of *critique* as it developed from German

33. See Gosden, *Social Being and Time*, 65–66.
34. Certeau is assuredly not the only thinker to have had insight into such reversals. We can find versions of such an epistemology in versions of feminist theory (e.g., "standpoint theory") which argue for the singular perspective on social existence provided by women's consciousness. See esp. Keller and Longino, *Feminism and Science*, in particular Harding, "Rethinking Standpoint Epistemology," 235–48; Haraway. "Situated Knowledges," 249–63; and Longino, "Subjects, Power, and Knowledge," 264–79. A similar reversal arguably occurs in Marx's account of the relation of Jews to the larger society (particularly to the problem of global emancipation) in "On the Jewish Question." Marx maintains that the supposedly marginalized Jews in fact stand for (and implicitly understand) *everyone*; that they have realized in their own consciousness and identity truths which remain veiled in the existence of the Christian majority. See Marx, "On the Jewish Question," 36–40, esp. 39. The question of the rhetoric and diction in this text is controversial. I read what some take to be Marx's anti-Semitism in this text as re/citational—as a bitterly satirical and antiphrastic rehearsal of what *others* say about Jews. In *History and Class Consciousness* Lukács, following Marx, attributes a corresponding insight to the working class that is structurally denied to their capitalist oppressors. See Lukács, "Reification and the Consciousness of the Proletariat," 83–222, esp. 164. Postcolonial theory offers analogous models of such reversal. See, for example, James, "Black Jacobins," 67–111, particularly the brilliant speech James composed for his protagonist, Toussaint L'Ouverture (77); Fanon, *Wretched of the Earth*; and Ashcrost, Griffiths, and Tiffin, *Empire Writes Back*.

Idealism in the Enlightenment and afterward, up to our own day. This is why it finds such a natural home in the models we associate with contemporary Postmodernism and in the kinds of reversal with which we have become familiar from deconstruction. The existence, the exercise, of critique always implies some form of difference, of perspectival externality. *Critique* is the intellectual register of differential irony.

We need others for many reasons. Certeau's work extends our understanding of this need. This is not *simply* a matter of ethical generosity. The force and scope of heterological understanding reinforces the urgency of a theory of materiality. What then comes to light is conceptualization of an inadequacy that makes the other's knowledge not just an indispensable complement to but a constitutive metadiscourse of our own. The sorts of ties that bind human individuals and groups deepen and complicate themselves in such an epistemological extremity, as a result of the combined opportunity and necessity of extending the grasp of our knowledge through crediting the knowledge of others precisely because *it is not ours.*

With that extended background I want to return to the squabble between reader and writer in the passage I quoted earlier. The adversarial relationship that our text manifests—recapitulating the sort of struggle for control of the story that in *Jacques le fataliste* extends over nearly three hundred pages—suggests that, however seductive it may be, the fantasy of linguistic and narrative liberation which Diderot was exploring in his fictions can never be totalized. If you are committed to textualism, you lose the battle if your readers *answer* what you write, if they come back at your text with any response at all. But that's the situation in which locutors *always* find themselves. This is what makes any projection of readers' incorporation into text—and thereby the reabsorption of the extratextual, social world for which they stand in—troubling, because of what it discards in its attempt to understand what is the case.

The point is not whether the intra-textual modality of otherness is somehow ontologically distinguishable from what it answers. Morphologically, the other's voice in a text looks just the same as ours. The point is to know whether the invariable medium of words is called to represent as present a perspective, an identity, an interest, a subjectivity, *extrinsic* to the text's locutor: something that could not be deduced from the subjectivity that generated it, something *she would not have said.* Otherness in that sense is the unanticipated and *unpredictable*: it is the intervention of difference into the identitarian world of the constant and the foreseen. That which I could not already say—the un-predictable—is what makes a strong conception of temporality and materiality indispensable for theories of human beings and doings.[35]

Wondering whether a heteronomous voice can be distinguished from the utterance to which it responds is like speculating in biology about whether you could tell by inspection if a particular tissue will be treated as histocompatible or as an invading antigen. The microbiological principles that govern identity and otherness are not deducible but always, and critically, contingent, situational, and specific. A protein that is native to one organism will act in another as a violent antigen and give rise to a potentially fatal immune response. Troping Derrida, we might say that in the microbiological world "there is nothing outside the DNA." Yet a body knows what is *self* and what is *other*.

So do texts. In the biological world as in the textual one more familiar to us in the interpretive disciplines, the universality of the medium by no means signifies the absence of critical conflicts, contradictions, and contentions within its register. So, while words might seem capable of anything, their freedom is never absolute. *Something always answers language.* Even as mischievous a writer as Diderot was constrained to register and react to the querulous independence of other subjectivities, despite the fact that often the explicit objective of his text (as with his efforts to "manage" the Marquis de Croismare through the text of *La religieuse*) was to neutralize them. Drawing the reader's objection and interrogation into the fiction, as in the passage I quoted earlier, might seek to outflank the force of others' difference from us by absorbing their pseudo-counter-discourses into our own text. We could then attempt to transform the reader, in proto-Barthesian terms, into nothing more than a writerly "effect." But such an operation can never succeed.

All texts register something outside their limits. They are driven or haunted by what exceeds them. The very urgency of their assertion makes no sense if there is no external and material world, uncontainable within them, with

35. There are regularities and patterns to the choices that culture makes available. Our sense of *anachronism*—which translates a deployment of our cultural knowledge—intervenes to tell us when we are neglecting the limitations that govern the elections that can be made. This is what makes the drama of time's "out of jointness" so uncanny. Derrida brilliantly discusses the phenomenon of such impertinent anachronism, focusing upon the para-chronological inappropriateness of the ghost's appearances in *Hamlet* and upon a parallel impertinence in the survival of Marxian thought in our so-called post-Marxist period. See Derrida, *Specters of Marx*. Fredric Jameson's version of this inhibition upon the absolute freedom of thought is characteristically pithy: "You can't manage to think about things simply by deciding to" (*Postmodernism*, 71).

which they must contend, against which they must react. Dialogism is the fundamental ground of utterance. Why would we have language if there were nothing *different* to hear?

So language can never escape bodies. The *others* are always there. Hence we are the text of our arrested attempt to textualize others. Then an agon like the one in the passage I've been discussing, or in so many places in Diderot's narratives, stands as more than a waggish anecdote manifesting the fears writers entertain concerning the querulousness, the restiveness, of their increasingly invisible and even unimaginable audiences. In its very structure such a gambit rather represents the force of the reversals of control which are irreducible in language because, despite fantasies of authorial authority, even sovereignty, language belongs to no one and responds to what is *not* its own.

Materiality, I've been suggesting, is the web of constraint which underlies such registrations of resistance. It bears upon and against any text. This happens as a result of the irreducible difference that underlies every speech situation, every use of language—the uncontainable voices, practices, perspectives, and interests that, at the very moment a text may seek to incorporate and neutralize them, explode its coherence and block its autonomy or totalization. Texts represent many forms of alterity. But the fundamental difference projected by the constraints that frame textualism is the one that counterposes against each other the semiotic and the material registers of the world—the one that brings into confrontation bodies and stories.

Modernity sees the world as language. What an adventure we have been having with it! Language suggests that we could say anything we want, that it could be made to do anything we choose. Remarkable insights about the world have arisen from this fascination with the linguistic. *But for modeling the world's social and material processes, language offers an inadequate paradigm.* When we use our seemingly weightless words to figure the world's material density, a crucial mismatch occurs. *Words* assuredly are not the same as *things.* But what is the dimension of their difference? As I put it elsewhere, inspired by Freud's reflections on the same problem, "language is compliant, things are resistant."[36] But that resistance constitutes our experience of reality and, because of its "compliance," language has fundamental trouble capturing this. We need to struggle against this paradigmatic disequilibrium if we are to draw the primordial weight

36. Terdiman, *Present Past*, 279.

of the world of real objects and real social existence into our representations, and express the refractoriness of materiality in the gossamer lability of words.

My reader doubtless recognized it some time ago, but in the—perhaps irritating—agon of my silent interlocution with her, it's well past time for me to acknowledge that the passage confronting author and reader which I quoted some time back, and which I've been burdening with these ruminations, is not by Diderot at all. Nor is it part of any Enlightenment reflection concerning the reader's place in the fictive illusion or the potential disruption or subversion of the latter. The text I cited is by Proust, written around 1921.[37] Diderot's antic exploratory efforts to understand the strange contention of language and materiality, of freedom and constraint, which are projected by writing and reading thus reappear here unexpectedly at the heart of high Modernism. But how did Proust find himself in *that* boat? What sense can we make of the reanimation in his novel of Diderot's concern with the freedom—and the limitations—of narrative?

The ambivalent relation to language—to its paradigmatic capacities and limitations—brings Diderot's early-modern reflections and narrative experiments into contact with Proust's formalist high Modernism and even with Postmodernism today. Of course, we cannot collapse these times into each other or compose a story of unproblematic connection across more than two hundred years of tense and stressful history. Yet the story written by the passage of these two centuries is not just a narrative of disjunction or parataxis. Across its heteronomy Diderot's problem with language converses with our own. Assuredly, even on this limited dimension of the languaging of the world, something crucial has changed. But it may not be what we might at first have thought. Since Diderot's period and even since Proust's, it is our sense of language's *other* which has been progressively orphaned. Increasingly, under the influence of a series of powerful writers and theoretical models, we have been mesmerized by textualism. How can we rebalance this seductive infatuation?

By the nature of the case what is eclipsed for us appears invisible. But this invisibility is not irremediable. What has been marginalized through a process of ideological exclusion can be recovered through the exercise of ideological

---

37. *Sodome et Gomorrhe II, À la recherche du temps perdu*, 3:51–52; my trans.; *Sodom and Gomorrah, In Search of Lost Time*, 4:69–70. No doubt in this passage Proust, with his talent for pastiche, was imitating Sterne or Diderot (whose texts he knew well). But the question is why this Enlightenment play with the reader seemed pertinent to him to begin with.

critique—using techniques that have their roots in the Enlightenment period in which the interrogation of language which concerns me here began to be acute. A period is never monological. Things are always richer and more complicated than they seem. More than the present is present in the present. Our experience of textuality today carries with it and has available within it the recollection of a view of language's relationship to materiality, to its fundamental other, which by revisiting Diderot's or Proust's problematics we can recover now.

Proust appears as a supreme exemplar of the aestheticism, subjectivism, and Idealism that distinguished Modernism and its vision of the text. He often underlined his own inclinations in such directions, as when he regularly defined art, in neo-Kantian or proto-Crocean terms, as *cosa mentale*—as a sovereign and fundamentally internal, self-referential performance, beholden to no limits or pressures beyond the agency of the artist.[38] Yet the skirmish with the reader which Proust fomented in the passage I quoted earlier is only one of a number of cases in *À la recherche du temps perdu* in which the insistent (if studiously marginalized) *subversion* of such an Idealist and subjectivist vision becomes perceptible. The result is that, in a surprising flash, the textual autonomy and absolutism that for Proust epitomized the art object and established its incommensurable value—and without which it would be hard to imagine Derrida's position—finds itself undermined from within the supposedly sovereign text itself.[39]

In his novels Diderot coquetted gleefully with narrative. In his stories narrative feels like a captivating new plaything. Playing with words can't do any harm unless—through a consequential solecism—we begin to believe that words are *all* we have to play with. This is an erroneous induction. One hundred and fifty years of Formalism have demonstrated that the pleasures of the text are extraordinary pleasures indeed. But they aren't the only pleasures or satisfactions we can enjoy. For Diderot, despite these intra-textual delights, alternatives still existed which seem to have been increasingly dissolved or abrogated in our

38. Among many examples of this favorite Proustian attribute for the aesthetic realm, see *À l'ombre des jeunes filles en fleurs*, I, *À la recherche du temps perdu*, 1:491.

39. Elsewhere I examined Proust's neo-Kantian ideology of aestheticism and analyzed a number of cases in which his own text subverts it; see Terdiman, *Present Past*, 160–63. The Proust passage I cited earlier is highly excerpted. The material omitted constitutes an extended disquisition on the difficulties of remembering *other people's names*. The passage thus represents in a different but parallel way the unavoidable limitations of any purely subjectivist view of consciousness, and its necessary entailment to elements of social existence which, more even than standing beyond its control, positively challenge it from a perspective that it is constitutively incapable of assuming or repossessing on its own.

period. Diderot's project presupposed and required a belief that, however complex and arduous it might be to cross the barrier that partitions the linguistic from the material realm, however long it might take to urge and finally to realize the sorts of transformations that analysis seemed to incite, this translation could in fact be striven for and realized.

Let us remember that in the eighteenth century such a pragmatic assumption was by no means a secure given. No doubt absolutism in France had become less absolute in many ways than it had been under the Sun King nearly a century before. But believing that ordinary people could scrutinize the secular world and use language to *alter* it was still an uncertain and hesitant notion. Reaching across the partition I evoked was difficult, but it also underlined the fact that there was something cognizable and potentially changeable *beyond* the world of language, usage, and the like.

But in our period (in much Postmodern theory at least) such forays into the extra-linguistic world have evaporated into flattened textuality. Such a construction evens out the sorts of differences which we might almost liken to topographic relief, that variegated character of the landscape which can give us, at different times, the experience of the seashore and the very different experience of the mountains. You might fancy the one or the other. The fundamental point is: they're both there in different places, and our experiences of them are not commensurable, not collapsible or transcodable one into the other. Postmodernism has proven one of the most capable paradigms we have for detecting the variations in our multifarious world. Yet something at its heart seems to dream of these differences as if they were ultimately marginal attributes—what medieval philosophers would have termed "accidents"—which could be resorbed into some all-pervading and inalterable substance such as the deity represented for older societies. The consequences of such a conception are simultaneously theoretical and practical. We choose our models, but nothing in logic or ontology commands us to credit only one side of the textual binary and discard the other.

The division of intellectual labor has fostered the increasing separation of these alternatives. Those who work at texts tend to write about their work with them in a way that gives circular justification for their activity and even its truncation with regard to other realms and other tasks. Issues of professional and disciplinary prestige circulate here in ways we need to tease out of the high-theoretical ratiocination by which we justify methodological choices. These motivations need not only to be identified but to be undermined.

But the alternatives potential in textualism and productive within its practices remain visible. This is so even when since the Enlightenment period what was perhaps the cardinal one of them—the materiality of all forms of social existence and interaction—has tended to settle over our horizon. For fully a century following (in novelistic realism, for instance), materiality's sun remained high in the socio-critical sky. But it has since become a dead star for many analysts in the cultural disciplines. Still, our suspicions of the progress myth would suggest that any notion that we have somehow passed to a state of higher understanding and linguistic self-realization since the period of Diderot's naive confusions must be viewed with doubt.

By Proust's period, following upon the textual solemnities of nineteenth-century Formalism, writing had become sacralized. Why would a novelist so doctrinally committed to the *autonomy* of narrative as was Proust disrupt his tale to project the irruption of a cantankerous and importunate reader into the textual field? The religion of the text can never be as infallible as divine revelation. Even as creedal an ideology as the theologization of the aesthetic carries the guilty knowledge of its own incompleteness. My question about Proust's disruption of his text then needs rather to be reframed and asked from the opposite direction: what real-world narrative situation could we imagine in which intervention from outside texts, from outside their subjective linguistic material, and adversatively answering it, would *not* insistently preoccupy writers—even (perhaps especially) those most committed to belief in the text's transcendence. Indeed, would not this situation of a hidden material world outside the text fundamentally define the conditions—and consciousness—of writers' "literary" activity? How, then, could they not register and represent it, even if, as in the notion of textuality itself, they did so through a version of Freudian denegation or some other oblique or camouflaged representation?

In their common commitment to a vision of reality coterminous with language, Proust's Modernism and contemporary Postmodernism lie on a continuum of preoccupation that arguably began with Diderot's Enlightenment language experiments. Here, despite the common view of him as epitomizing the most detached and historicophobic of high Modernisms, Proust can serve as an illuminating intertext or transition figure. Modernism and Postmodernism exhibit a genus similarity and a species differentiation. What enables both attitudes is a notion of texts as separable objects—language with no incorporated referentiality, no attached *body*. But Modernism believes this separation exalts the ideational field, segregating it from the contaminations of a debased world. Postmodernism undoes this hierarchized valuation. The Postmodern text is . . . just text. It is movable and alienable, recyclable, fungible, reinterpretable, available without distortion or injury for troping and manipulation.

Thus it lives its detachment from bodies in a different mode from the Modernist text. Modernism makes the text's separation *serious* and *exalting*. Postmodernism thinks of it as a divertissement, off in its own locus of amusement. The Postmodern text thus sheds its ethical or aesthetic ponderousness in order to construe its bodylessness as enabling the enjoyment of a game. This inconsequentiality is the result of the detachment from bodies which was already being explored in Enlightenment narrative experiments then was adumbrated, but not fully realized, in Modernism. The deep intellectual and libidinal connections humans make with their environment, what Deleuze and Guattari term "investment," are thereby suspended.[40] The process both frees but also evacuates the texts it reconceives.

In his hypostasis of language's sovereignty Proust aligned himself proleptically with Postmodernism. But like Diderot, he retained a perceptible skepticism concerning what such a construction implies or portends. This skepticism subverts or unsettles Formalist doctrinal positions for which many cite him as inspiration and authority—it reminds us to remember Proust's often-marginalized "Balzacian" side. Whence the powerfully deconstructive *materialism* of the sentence excerpted from the same passage in *Sodome et Gomorrhe* which I quoted as one of the epigraphs to chapter 5: "The activities of our mind are effortless *so long as they are not obliged to answer to the real*" (*À la recherche du temps perdu*, 3:51; emph. added).

What plays out in the narratives of Proust, as of Diderot, is not really a contention between readers and writers but one between modes or models for understanding the place of language in the constitution of the reality we answer to. The deep question is how we should construe the seeming autonomy of texts, the paradoxical and ambivalent authority of authors. As language users, it can seem (as it did at times to Diderot in constructing the fictions of *La religieuse* or of *Jacques le fataliste*) that we may be constrained by nothing at all. "What's to prevent me from marrying off the Master and then cuckolding him? Or shipping Jacques off to the Indies?" (*Jacques le fataliste*, DFPV 23:24–25). What

---

40. Deleuze and Guattari, *Anti-Oedipus*. Deleuze and Guattari dispute Freud's axiom that the social field cannot be "invested" in directly. Jameson extends the concept in his notion of "libidinal apparatus"; see *Fables of Aggression*. See also Buchanan, *Deleuzism*.

indeed? Nothing in the world would seem to resist such an initiative on the part of language. That is the sort of puzzle that frames our own Postmodern perplexities.

But to us as actors in a social and historical world the experience of *limitation* seems a cardinal and untranscendable element of existence. How can we theorize such constraints, particularly as they bear upon us in the seemingly *un*-limited world of signs and language? Thus arises in textual practice our consciousness of the paradigmatic mismatch to which I referred in chapter 2, between the model of the labile world which language projects and the refractory material world outside or alongside it. This is an incompatibility that versions of textualism seeking to collapse the multifarious registers of existence back into language induce us to misrecognize.

In the face of the strictures that materiality imposes, it has taken a great deal of concerted ideological work to sustain contemporary textualist visions of the signifier's free play and of the autonomy of language. Indeed, we might wonder how, with regard to this model of sovereign textuality, Postmodern orthodoxy has been able to bear up at all. For it constantly confronts the subversions that texts *themselves* perform of their own ideologically determined pretensions to autonomy—like the ones mobilized by Diderot's and Proust's representation of an agon that opposes their readers' wills, needs, and desires against their own authority. Such presences within the text unmistakably undermine its absolutism. At the hands of the text's own internal processes textualism then seems to turn inside out to demonstrate how it is determined by and ultimately dependent upon the very externality it denies: upon the one thing that it cannot incorporate or neutralize, the uncompassable difference that delimits its claims to totalize the world. Even textuality can be deconstructed with Derrida's own toolbox.

How can this subversion not have been obvious to the theoreticians of textuality? If we look at the history of criticism over the past few decades, it seems apparent that their attention was elsewhere. When we grant them the grounds on which they chose to make their argument, then Derrida's *il n'y a pas de hors-texte* and parallel notions become unanswerable. For perception and cognition are obviously textual modalities. If they are all we have to work with in thinking about the world, then everything is text. The *Ding-an-sich* may exist, but our access to it assuredly passes through language.[41]

41. As Rorty puts it, "The world is out there, but descriptions of the world are not" ("Contingency of Language," 5).

So texts mediate our relation to everything in experience. From this starting point it seems an easy further move to suppose two things: first, that because texts constitute our immediacy, we may as well ignore or forget about what they *mediate*, since to that realm we can never get clear passage but, rather, will only find ourselves in an infinite regress; and, second, that from the point of view of authority or reliability (or their consequential absence) any given text must be considered the equivalent of any other text, hence none can be granted privilege or priority. For where, at what impossible Archimedean point, might someone stand to assert such authority? If texts are everything, then nothing frames or controls them. Our customary analytical reflex to locate the *meta-* and *infra-* levels that embrace any conceptual entity then loses all pertinence. Under such a construction trying to reach outside the text leads you at best to yet more texts, at worst to fundamental misunderstanding of the conditions of knowing since Kant focused upon the question (the first edition of the *Critique of Pure Reason* appeared in 1781, three years before Diderot died). Deborah Jenson summarizes the situation aptly: "viewing representation as real has taken on the status of a . . . primordial error."[42]

But do we really experience texts and language in this absolutizing way? Is this the most capable paradigm we can devise to model our experience? That is the question I have been putting in Diderot's mouth in this book—or rather, that is the paradox I want to claim he was himself exploring. He was persuaded that language was tightly bound to the material and social world and yet unable to conceptualize how that might be. His contradiction can help us take some critical distance from our own contemporary doxa concerning this problem.

The Postmodern construction of the question depends upon making the meaning of *text* so general and abstract that everything is corralled within it, while outside it there is nothing. Then textuality delimits the world. Such a notion of text creates a conceptual version of Edwin Abbott's "flatland."[43] Its two-dimensionality might give us pause, since it is a characteristic of definitions encompassing all referents that in practice they are useless: unexceptionable but vacuous. In effect this is the point that Richard Rorty (though often sympathetic to Postmodernist positions) makes with regard to textualism:

> As usual with pithy little formulae, the Derridean claim that "There is nothing outside the text" is right about what it implicitly denies and wrong about what it explicitly asserts. The *only* force of saying that texts do not refer to nontexts is just

42. Jenson, *Trauma and Its Representations*, 5.
43. See Abbott, *Flatland*. The book has been widely reprinted.

the old pragmatist chestnut that any specification of a referent is going to be in some vocabulary. Thus one is really comparing two descriptions of a thing rather than a description with the thing-in-itself. This chestnut, in turn, is just an expanded form of Kant's slogan that "Intuitions without concepts are blind," which, in turn, was just a sophisticated restatement of Berkeley's ingenious remark that "nothing can be like an idea except an idea." These are all merely misleading ways of saying that we shall not see reality plain, unmasked, naked to our gaze. Textualism has nothing to add to this claim except a new misleading image—the image of the world as consisting of everything written in all the vocabularies used so far.[44]

The problem with the uses to which the concept of textuality thus deplumed by Rorty has been put in our own period is that this ontological universality of the cognizable ("everything is text") has been transmuted into a very different proposition, with very different implications. The effect of this latter move is to call into question the possibility of priority, hierarchy, or determination *within* the formation thus defined. This is what has given rise to broad and often confused speculation about the constitutive autonomy of texts. The argument is familiar: if there is nothing but text, then there can be no meta-level to which we could appeal to norm or control the textual. This is conceptual flatland. In that case how could any text be said to have authority over any other? Consequently, the world, properly seen, becomes a relativistic or random accumulation of stochastic and disjointed language fragments—constrained by nothing, since there can be nothing endowed with the capacity to adjudicate between individual textual entities. At the limit there *are* no meanings. In which case we're free—but we're also disconnected from anything that might make our freedom useful or pertinent.[45]

But the logic of a "flat" textuality is misleading. To begin with, the notion that everything cognizable occurs in the form of texts by no means signifies that there can be no internal structure, hierarchy, or determination within the textual formation itself. The notion of an all-encompassing, wall-to-wall textuality thus takes anti-essentialism and anti-authoritarianism to an extraordinary limit. It is out of such a logic that the vexed issue of Postmodernism's politics ultimately emerges.

44. Rorty, "Nineteeth-Century Idealism and Twentieth-Century Textualism," 154. It is important to be clear about the fact that Derrida's critical practice (and "deconstruction" most centrally within it) is far from blindly falling victim to the unexplored flattening of all texts into random and disconnected fragments. Indeed, from this perspective the purpose of deconstruction is precisely to demonstrate the profound but mystified *entailments* by which texts are bound to others.

45. On the meaning of such "meaninglessness," see Terdiman, *Present Past*, 67–69.

CHAPTER SEVEN

Materiality, Resistance, and Time

There seems to be virtually no case in which the soul can act or be acted
upon separate from the body [*aneu somatos*].
                    —ARISTOTLE, "On the Soul," 403a, 1:642

Mon corps est là où il y a quelque chose à faire.
[My body is where there is something to be done.]
                    —MERLEAU-PONTY, *Phénoménologie de la perception*, 289;
                                        Phenomenology of Perception, 250

What is remembered in the body is well remembered.
                    —SCARRY, *The Body in Pain*

Reality happens without waiting for our theories—that was how I began this
book. Thought always runs behind. But some theoretical paradigm—Poststructuralist models among them—can't well capture this hysteresis. For them the
"world" can't "run behind" understanding because the world is no different
from language. The result is that our relentless experience of difficulty and
delay cannot rightly be cognized at all.

But if experience and language had no gap between them, how could we not
already have understood what we seek to formulate as theory to begin with?
This sense that there is a need to fulfill which is not *already* fulfilled, this sense
that our understanding is always out of phase with *something* it needs to comprehend, is the reflex of our immersion in constraint, of our limitation by
materiality and by an ineluctable temporality. Life doesn't unproblematically
give in to language.

So we need a way to theorize *difficulty*. We need a model of the *refractory*.
Why is finding such a model thorny? The problem arises in part because, since
the Romantics, we have heard so much about the imagination's possibilities
that we have tended to forget about its constraints. But the principal cause of

our inattention is the foundational mismatch between language and the extra-linguistic world, between the ideational and the material—or, to use another vocabulary, between the *écrit* (writing) and what Jean-Luc Nancy has termed the "excrit." Nancy explains his charming neologism this way:

> The word [*excrit*] came to me in reaction to a whole infatuation with *écriture*, text, salvation through literature, etc. There is a phrase of Bataille's: "Only language can indicate the sovereign moment when it is no longer valid [*où il n'a plus cours*]". . . . There is only language, sure, but what language refers to is the non-linguistic, things themselves, the moment when language is no longer valid. It reminds me of a conversation with [Paul] Ricoeur long ago at his house in Chatenay. He had just read my first book on Hegel and, opening the door to his garden, he said: that's all fine, but where's the *garden* in it? I never forgot: the *excrit* is the garden, the fact that *écriture* indicates its own outside, decants itself [*se transvase*], and reveals *things* [*montre les choses*].[1]

Nancy's "decantation" is an alternate figure for what I've been terming the "phase-change" between ontological states (from materiality to ideality and back again) which is the most constant practice in human cognition, under-standing, and action. Some would say—yes, this is all very well, but our words cannot become the garden. So we cannot theorize *it* or the *Ding-an-sich* or, indeed, any part of the realm of the *excrit*. Some even conclude from this that there is no point even trying to speak about what exists beyond words, since words—which, in this view, are *us*—can never go there. Such a position author-izes (or mandates) sanctuary (or claustration) in the language-world alone.

The answer is that Kant, Nancy, many others, and language itself are *already* doing what such theoretical restrictions on our practice allege cannot be per-formed. It's like a familiar joke. Asked whether she believes in baptism, the interlocutor replies "Believe in it? why I've *seen it done*." Accusations of "pri-mordial error" are leveled by some Poststructuralists against any system that suggests that language may *not* be all there is.[2] Some contemporary versions of textualism in effect claim never to have "seen it done." But to think so, you'd need to close your eyes very tight: it's "done" every time we speak, and if it were not done we couldn't exist.

---

1. "Le partage, l'infini et le jardin," interview with Jean-Luc Nancy by Jean-Baptiste Marongiu, *Libération* (Paris), 17 February 2000, sec. "Livres," 3; my trans., some emph. added. For more on Nancy's "exscription," see "Exscription."
2. See the passage I cited in chap. 6 from Jenson, *Trauma*, 5.

So, we need to subject the "infatuation with *écriture*" which Nancy evokes to the same critique we would deploy for understanding *any* cultural ideology or practice. Human usages and conceptions develop from practical life. If we base ourselves in the quotidian behaviors and beliefs of human beings doing their work, living and acting in the world, it would seem impossible to sustain the notion that the corporeal, material existence indispensable for getting work done could be so severed from or absorbed within the linguistic realm that the overwhelming weight of the former could lose itself in the relative weightlessness of the latter.

Nancy's *excrit* projects the de-reification of textualist absolutism, including the strain many have associated with Derrida since *Grammatology*—a development all the more interesting because Nancy has long been closely identified with Derrida himself. In a salutary deconstructive spirit the *excrit* maps the outside of *écriture*, what is external to it and fundamental for constituting and stabilizing it as a concept. It explores what cannot be recontained within language, what always remains the "excess" or the "dangerous supplement" that theorists such as Bataille and Derrida themselves have argued can never be exhausted or reabsorbed in discourse.[3] This is a powerful extension of deconstruction: *deconstruction deconstructing textuality*.

In the tradition of *Ideologie-Kritik* from the nineteenth century to Poststructuralism, Nancy's analysis thus *re*-constructs how the *écrit*—"writing"—was constructed to begin with. It takes the notion's determinants apart by restoring what is not available in them on their face or by inspection but is nonetheless indispensable for their intelligibility. Thus, the *excrit* "reverse-engineers" the seemingly self-evident concept of sovereign writing in order to bring its historical and conceptual formation—and its consequent contingency—back to light. It remembers what textualism (in Rorty's sense) forgets. Mapping the place where words pass over into things—*se transvasent*, in Nancy's vocabulary—makes the shape of the word system clearer. Indeed, it is a necessary move for cognizing the system itself.

Nothing exhausts reality. Everything has a limit and an outside. This externality or otherness may be temporal, spatial, conceptual, or material, but it always exists. The entity that would comprise all entities, the concept that would totalize all concepts, always comes up short. It will fail in its objective

3. For Bataille, see "Critique of the Foundations of the Hegelian Dialectic," 105–15; and "Notion of Expenditure," 116–29, in *Visions of Excess*. For Derrida, see ". . . That Dangerous Supplement . . . ," in *Of Grammatology*, pt. 2, chap. 2.

because, in proportion to the increase of its capaciousness, its generality will tend toward loss of definition, discrimination, or conceptual bite. Totalities are always partial; difference can never be suppressed. That's what's wrong with trying to absorb materiality entirely into language. Moreover, the same limitation plays even within the ontological registers around which my discussion turns. Thus, we will find no materializable word for all words and no cognizable thing that everything can be part of. Notions only emerge, perception is only possible, when their referent or their object is relativized and contingent, when something *else* sits on the other side of its margin.[4]

When people suppress the indispensable margin and enclose themselves within writing or textuality, then whatever seems incommensurable with these appears as *noise* that can be ignored because it disturbs language's systematicity.[5] Textualism's reduction refuses or repels the force of what exceeds text. No wonder it doesn't talk about it. Consequently, the extra-linguistic, the *excrit*— what cannot be converted to words—is devalued. But restoring the boundary of language both rematerializes externality and revalues its importance. The *excrit* insists upon the necessity of crediting what—in the image of Paul Ricoeur's garden—is *not* language. More than that, it rehabilitates the notion that the world of human work and material objects determines the world of words *from the outside* at the same time that it is determined by it.

For thinking, such interdetermination is deeply puzzling. What mysterious ether can we posit as the medium by which, according to Nancy, such influence passes over *(se transvase)*? What could account for, and how could we understand, the uncanny phase-change that I evoked for characterizing this process? Our images always get stuck in an oxymoron. We will never get an absolute solution to this problem, nor will it ever go away. The reason is that the problem incorporates just the incompetence it seeks to overcome. It begs (or stumbles over) its own question. Any solution to it would have to be framed in words and concepts. But that was the difficulty to be resolved in the first place. So to solve it you'd have to have solved it already. To borrow an image of Stendhal's which evokes the problem, eyes can't see themselves. The *tool* we need to use thus devolves into the *job* we need to do. But words will never "do" objects, will never encompass or recontain them. This is the place where language won't work.

Yet a different perspective is possible. Materiality and language are indeed

---

4. For a fuller discussion of this point, see Terdiman, "Marginality of Michel de Certeau."

5. In chapter 5 I quoted Viggo Brøndal's characterization of the extra-systemic as the "great impediment to any rationality." See Timpanaro, *On Materialism*, 159.

other to each other. But this "otherness" does not signify incommensurability or absolute disjunction. Otherness is not opaque and uncognizable but constitutively *relational*—indeed, as experience constantly demonstrates in manifold realms, it is a powerful and consequential form of relationality. Deconstruction would even say it is the most *general* form of association between entities or words—it is the heart of *différance*, of how the world works and flows by constantly changing *and yet constantly connecting across change*. This is why deconstruction empties out the category of "presence" and substitutes for it the time-contingent category of "dissemination."

If we take the notion seriously, otherness then means that neither element in a two-part relation can ever provide by itself the medium for apprehending both of them or their connection. *Connection* is a mode of relation on its own. It cannot itself be transcoded or resorbed back into either of the terms that confront each other in its functioning. If it could—if difference could be recontained, reinterpreted as a previously disguised or mystified version of sameness—there would be no otherness to begin with.[6] But in the multifarious world that we are increasingly aware of living in, an ethical and theoretical responsibility of honoring and conceptualizing otherness seems critical.

The resources for doing so are available. What experience gives us can surely be theorized. In daily life as in high-level conceptualization, things "change phase" constantly—not just water becoming steam but also print or speech becoming meaning, desire or project materializing itself in behavior: *different* things becoming perceptible and cognizable despite their difference. In every act of semiosis—in every human act—either a material signifier transforms into an immaterial signified, or the phase change works in the reverse direction. There is a constitutive connection between the realms or phases of existence—centrally, between language and materiality. Everyone lives this connection constantly, and no one could live without it. The fact that it's difficult to capture in language doesn't mean it doesn't occur.

But, despite our universal practice of this quotidian relation, we do find it difficult to theorize. There must be and there *is* passage from one realm to another. When both terms are linguistic, then language can encompass their connection. But often they are not both contained within language. Then lan-

6. Elsewhere I considered a local example of how such attempts at recontainment, characteristic of the New Historicism among other methodological families, falsify or weaken the power of "difference" or "otherness"; see Terdiman, "Response of the Other."

guage bumps up against the *excrit*. The garden is always there. Standing in Ricoeur's living room, Nancy and Ricoeur both experience it. They experience the insistence of its challenge to conceptualization, even though—or precisely *because*—the garden isn't words. As Mallarmé put it in his prose poem "Conflit" concerning his confrontation with an analogous materiality, "Impossible de l'annuler, mentalement" (Impossible to erase it by [an act of] mind [*Oeuvres complètes*, 357]). Despite how much it could simplify our theory, we can't abrogate the force of what, like Ricoeur's garden, insouciantly declines to be *just* language.

The solution cannot be to conceive thought or language "reaching out" to materiality to the point of enveloping it, for that only evades the foundational problem—the *separation* of the two worlds between which experience constantly mediates. If I seek to cognize and comprehend *relationship*—an inherently complicated problem—in the effort to simplify I might be tempted to efface one of the terms that compose it. Reductions are essential and can be salutary. But *that* particular reduction is an amputation. With the disappearance of one of the terms of the dyad, the problem isn't cracked; it's *crushed*. But how did *écriture* come to seem absolute in the first place? What was the construction that Nancy's *excrit* proposes to deconstruct?

In 1852 Flaubert famously fantasized writing a "book about nothing." But, in the very thought of overcoming or abolishing outward referentiality, his goal of purging it perversely reinscribed the margin that it sought to overcome or obviate.[7] The *excrit* thus re-materializes a consequential margin, the one that delimits the complex of writing- and language-based paradigms themselves. These paradigms have been influential since nineteenth-century formalism propelled language, ideas, style, and similar concepts toward the position of supreme—and ultimately of unique—value in cultural practice. Over time, as is typical when concepts are internalized and institutionalized, the margin and what lies outside of it became increasingly veiled. In the century and a half since Flaubert, the power of the nonlinguistic to constrain and put pressure

---

7. Letter to Louise Colet, 16 January 1852, in Flaubert, *Correspondance*, 2:31. The theme continued to obsess the avant-garde throughout the nineteenth century. Mallarmé foregrounded "nothingness" in "Un coup de dès" (1897); see *Oeuvres complètes*, 459–77. The poem begins with the word "JAMAIS" (459), and the phrase "RIEN . . . N'AURA EU LIEU . . . QUE LE LIEU" (474–75) is virtually the last thing in it. The general development of the concept toward which this theme points is the subject of Jameson's influential book, *Prison-House of Language*. I discussed the problem of referentiality and self-referentiality (with particular attention to Mallarmé) in Terdiman, *Discourse/Counter-Discourse*, 306–21. On Flaubert's reading of Hegel, see Cajuerio-Roggero, "Dîner chez les Dambreuse."

upon language has quietly been floating out of sight. But we have yet to see the margin.

We need as well to remember that for Flaubert or for Mallarmé, the absolutization of language, of poetry, or of style was far from self-evident. It was a utopian horizon, a project toward which one worked—not an ontology or a transcendent or transhistorical fact. On the other hand, contemporary textualism has moved so far beyond recollection of such struggle that, as Rorty characterized the situation, today people *talk* "as if there were nothing but texts."[8] The point is not that premodern thinkers believed their language could *become* the thing it referred to, as if Mallarmé's stone palaces could somehow magically take up residence within his poems after all. No one ever seriously thought that *that* was the objective. What differentiates their nineteenth-century conception from the reductions of Modernism is the availability in their conceptual practice of a notion of *practice* itself—and of practice's arduousness.

Words *do* express and *can* refer to the moment of their difficulty, their inadequacy, or their disability as they reach the edge of the garden, the margin between language and materiality. And they have been doing so for a long time. Of course it's not easy, and recently it has become doxa simply to renounce the effort. But we don't need to sell language so short. Words do have trouble rendering the obtuse materiality of what resists us in the world. The fit between *language* and *things* is indeed awkward. *Things* forestall our desires and withstand our efforts to transform them, and *words* are too labile, too weightless, to represent this disparity well or to push very hard against it. *Words do badly at bodies.*

But that's not the same as saying that they can't do anything at all, that there can be no connection between these disparate realms of our existence. In my projection—with their commitment to the world-changing power of language practice and their simultaneous recognition of language's wanton propensity to detach itself from any material referent—this is what Diderot and the Enlightenment have to say to Postmodernity. Diderot's metonymic example deconstructs or deterritorializes the hypertropic exaggeration of the linguistic realm. For Diderot language is a world-transforming *practice*—complex, ambiv-

8. See the passage I quoted as an epigraph to chap. 5; Rorty, *Consequences of Pragmatism*, 139. This is not, however, an accurate account of Derrida's position or practice. His *Specters of Marx* makes clear his debt to materialist critique of ideology and his belief that deconstruction carries on this work (12–15). One of his early students claimed that Derrida "always thought of his work as a continuation of Marxist ideology critique" (Michael Ryan, pers. comm., winter 2001). On this point, see Derrida, "Marx & Sons," 256–57.

alent, fractious, and refractory but practicable nonetheless. His life is a tribute to his belief in the pragmatic effectiveness of thought and words. His texts are a repeated, intricate testing of the problematic margin between the *vraisemblable* and the *veridical*, between self-focused and outward-focused language.

Talk is cheap: the familiar adage captures a critical element of the intersection between the two registers of experience which I have been terming "language" and "materiality." How do we know which of these modalities we are occupying—or which is occupying us? There is a simple test that can answer this question and map the difference between these fundamental registers. In the realm of language the force of determination—what we feel as the world's resistance to our desire or our initiative—is uncannily inhibited, interrupted, or canceled. Then words and texts discover in themselves the power to conjure up referents—even pink elephants or present kings of France—whose existence material reality, on its dull and stolid side, unimaginatively withholds.

The referential world (as Diderot kept astonishing himself by discovering) seems to have no power to inhibit or channel its representation. You can say anything; the real-world facts, the material objects you refigure or fantasize, don't demur. They rather appear to manifest themselves obligingly on the stage of your linguistic theater. Look at that blue table over there. Yet the intense body experience and body memory to which Elaine Scarry refers in one of the epigraphs at the head of this chapter, and which dominate her luminous book on *The Body in Pain*, help us frame a refractoriness in the corporeal register which somehow is never quite parallel in the linguistic realm.[9]

The temporality and the atmosphere of fantasy or dreams in which, from our earliest experience, phantasmagorias are produced and entertained, enables our participation in the enraptured world of texts and language—a world that, simultaneously, the register of materiality seeks to constrain to the limits of possibility and contingency.[10] This is a fundamental dialectic, neither of

9. There are exceptions. Speech act theory, as is well-known, defines a category of sentences called "performatives" which make material things happen. Simmel (as I mentioned in chap. 5) argued in a *non*-Idealist sense that the *notion* of society itself makes social cohesion possible. This is the insight upon which Benedict Anderson built in *Imagined Communities*. These do not, however, erase the sometimes dispiriting distance between *wishing* and *having*. This separation defines our notion of time and perhaps of life itself.

10. Freud always insisted upon the absence of "reality testing" in dream thoughts: "Real and imaginary events appear in dreams at first sight as of equal validity"; see *Interpretation of Dreams* (1900), *SE* 4:288. However, it is important to underline that for Freud this blending of the veridical and the imaginary—the material and the textual—characterizes not just dreams or hallucinations but

whose terms can rightly be considered in isolation. Such a dialectical logic undercuts and resolves a long history of squabbling about which of the terms that compose it ought to be conceived as prior or as cardinal. The answer is: *neither.*

On this view the world is neither "material" nor "semiotic" (as I am using those terms here): it is both, and it can be productively conceived from within either register.[11] It is harder to justify a methodology that suppresses the term it does not favor, that seeks its liquidation. We may work fruitfully within either of the paradigms that base themselves in the dual registers I've been framing. Inevitably when we do so, we de-privilege the other one to some degree. But to move from such pragmatic abstraction of the other term of the dialectic to the theoretical postulate that it is irrelevant or nonexistent is a disabling move.

This is the tendency that textualism embodies (vulgar materialism would be equally culpable of it). But the textualist reduction is not only truncated; it is *reactive*. It has been overdetermined by a rejection that it does not, and perhaps cannot, acknowledge. So it appears in the form of *denegation*, as a cardinal counter-discourse. Its need is to repudiate the impulse toward resolution which seems fundamental in Hegel's model of reason and of history. Textualism recoils from Hegel. It refuses the moment of closure or synthesis which, through a paradigmatic *Nachträglichkeit*, in Hegel seems retroflexively to decide the meaning of any preceding moment. (Of course, this view has been available to metaphysical reflection since Aristotle articulated his doctrine of final causes.) In such a construction things mean *where they are going*—meaning that their meaning is determinate. But since for textualism there is no register outside of language which could exercise determination to begin with, it repudiates *this* determinism with particular energy.

Consequently, we need to examine how the textualist abreaction against determination reads the Hegelian impulse to determination and how it can be read by it. Hegel might at first seem an easy case. He appears to project finalities

---

all psychic representations: "*Psychical* reality is a particular form of existence not to be confused with *material* reality" (*SE* 5:620). From the point of view of cultural theory the absence of any secure distinction between "psychical" and "material" reality determines the impossibility of distinguishing between a semiotics of the "real" and a semiotics of the "imaginary"—an absence of distinction which constitutes semiotics to begin with. Umberto Eco makes this clear in *Theory of Semiotics*: "Semiotics is concerned with everything that can be taken as a sign. A sign is everything which can be taken as significantly substituting for something else. This something else does not necessarily have to exist or to actually be somewhere at the moment in which a sign stands for it" (7). For discussion of this issue, see Terdiman, *Present Past*, 208, 258.

11. In my last chapter I will analogize this multiplicity to Niels Bohr's theory of "complementarity."

everywhere. Concepts such as "absolute freedom," ontological states such as *"pure* self-identity" (*Phenomenology*, 361) appear to posit (indeed, to celebrate) unsurpassable closure. The textualist tradition has long convicted Hegel of such rigidity and absolutization. And the argument against his position is comprehensible. We are in a time of history still being made. How could anyone in such a period countenance a vision of history at a standstill? How could anyone committed to multiplicity, pluralism, and reform—not to speak of dissemination—not be shocked by the apparent monologism that appears to be the horizon of Hegelian thought?[12]

Moreover, the anti-Hegel argument continues, the *political* implications of such a supposed supreme unification are dangerous. The reign of terror—in which the twentieth century has catastrophically outdone the Terror itself—has only made such absolutist concepts seem the more perilous. Many thinkers have found this absolutizing Hegelian dynamic intolerable. For them just over the horizon of "the ultimate," of "resolution," of "synthesis," lies *violence.* Whence the powerful reaction to the identitarian, finalist drive in Hegelian epistemology. Nowhere is it more resonant than in Lyotard's stirring repudiation in "What Is Postmodernism?" of Hegel and those (particularly Marx) supposedly inspired by him: "The nineteenth and twentieth centuries have given us as much terror as we can take. We have paid a high enough price for the nostalgia of the whole and the one. . . . We can hear the mutterings of the desire for a return to terror, for the realization of the fantasy to seize reality. The answer is: Let us wage war on totality. . . . Let us activate the differences and save the honor of the name."[13]

This influential passage focuses the issue splendidly. The stakes arise in a fundamental interpretive problem for intellectual and cultural modernity: how should we understand the Hegelian dialectic? Finalist or limitless? Absolute or relativist? Prussian state or open society? Ongoing story or end of history?

Here is the passage from the *Phenomenology* from which I excerpted the stigmatized Hegelian terms I just quoted : "Absolute freedom as *pure* self-identity of the universal will thus has within it *negation*; but this means that it contains *difference* in general, and this again it develops as an *actual* difference." The thought is complex and appears almost self-refuting. It passes beyond the fa-

---

12. A fuller discussion of the concept in question here can be found in Cooper, *End of History.* Plotnitsky makes this critique a central point in *In the Shadow of Hegel.*

13. Lyotard, "Answering the Question," 81–82.

miliar riddle of "paradox" toward the far reaches of the paralogistic.[14] But in my reading of it, that is the point. Hegel wants to assert that even in its most ultimate or finalist mode the resolution of contraries (as in "absolute freedom") *still contains contraries*. The propositional contradiction this entails will drive literalists or analytic philosophers crazy. But, while it would take a long argument to develop the point adequately, what I think is happening here is Hegel's effort to deconstruct his own finalism. Despite his formation within Christian eschatological thought,[15] despite the homology between such a vision of history and his own projection of it, he subverts his own paradigm in the most dramatic way possible—by positing that even *this* ultimate resolution is provisional, partial, and counter-teleologized. *Finality itself isn't final*. The paradox is made strikingly visible in the paradigmatic tension that animates the *Phenomenology*'s final section. Its title is "Absolute Knowing." But its last word, and the concluding word of the book, is *Unendlichkeit*—"unendingness" or (in Miller's rendering) "infinitude" (493).

What this means might seem deeply obscure. But I think the energies that produce the obscurity are clear. Hegel is struggling to contain something that is uncontainable in logic or concept. In chapter 6 I began to argue that the Hegelian paradigm is never flat-footedly single-voiced. One master-impulse in Hegel is emphatically teleological.[16] Another, however, pulls hard *against* finalism—just as one might expect in the case of a consummate dialectician. In a dialectical system, if things are sitting still, we can suspect that such immobility has been achieved *against* the logic of the system itself. The quiddity of dialectic is to *resist shutdown*.

This makes common sense. The world never stops to let us off. When, in fundamentalisms or dogmatisms, we find thought satisfied with *where it already is*, we will tend to feel that things have not been resolved but rather *arrested*. We

14. Hegel, *Phenomenology of Spirit*, 361. "Die absolute Freiheit hat also als *reine* Sichselbstgleichheit des allgemeinen Willens die *Negation*, damit aber *den Unterschied* überhaupt an ihr und entwickelt diesen wieder als *wirkichen* Unterschied"; *Phänomenologie des Geistes*, 438. Adorno provocatively discusses how we should—and should *not*—make "sense" of Hegel's notorious difficulty; see *Hegel*, 95–109.

15. This is a point that Derrida re-emphasizes in his discussion of the irreducible "religiosity" of Hegelianizing notions such as "ideology" in Marx. See "Marx & Sons," 256–57.

16. For a compelling example, see a passage in the *Encyclopedia* (*Logic: Part One of the "Encyclopedia of the Philsophical Sciences"*), 1:351–52. This passage and the general finalist dynamic are brilliantly discussed by Adorno (*Hegel*, 92–95). For the French Hegelian tradition it is Kojève's influential interpretation of the "end of history" which lays behind the struggle *against* the notion that has occupied thinkers such as Bataille, Derrida, and others, as I will discuss later.

could think of this expectation as the affective register of the Enlightenment's own program of critical skepticism about all authority and doctrine. This is the nub of Poststructuralism's argument with Hegel. To analyze this further, I need briefly to trace the inheritance of Hegel's ideas within the French orbit in which Poststructuralism itself emerged beginning in the late 1960s.

The filiation of French Hegelianism and of the reaction against it have been examined in a number of important books.[17] The French take on these matters is important because the "textualism" I am interrogating found its most resonant expression among French Postmodernists. "French Hegel"—the influential interpretation of Hegel which was developed in Paris in the 1930s and afterward by Jean Hyppolite, Alexandre Kojève, and Eric Weil—is the Hegelian avatar against which Poststructuralism in France projected its theoretical energies.

The influence of a series of charismatic Parisian thinkers in the late 1960s and afterward roots here (if only through denegation) in the interpretation of Hegel, whose most notable exponent was Kojève. More than any other scholar or teacher, it was Kojève who foregrounded the theme of history's *end* in Hegel. In the celebrated seminar he taught in the Section des Sciences Religieuses at the École Pratique des Hautes-Études, Kojève's students included Georges Bataille, Jacques Lacan, Eric Weil, Raymond Queneau, Maurice Merleau-Ponty, Jean Toussaint Desanti, and numerous others.[18] These figures, in turn, influenced or taught those who would become the leading Poststructuralists in France.

It would be absurd to conceive Poststructuralism as no more than a reflex of the intergenerational anxiety of influence or simply as a covert desire to kick free of Hegel. But, if the concept of literary or theoretical generations has any explanatory value—and the elitist concentration of French higher education in a small number of Parisian lecture halls and seminar-rooms could lend particular credence to the notion—then it makes sense to think that phenomena such as *influence* and *reaction* were often mediated in particularly direct and intense relationships between teacher and student.[19]

So, Kojève's analysis of Hegel takes on particular consequentiality in its *own* teleology—that is, in its influence upon the Poststructuralist generation in Paris. Kojève's interpretive emphasis focuses the finalist dynamic in Hegel with par-

17. See, particularly, Butler, *Subjects of Desire*; and Roth, *Knowing and History*.

18. Appendix to Roth's *Knowing and History*, 225–27.

19. On the reaction and reinterpretation in general, see Roth, afterword, *Knowing and History*, 189–224. Roth writes: "In this shift away from Hegelianism we witness one of the crucial transformations in modern intellectual history" (190). In chap. 6 I considered a similar agon involving Derrida and his teacher Foucault.

ticular force: "Man can be truly 'satisfied,' History can end, only in and by the formation of a Society, of a State, in which the strictly particular, personal, individual value of each [person] is recognized as such, in its very particularity, by *all*, by a Universality incarnated in the State as such; and in which the universal value of the State is recognized and realized by the Particular as such, by *all* the Particulars."[20]

While one could interpret this passage as merely reaching toward the horizon of an *impossible* reconciliation, it coheres both with the political intention of Kojève's interpretation and with the subsequent uptake of his teaching and writing, in its emphasis not on the *unfeasibility* of such a communitarian or communist resolution but, rather, on the *necessity*—conceptually and politically—of striving to achieve it. Kojève was assuredly not seeking to universalize the Prussian state that Hegel is accused of apotheosizing in *The Philosophy of Right* and elsewhere.[21] Rather, he was Marxianizing Hegel's theory in order to justify the eventual political and historical triumph of the proletariat.[22]

20. Kojève, *Introduction to the Reading of Hegel*, 58. It's helpful to remember that the portentous terms carrying their magnifying majuscules ("History") in French or English translations or interpretations of Hegel seem less aggressive in the original German, in which all nouns are capitalized.

21. The controversy over the long-discussed issue of the Prussian state is considerably clarified in Kaufmann, *Hegel's Political Philosophy*. Kaufmann's introduction (1–9) lifts the shadow cast by some influential but absurd mistakes on the level of simple philology—such as the celebrated statement in *Philosophy of Right* (sec. 258), in which Hegel is supposed to have asserted that "the State is the march of God through the world." This version lent fuel to Karl Popper's influential but "gross" misreading of Hegel in *The Open Society and Its Enemies* (see Kaufmann, "Hegel Myth and Its Method," 141). In fact, the statement about God and the state was simply misattributed by German editors and mistranslated by foreign ones. The German sentence can only mean "God's way with the world is that there should be a state" (4). But in any case this widely and fiercely stigmatized dictum *was not written by Hegel at all* but, rather, by the first editor of his *Philosophy of Right*, Eduard Gans. It was then carelessly taken over into English by the translator of Gans's defective text. The succeeding articles in the Kaufmann volume, by T. M. Knox, E. F. Carritt, Sidney Hook, Shlomo Avineri, Kaufmann himself, and others, helpfully demystify the issues. In particular, the notion that Hegel's theory of the Prussian state represents his apotheosis of politics itself—still less constitutes the "end of history"—is persuasively confuted in the analysis by Knox ("Hegel and Prussianism," 13–29). Paul Ricoeur's ringing and angry comment about the perverse misreading of Hegel by his opponents is apposite: "For the history of ideas, the incredibly rapid collapse of Hegelianism, as the dominant mode of thought, is a fact that stands out like an earthquake. But that it happened and happened so quickly is clearly not proof of anything. This is all the more true in that the reasons for this downfall alleged by Hegel's adversaries, those who in fact replaced his philosophy, appear today as a monumental case of misunderstanding and malevolence, given a more careful reading of the Hegelian texts" (*Time and Narrative*, 3:202–3; cf. 239).

22. The junction between Hegel and Marx in Kojève's work, and its relation of the "end of history," are intelligently clarified in Roth, *Knowing and History*, 117–18, and chap. 6 (125–46, esp. 134–36). The overwhelming need for *finality* which is a primary dynamic in Hegel—but, as I continue to emphasize, *not* the only one—refracts through Marx as well. This is why Derrida speaks in *Specters* of the "quasi-paternal figure of Marx," whom he claims is at the origin of a tradition "in which the Marx-

That conflation in Kojève's seminars in the 1930s, between Hegel's writing and the 1930s socialist project, was probably the most important spur for later turning a tradition of interpreters against Hegelian and Marxian finalism. It caused them to treat such positions *allergically*. The Hegel and the Marx who emerged from this reinterpretation are impoverished, to the point that Fredric Jameson claims in his foreword to Lyotard's *Postmodern Condition* that the real (if unacknowledged) antagonist of Postmodernism was the loathsome Stalinism of the French Communist Party (CP).[23] This, too, is a rhetorical exaggeration. But, like the position it seeks to clarify, there is truth in its oversimplification.

Now, however, with the effective demise of the French CP and the disappearance of the Communist regimes of Central Europe and the USSR, it becomes possible to consider the foundations of the doctrinal argument more dispassionately. In particular we can now maintain with less fear of some imagined complicity with totalitarianism that Hegel and Marx both struggled with the notions of determination and of the resolution of contraries—that is, with the practices of power and of politics—in ways that remain not only apposite but conceptually critical today. And, though the stakes in my interpretation here may seem distant from an apparently local and increasingly irrelevant doctrinal struggle in 1950s and 1960s France, the question of Hegel bears immediately upon the question of language and materiality which is central to my argument in *Body and Story*.[24] In any case, in the reaction against the supposed closure of the Hegelian system—and of its supposed successors in European Communist parties—Poststructuralists deprived themselves of a foundational resource: the conception of the pressure that *hors-texte* or non-text can exert upon language.

My argument here is simple. Hegel seeks to hold irreconcilable postulates in tension. That is what dialectic always seeks to do. This tension is *logically* unresolvable. It can only be worked out in some mode other than language. Luckily, we have materiality. But the tension in question here is the paradigm that I hope can model for understanding how multiple, irreconcilable theoretical orientations (such as Diderot's reformist materialism and Poststructuralism's linguistic idealism, which I have been trying to bring into emblematic contact

---

ian inheritance was—and still remains, and so it will remain—absolutely and thoroughly determinate" (13–14). And Derrida goes on to say: "We all live in a world . . . that still bears . . . the mark of this inheritance" (14).

23. In Lyotard, *Postmodern Condition*, x.

24. Judith Butler provided a thoughtful examination of the uptake—and inversion—of Hegel by French postmodernists in "Questionable Patrilineage," 177–86.

in this book) neither transcode one into the other nor mutually vaporize in some version of the collision between matter and antimatter. They just go on being in conflict.

Hegel holds *two* positions.[25] The first posits the progressive movement of Negativity until the point at which all contradictions are finally resolved. The second intuits the theoretical incoherence of such resolution, the impossibility of its eventuation. The first of these visions of history and social process tends toward the frozen absolutism for which Hegel has been condemned. But the second, equally insistent in his model, equally necessary for the realization of its insights, has a double bearing in its termless churning of difference. It proposes the theory of a process that can never achieve closure or reconciliation. Long before Derrida made the concept (of course very different in his usage) compelling, it projects a version of unceasing "dissemination." But, much more significant for my argument here, it suggests how, in the theoretical impossibility of closure, there are just what we have experienced throughout the period since Modernity arose: multiple perspectives, subjectivities, paradigms, and models. Multiple *theories*. And, as Bataille suggests in his influential notion of "general economy," there is always more than any theory can capture.[26]

It is important to notice how Hegel's second dynamic—toward termless contradiction—comforts his first one even while it repudiates its substantive claim. It justifies the existence even of its own challenger. While there is a sense in which these two dynamics coexist on a plane of propositional equality, from another perspective—itself inherent in the model—the second paradigm (*Unendlichkeit*) functions like the pair's superset, its own meta-theory, in which both dynamics find their place. The first model ("end of history") sees the world that the second projects only as a provisional, if necessary, mistake. But the termless second model gropes toward an understanding of *how* this situation of multiplicity, of authentic heterology, can and must always be real, present, and effective. The first model is blind to the necessity of a contrary paradigm. The second *insists* upon it. What, then, is inevitable in Hegel is not the *end* of history but its *continuation*.

This limitless and heteronomous potentiality within Hegel's thinking de-

---

25. Not that he's the only thinker to do so. Here is the dialectical Derrida: "My own conviction is that we must maintain two contradictory affirmations at the same time" ("Dialogue with Jacques Derrida," 113).

26. This point will be central to my discussion of theory's *ethics* in my concluding chapter. For Georges Bataille's "general economy," see *Inner Experience*; and *Accursed Share*.

velops most productively in Adorno. Julia Simon puts this clearly: "Whereas Hegel's idealism highlights the moment of synthesis, Adorno's materialism perpetually staves off synthesis, because there is always a remainder that resists sublation. In other words, there can never be final synthesis for Adorno because matter (object, thing-in-itself) always resists adequation to its concept."[27]

In light of the foregoing, let me draw some tentative conclusions concerning the "theory wars" that we have been living for a long time. The bearing of the second dynamic in Hegel—which I would argue *is* his model in its most capable development—is to make the disputation of theoretical paradigms, visions, methodologies, and positions *itself* paradigmatic. It projects the world in which the interpretive disciplines have been living since the Enlightenment.

If we accept this postulate, then any number of familiar but fruitless doctrinal battles—say, between various strains of aestheticism or formalism or Idealism, on the one hand, and diverse varieties of Materialism or of socially or politically committed criticism, on the other—are obviated or outflanked. Then it becomes necessary for any reading to justify the approach it brings to bear on the grounds of its analytic intention, not on those of some transcendent rightness of the approach utilized or on the spuriousness of the approaches it repudiates.

Sometimes in cultural history the equilibrium of this dialectical structure becomes unbalanced. Such a tectonic movement was beginning in the Enlightenment. Then we might conceive the strains of Modernity and Postmodernity which have dominated discourse in the recent period as an instructive case of an increasing hypertrophy of the *language* term of this pairing. And Diderot could stand as a counter-discourse *avant la lettre* of an effort early in the modern period to rebalance the equilibrium of the terms under the pressure of an increasing perfusion of the socioeconomic and cultural world by the conjuring power of signs.

With these considerations in mind we could reconceive the cultural meaning of the two theoretical paradigms that have most regularly presided over reflection concerning the experience of Modernity, those of Marx and Freud. Marx and Freud can be figured together as the great and concerted theoretician of *materiality*—understood here not in any exalted ontological sense but, more

---

27. Simon, *Mass Enlightenment*, 118. The conceptual convergence between Adorno's position and Bataille's is striking. In the late 1930s Adorno (along with Walter Benjamin and Max Horkheimer) attended lectures at the famous Collège de Sociologie, which Bataille, Roger Caillois, and Michel Leiris had founded. On Adorno's participation, see Surya, *Georges Bataille*, 271–72. On the Collège de Sociologie, see intro. by Allan Stoekl, in Bataille, *Visions of Excess*, xx–xxiii.

simply, as register of the forces in experience which constrain possibility and produce our sense of the frustrating viscosity or inertia of existence.

This refractoriness is theorized everywhere in Marx, notably in his often-disparaged "base/superstructure" model of 1859.[28] There are rigidities in the model. Its fundamental insight, however, is to reconceive the Materialism-Idealism dyad not as an opposition but as an *array*. Its purpose is to sort out entities and processes according to the degree of what might be called the *experiential inertia* that they demonstrate. The dyad thus opens up into a matrix that links aspects of social existence to each other and sorts them based upon their susceptibility to the exercise of human will. The elements of the base, then, are those that confront us with settled and refractory materiality. They are *hard* to change. They have the staying power of something like the "constant capital" of social existence.[29] Conversely, the inhabitants of the *Überbau*, the superstructure, are located there because of their relative *mutability* and *lability*—because they can be changed without our needing to lift and move the massive, constituted weight of the machinery by which societies self-reproduce and persist.

This is a model of determination which thinks causality through the relative power of differential elements, through a vector that links, rather than logically *opposes*, the two realms traditionally identified as *material* and *ideal*. My notion of *experiential inertia* inevitably invokes temporality. What is differential here is *the time it takes*—to alter the givens of existence, to change (in however modest or global a way) the world. This distinction nicely differentiates *representations* from what used to be called the *real*. This latter is a term that, in the sense defined by this process of sorting out the diverse elements of experience and environment, could usefully be reconsidered.

What is at stake from this perspective, then, is the *persistence* of practices and social arrangements fundamental to the production of social existence itself—and, conversely, the relative *lability* of conceptual entities. Marx's insight was to conceive the weightiness of the former not as a kind of dumb materiality but as having causative influence proportional to their massiveness. If we want to know what is the case, such a sorting would seem indispensable.

Marx's central conceptual projection of the "mode of production" then becomes a model of what is deeply settled and refractory in life—of everything, from history to habit, from constituted power to the technology of the instru-

---

28. See Marx, *Contribution to the Critique of Political Economy*, 20–21. Raymond Williams has insightfully examined the model. See *Marxism and Literature*, 75–82; and his important 1973 essay "Base and Superstructure in Marxist Cultural Theory."

29. Concerning "constant capital," see Marx, *Capital*, pt. 3, chap. 8.

ments of production to infrastructural ideology, which restricts our freedom with the force of what the tradition of thinking in the Marxian mode has termed "necessity."[30] (Coordinately, we could construe this pattern of reflection as an indispensable accompaniment and continuation of the Enlightenment's meditations on liberation and its thinkers' exploration of what they conceived as the fundamentally *political* character of the restraints that inhibited it.)

Then, in this paradigmatic contrast, we could see the register of experience framed and illuminated by Freud's great construction as converging with what I have been designating as "language"—the world of words, texts, and their seemingly instantaneous and unconstrainable transformations. Freud's paradigm for the refractory parallels Marx's precisely in its grasp of the ineluctably structured time-differentials that determine the possibility of human change. For Freud the equivalent of the perverse persistence of the Marxian "base" is what he termed "system *Ucs.*," the unconscious in its successive theoretical avatars. From this perspective the salient feature of the unconscious (and one Freud insisted upon strenuously) is its *permanence*. "It is a prominent feature of unconscious processes that they are indestructible." "In mental life nothing which has once been formed can perish."[31]

Marx and Freud were seeking paradigms that could explain the apparently ineluctable experiences of *resistance* and *persistence*—in Marx's case, of the structures of socio economic life, the mode of production; in Freud's, the perverse obstinacy of neurosis and other psychological maladies. In the Structuralist period each of these systems was transformed into a linguistically based or linguistically inflected model—for Marx, in Althusser and in Tel Quel; for Freud, in Lacan. In this transformation the capacity of the models to explain *persistence* and the weightiness of the elements of existence was coordinately weakened or lost. These latter elements won't instantly dance when we command them to. Recall the last time you picked up a carton of groceries or pushed your stalled car to the side of the road. The corporeal strain that such efforts entail—

---

30. The celebrated phrase about freedom being the "recognition of necessity" is a paraphrase of Engels's discussion in Engels, *Herr Eugen Dühring's Revolution in Science*, chap. 11. In turn it seems that Engels adapted the idea from Hegel's *Introduction to the Philosophy of History.* Hegel writes: "Philosophy is the objective science of truth, it is the science of necessity"; and "the higher point of view is that Mind is free in its necessity, and finds its freedom in it alone, since its necessity rests on its freedom" (26). In the *Logic* he put it this way: "Necessity is blind only so long as it is not understood" (209). Jameson paraphrases the fundamental insight in a passage I will discuss further. It begins: "History is therefore the experience of Necessity" (*Political Unconscious*, 102).

31. *Interpretation of Dreams*, 1900; *SE* 5:577–78; *Civilization and Its Discontents*, 1930; *SE* 21:69. In *Present Past* I analyzed Freud's model of the indestructability—hence, the refractoriness—of the unconscious (see chaps. 7–8, esp. 269–87).

and which everyone knows *in their bodies*—gives us the master-metaphor for the refractory. "What is remembered in the body is well remembered," as Elaine Scarry put it in one of this chapter's epigraphs.

Conversely, the instantaneous and seemingly effortless transformations and shifts that happen in what seems the world's *other* register—the increasingly accelerated exchanges that were already visible in Marx's model for capitalism and which only developed further in Georg Simmel's analysis of the stock exchange,[32] and in our familiarity in the contemporary period with cyberspace transfers of all kinds, whether of money or of information—engender the sense that language can indeed model the world. Here, in contrast to the figuration of *weight* which seems constantly to arise when materiality must be represented, a metaphorics of the *miraculous* in something like the image of angelic teleportation offers itself in our attempt to capture the instantaneity and effortlessness of these transformations.

For Freud this counter-register would arise in the instantaneous operations—those he first taxonomized in *The Interpretation of Dreams*—of what Peter Gay called Freud's dream work tool kit.[33] In condensation, displacement, projection, and negation, the contents of the psyche mutate with the unaccountable facility of supernatural metamorphosis. Would that the neurotic contents that bind the patient to damaging repetition could be so easily superseded! But this resistance to resolution—to the *cure*—was what Freud needed most centrally to model. It is the emblem of the refractoriness that in Marx, Freud, and numerous other systems sorts out the forms of existence which resist human will, desire, effort, or hope and can make human time so painful. Such paradigms, and such a taxonomy, are seeking to frame our experience of what, despite a long history of repudiation of the concept, we may still be attracted to calling the "Real."

> "The Real is what *resists*."   —KOJÈVE, citing Pierre Maine de Biran, in
> *Introduction to the Reading of Hegel*, 156

Epistemology of the Refractory: My phrase seeks to identify a mode of apprehending the world of language and of materiality which might help us rebalance the claims each of these registers makes on understanding. Most of us

---

32. "The stock exchange and its representatives have achieved the closest possible local assembly in order to carry out the clearance, distribution and balancing of money in the quickest manner possible. This twofold condensation of values into the money form and of monetary transactions into the form of the stock exchange makes it possible for values to be rushed through the greatest number of hands in the shortest possible time" (Simmel, *Philosophy of Money*, 506).

33. Gay, *Freud*, 113.

have an intuition that *something* constrains language and utterance and that, for capable comprehension of the world, some register of causality or determination is indispensable. We know you *can't* do just anything with words.

Yet much in our disciplinary culture disables this intuition. Nineteenth-century Formalism was already organizing a defense against the notion of the imagination's constraint. It did so first by deploring and dismissing the influence of secular practicalities. The emblem of such a strategic ideological deflation might well be Flaubert's corrosive imprecation "bourgeois!" This castigation of the world of practical activity exiled far from elevated spheres of thought, form, and language the realm where limitation operates. This stuck the others with the problem and projected an aesthetic realm that could transcend materiality. It was a brilliant move, and its influence has been both persistent and profound. Today the tunneling of our vision which was adumbrated in such defensive Formalism in the first half of the nineteenth century has become even more efficacious and hermetic.

Yet, if in some suspension of contemporary doxa we are brought to think about it, we will probably sense that the countervailing register of materiality cannot be evaded in language. Thus, the *Real* rematerializes. It had suffered Modernist anathema. But against all odds it has remained lurking just beyond the horizon ever since, in a memorable malediction, Théophile Gautier expelled it from aesthetic respect in 1834: "The only beauty is what is useless; everything useful is ugly, for it is the expression of some need, and the needs of human beings are base and repulsive [*ignobles et dégoûtants*]."[34]

How has the real remained marginalized? Contemporary doxa has so shadowed the constraints that play on language, and so puffed up the pleasures of the text, that it is rare to find anyone wondering what might be urged as a mechanism or modality limiting their supposed sovereignty. The eclipse to which I referred earlier of Hegel and deterministic systems more generally is both a symptom and a cause of this incuriosity. Thus, the enterprise of theory which in the past few decades has flourished within the discipline of literary and cultural studies—particularly in its deeply influential Poststructuralist and Postmodern strains—has directed its attention *away* from the elements in practice and in experience which might undermine the seductive theses that sustain textualism.[35]

---

34. Gautier, preface to *Mademoiselle de Maupin*, 57–58; my trans. See also Terdiman, *Present Past*, 133–34.

35. My analysis here tries to instantiate the mechanism it discusses: it suggests that the sorts of factors—ideological, in this case—which constrain supposedly free language production function in

The counter-argument is less exalted than was Gautier's celebrated proscription. Here is how it appears in an epigram of Philip K. Dick's: "Reality is that which, when you stop believing in it, doesn't go away."[36] That's a nice image of what I mean by "refractory." But how might we conceive, how might we theorize, the interaction or inter-determination of these two realms: of "belief" and of what is relatively autonomous—if not cantankerous—in relation to it?

This new avatar of the mind-body disjunction is not easier to resolve than were its classical predecessors. It seems evident how the force of the semiotic can determine not only our perception of the material world but even its behavior. We have an effect on the world around us, and it is surely inflected in a different way by the manner in which we conceive it. But how (in the contrary direction) can materiality constrain signs? how can the bodies about which stories are told put pressure on the stories we tell about them? If there is a *Ding-an-sich*, we can't get access to it directly. However, this blockage is not bidirectional. Reality does access *us*; it can dominate and determine our possibilities. But it is not obvious how this happens.

To understand the stakes and the strategies by which we might rethink these issues, my approach has been to return to the Enlightenment period, in which, with Diderot and for good historical and social reasons, I've been claiming that reflection on these issues became acute. But as is well known, Diderot was far from being alone in such a consideration. To examine how it developed and how it might be brought to bear upon our current perplexities, we could best return again to Hegel, whose theoretical work carried the exploratory and dialectical impulse at the heart of Diderot's conception of the world powerfully—I would argue epochally—forward. Diderot was "onto" textualism. Hegel theorized its attractions and its costs.

With Hegel the issue that has concerned me in this book is deliberately joined. Diderot puzzled over the lability of thought and language, of texts and stories. Hegel proposes a resolution for the problem. What worried Diderot, I argued, was that in the story world material reality appeared uncannily to lose traction, so that you could write anything about anything. Then human undertakings—including the sort of transformative activity the philosophes were conceiving in the face of the world's irrationalities and abuses—seemed to forfeit their warrant and perhaps even their means of action. How could you

---

such a way that it becomes legitimate to talk about a "period style" in theory and criticism, both in terms of what it ratifies and in terms of what it marginalizes or excludes.

36. Dick, "How to Build a Universe That Doesn't Fall Apart Two Days Later," 261.

imagine using writing to change the world if language turned out to be as unattached, as "frictionless," as Diderot had discovered it appeared to be?

Hegel provides a model for how understanding and practice, how language and materiality, might be brought back into relation with each other. As the supreme and absolute Idealist, Hegel is often thought of as privileging the priority of thought. But in relation to this issue I believe we need to see him as a materialist quite as resolute as Diderot himself.[37] In response to Diderot's puzzled interrogation of fiction and textuality, what I would like to draw from Hegel is a modestly new perspective on our modalities of knowing—what I called earlier the "epistemology of the refractory." To begin to explain it, let me examine the alignment between Diderot's problem concerning fiction and Hegel's more abstract projection of a theory of knowledge.

The terminology utilized in the two cases is quite different. I've cast the distinction that becomes acute for Diderot in terms of a conflicted convergence of *bodies* and *stories*. Conversely for Hegel, the apposite distinction emerges, precisely at the conclusion of the *Phenomenology*, as an opposition between *Space* and *Time*. In a characteristic dialectical move Hegel sees this opposition as comprehending or determining the world.[38] How does it do so, and what can we develop out of this duality in connection with the problem that concerns me in *Body and Story*?

Let me momentarily play the game of attributing intention to a part of speech. Then I would note that the conjunction *and* at the center of my title is meant to evoke not an inert accumulation or succession but an active con-

---

37. It is striking that, despite the customary view of Hegel as high priest of the impalpable, of thought's priority over material existence, he has never been embraced as a forebear of the doctrine of textuality. The overdetermined Poststructuralist anathema that I discussed earlier has much to do with this exclusion. The notion of *Geist* might seem to carry within it something of the same spirit of language's sovereign liberation. But the exponents of textualism in the Modern and Postmodern periods have clearly sensed that Hegel remained resolutely committed to a dialectic *between* thought and materiality dissonant from their own understanding. With regard to Hegel's "Idealism," Kojève argued forcefully that Hegel, rather than embracing such a position concerning the priority of subjectivity and thought, repudiated it and painstakingly sought to differentiate his own dialectical view—framing the indispensable *co-determination* of both registers—from outright Idealism, particularly that of his predecessor Fichte. Kojève's name for Hegel's view is "Realist"; its effect is to rebalance the customary notion of Hegel's Idealism with the strong injection of a Materialism that brings him much closer to eighteenth-century French materialists like Diderot than is usually supposed. For Hegel the dialectic of subject and object is effected inside the subject but is only meaningful if we suppose the existence of an objective world external to and independent of the subject. This objective world, Hegel argues forcefully, must attain "its complete freedom [*seine völlige Freiheit*]" if such a dialectic is to be authentic, as he insists it must (*Phenomenology of Spirit*, sec. 807). On these points, see Kojève, *Introduction to the Reading of Hegel*, 152–55.

38. See Hegel, *Phenomenology of Spirit*, chap. 8 (final chapter), esp. sec. 800 ff. The distinction between Time and Space occurs in sec. 807, the penultimate paragraph of the *Phenomenology*.

frontation and inter-determination of these terms and what they designate. It seeks to express the maintenance and the effectivity of both of the referents that it links. But, as I've suggested, to maintain both registers is *not* to say that they can be transcoded into each other or merged in an unproblematic or indifferent identity. A fundamental distinction, a fundamental resistance operating between these terms, lives in and is enabled by their duality.

A similar, and similarly refractory, duality frames the problem with which Hegel concludes the *Phenomenology*. This difference resists any transcoding. To call time a "version" of space is always possible. The imagery we use to express temporality—"stretch" or "flow" or "extent" of time; "long" time—incorporates the intuition that the daunting impalpability of time can be made more manageable through the language of Cartesian *res extensa*, of experiential physicality and materiality. But we can become dupes of our metaphors unless we subject them to critical examination of what they *don't* adequately convey, of where and how they fail. If we unthinkingly conflate with spatiality itself the spatial language by which we often represent time, most of us would sense the irretrievable loss of a fundamental element of what makes time a cardinal register of experience. From Augustine forward, the refractory "distention" of temporality has defined the difference that makes time incommensurable with any other modality of experience.[39] This protraction resists being telescoped or elided. Without it you don't have time.

Yet contemporary theoretical paradigms and patterns of conceptualization propel many people toward a conflation of time and space or even toward the former's effacement by the latter. Fredric Jameson puts this tendency clearly when he talks about Postmodernism's characteristics: "The waning of affect . . . might [be] characterized . . . as the waning of the great high modernist thematics of time and temporality, the elegiac mysteries of *durée* and memory. . . . We have often been told . . . that we now inhabit the synchronic rather than the diachronic, and I think it is at least empirically arguable that our daily life, our psychic experience, our cultural languages, are today dominated by categories of space rather than by categories of time, as in the previous period of high modernism."[40]

"Waning of affect" and suppression of temporality seem to Jameson comprehensible as different manifestations of the same determinant. The reason is that the former—whether it is expressed in the mode of inconsequential play or

39. The classic analysis is that of Ricoeur, *Time and Narrative*, vol. 1, chap. 1.
40. Jameson, *Postmodernism*, 16.

arises in some cultural analogue of psychological depression in which affect peters out in hopelessness—proceeds from disinvestment in outcomes and consequences. Then the materiality and consequentiality of time, the dynamic that carries us toward forward-looking objectives, drops out of thought. Either our objectives appear instantly attainable—as in the cybernetic ecstasy that contemporaneity has projected (for privileged consumers at least), or else they feel as if they are absolutely out of reach—as in the chronic consumerist sense that *something* always lies "beyond," leading to a practice of interminable substitution of "goods" for some *other* Good whose absence we vaguely sense but whose possession we cannot attain.

What we call "resistance" or "the refractory" functions in a middle zone between these monothetic extremes. This space is the one in which our lives are largely lived. We are mostly poised—or stretched—between *impossibility* and *attainment*. These polar categories are abstract, and probably they have little reference to the world of lived existence. Hardly anything in that world—our world—is ever absolutely impossible; contrariwise, hardly anything is ever absolutely realized. With these notions we are in the realm of Pascal's two infinities: we cannot touch those poles at all.[41] They exist in the static, metaphysical realm of being, not in the more frustrating and untidy everyday world of becoming—of desire, hope, or project. More than ideal types, they are ontological kinds. As such, they are insensitive to temporality or history.

But as Jameson put it in one of his most memorable formulas, "History is what hurts."[42] This irruption of the phenomenology of *pain* puts us back in the flawed but familiar world of resistant temporality which defines us, our desires, our accomplishments—and our losses. To restore time's inexorable density, we need to be able to model why and how the world constrains and re-contains the seemingly limitless lability of our discourse about it which was simultaneously fascinating and alarming Diderot. For, as Jameson argued in the same passage, it is the world's *resistance* to us—and, hence, to our freedom to capture it in language—that we experience most fundamentally in time's intractability. Between our *saying* and our *doing* an arduous distance opens.

This *resistance* is fundamental to the distinction between the registers of

---

41. Pascal, *Pensées*, 1:136–58 (*pensée* 197).

42. Jameson, *Political Unconscious*, 102. The passage runs: "History is therefore the experience of Necessity, and it is this alone which can forestall its thematization or reification as a mere object of representation or as one master code among many others. Necessity is not in that sense a type of content, but rather the inexorable *form* of events. . . . Conceived in this sense, History is what hurts, it is what refuses desire and sets inexorable limits to individual as well as collective praxis."

language and of materiality. We need a way to conceptualize the most common and constant of our forms of experience, the gap between intention and realization, between desire and fulfillment, between that which we can conceive and that which we can achieve. Such separations haunt our activity and seem to constitute our experience. In his play with texts Diderot found a trapdoor in existence through which it seemed you might overcome the resistance that governs such separation. The emblem of his "discovery"—or of his perplexity—is the innocent-sounding sentence from *Jacques le fataliste* which has recurred repeatedly in my discussion: "It's so damn easy [*facile*] to make up stories!" (*DFVP* 23:25). When we counterpose this "facility" against the resistance that defines time's distention, we find ourselves translated into the distinction between Time (or becoming) and Space (or being) with which Hegel concludes the *Phenomenology*.

Here is a more complete version of the quotation from Kojève which I placed as an emblem at the head of this section: "I do not believe that the *Real* properly so-called can be defined otherwise than it has been by Maine de Biran (among others): the Real is what *resists*. Now, it is perfectly wrong to believe that the Real resists Thought. In point of fact, it does not resist it: it does not even resist false thought; and, as for true thought, it is precisely a coincidence with the Real. The Real resists Action, and not Thought. Consequently, there is true philosophical 'Realism' only where philosophy takes account and gives an account of Action—that is, of History—that is, of Time."[43]

In this passage Kojève refers to François-Pierre-Gonthier Maine de Biran (1766–1824). Maine de Biran was a Royalist politician. Initially, he was a member of the circle of the Idéologues (a movement named by Stendhal's friend Destutt de Tracy and counting as members Condillac, Cabanis, and Condorcet). The Idéologues were empiricist "sensationalists"—in this they followed Condillac's terminology—who sought to derive the totality of psychic, ethical, political, and spiritual sentiments from sense data. But after his initial attraction to these ideas, Maine de Biran began a protracted analysis of the shortcomings of his former position. This analysis centered in his position that human *will* was a necessary concept for explaining human thought and action. It was the will that could cause bodies to move. In effect the view he advocated coupled the relative passivity of empiricist sensationalism with a strong vision of human agency. It was out of this dialectic that his reflection on the Real and its

43. Kojève, *Introduction to the Reading of Hegel*, 156–57.

resistance to human agency developed. This view has compelling force: for "agency" would not have any meaning if it came for free. For it to have traction at all, there has got to be a countervailing, material force.

This is why Kojève was attracted to Maine's position. Through its assertion he identified a crucial difference between the views of Fichte, on the one hand, and, on the other, those of Hegel which he sought to advance. For Fichte, he wrote, "this relation of the Subject and the Object is effected within the Subject, the Object being but one of the aspects of subjective activity. For Hegel, on the other hand, the dialectic of the Subject and Object, which is effected inside of the Subject and is described in the *Phenomenology*, is meaningful only if one supposes the existence of an Object properly so-called—that is, and Object external to and independent of the Subject. Or, as Hegel says, one must give the Object 'its full freedom [*seine völlige Freiheit*].' "[44]

The Real in Hegel's terms (or at least in Kojève's interpretation of them) weighs against our agency. It resists action. But, by setting limits and constraints to our possibility, it tells us who we are and what we can do. There would be no epistemological benefit to us if these limits did not have significant independence from our will, if they merely projected or activated our own fantasies. In *Present Past* I discussed a convergent epistemology that Martha Nussbaum drew from reflection on Proust. Nussbaum asked what might be the attraction of the "involuntary" (as in Proust's celebrated "involuntary memory" or in Freud's parapraxes). The answer is that what we do *not* choose has an epistemological privilege because it seems to reach us exempted from our mind's manipulation, rationalization, and falsification. Subjective determination is *too damn easy*. In an early-twentieth-century world that was becoming hypersensitive to the naturalization of habit and ideology, to human defenses and rationalizations and the other mind games people play on themselves, this projection of a relative independence in the determination even of our own experiences (whether the Proustian *madeleine* or the Freudian "slip") projected an "outside" to subjectivity which could be conceived as norming and framing it.[45]

The servitudes of the body are likewise relatively independent of subjectivity. Despite fantasy, short guys *can't* slam-dunk. Bodies are resistant to speech acts—not *impervious*, to be sure, else the mind-body problem would be entirely intractable. But the most universal experience of humankind is the insubor-

---

44. Kojève, *Introduction to the Reading of Hegel*, 151–52. The Hegel reference is to the penultimate paragraph of the *Phenomenology* (492).

45. See Nussbaum, *Love's Knowledge*, 261; and Terdiman, *Present Past*, 202–4.

dination of the world to our desire—which we could re-code as the resistance of materiality to language. Our bodies put a fence around our possibilities which constrains the *too-damn-easiness* of stories and of language in general.

"My body is where there is something to be *done*," Merleau-Ponty wrote in another of this chapter's epigraphs.[46] *To be done*: the temporality here is worth considering. The future infinitive represents in syntax the mystery of human contingency and of the future itself. Something is to happen, *but it hasn't happened yet*. How can that be? Only because of the materiality of effort and the imperfections of corporeality. But language models can't easily conceive why what is *to be done* hasn't been done *already*. In their frictionlessness they don't do well at the separation between intention and accomplishment, desire and fulfillment, potentiality and realization.

But our bodies know well how this distance opens. From our earliest sentient moments the phenomenology of our body experience gives us the paradigm of all of our subsequent familiarity with refractoriness and resistance. Our bodies' weight and the burden of the things we seek to move using its muscles are where we learn our originary sense of possibility and our paradigmatic acquaintance with difficulty. In school we are taught the equations that govern categories like acceleration, velocity, time, energy, and mass. These notions in physics can seem entirely detached when we are asked to calculate how long it will take for a spacecraft to reach the Moon. But think about carrying that heavy carton of groceries in from the car. Then the abstract operators in $s = vt$ or $F = ma$ materialize in the corporeal, visceral, millennial experience of human effort.

The job of bringing the groceries in confronts us. We have to do that job. Nonetheless, we temporize and hope someone else might do the carrying. We delay because of the effort, the labor, or the time—and these might be the same—which are irreducible in bringing even a banal task to completion. The model of cultural analysis which we need must be able to capture this putting-off of the task and, beyond it, the quotidian, constitutive *resistance* that forestalls the instantaneous and cost-free accomplishment of any possibility. The model of action and of analysis which we seek needs to comprehend the refractoriness of human existence and understand why, in the face of our most intense aspiration and our hope, things still *take time*.

---

46. Merleau-Ponty, *Phenomenology of Perception*, 250; trans. modified.

An Ethics of Theory

L'ineptie consiste à vouloir conclure. . . . Oui, la bêtise consiste à vouloir conclure.

[*It would be stupid to try to conclude.* . . . Yes, attempting to conclude is moronic.]

—FLAUBERT, letter to Louis Bouilhet, 4 September 1850, *Correspondance*, 1:679–80

Prenez le plus fameux party, il ne sera jamais si seur qu'il ne vous faille, pour le deffendre, attaquer et combatre cent et cent contraires parties. [Consider the most prominent position, it will never be so certain that in order to defend it you will not be obliged to attack and oppose hundreds of contrary ideas.]

—MONTAIGNE, "Apologie de Raimond Sebond," *Essais*, bk. 2, chap. 12, 561

Au demeurant, qui sera propre à juger de ces différences?
[And in the end, what court could properly adjudicate these conflicts?]

—MONTAIGNE, "Apologie de Raimond Sebond," *Essais*, bk. 2, chap. 12, 678

What is reality? And who are [its] judges . . . ?

—WOOLF, "Mr. Bennett and Mrs. Brown," 327

My own conviction is that we must maintain two contradictory affirmations at the same time.

—DERRIDA, "Deconstruction and the Other," in
Dialogues with Contemporary Continental Thinkers, 113

So Diderot and Derrida disagree about the relationship between language and the "real world." Then it would appear important to ask which of their models— the Enlightenment-dialectical or the Postmodernist-deconstructionist—is right. Could they *both* be right? But this would seem problematic, since the two paradigms seem to cancel each other out. How, then, should we proceed?

The puzzle of how to adjudicate between models of the language-referent relationship leads beyond itself to an even more fundamental question which is my concern in this counter-conclusory conclusion. My question is this: what and how should we think when discrepant theories appear irreconcilable? How should we understand, and how practice "theory" in a world of seemingly endless difference and disagreement?

People have thought about these questions before. I want to consider some strains of this reflection—particularly a long tradition of philosophical skepticism which has not been much attended to today, and modern versions of it such as Niels Bohr's theory of complementarity. The fundamental problem is to think about the epistemological and ethical resonances of the phenomenon of *contention itself*—exemplified for many of us in the interpretive disciplines by the "theory wars" that in recent decades have focused so much energy and spilled so much ink. The purpose of such reflection is not to conclude which side is the right one but to deepen understanding of the ubiquity of "sides" to begin with.

The problem of conflicting positions has always been difficult. But today the world seems to mass-produce contention, to be rife with division. Agon has become quotidian and omnipresent. Even beyond traditional elites in the North and West, the competition for increased market share on the bourse of intellectual capital and the cultural and individual profits that attend such increase have grown considerably. This matters. Today globalization has made more voices consequential; technology has made them more audible; and the politics of a world of unequal resources and discrepant life chances has made them more contentious. This is the world in which we live. But what could be the meaning of a world in which contention is everywhere?

In thinking about this question, I want to start out from two perceptions: that the world is alive with diversity and with potentials; and that ideas constantly clash. These twin recognitions about how understanding intersects with existence provide a basis for thinking about theory itself.

We have long and almost uninterrupted experience with paradigmatic contention. Such conflict seems to be the normal state—the history—of intellectual and cultural discourse. The content of these controversies varies, but their form remains surprisingly regular. From the pre-Socratic argument between Parmenides' doctrine that existence is unchanging and Heraclitus' contrary vision of the world as unceasing flux; to the medieval disputation between realists and nominalists; to "creationist" versus "evolutionist" arguments between figures such as Huxley and Wilberforce in the nineteenth century; or (later but still within the philosophy of biology) to conflicts between "mechanists" and "tele-ologists" over the causal foundations of Darwinian theory—but a list of such contentions could go on for pages. Such superfluity of examples is my point. I believe the question we need to ask about it is, what does this pattern of universal argument *itself* mean about our modalities of understanding?

In the interpretive disciplines contention is the way of the world. We need to understand better why this should be so and how it might help us to comprehend our own activity. In the modern period an extended series of *querelles* has conditioned the history of thinking about interpretive understanding. A diagnostic case might well be the venerable seventeenth-century "Battle of the Books." It has the advantage of not engaging much passion today. So perhaps we can see more clearly what was really going on in this paradigmatic melee.

The Battle of the Books (in France, the *Querelle des Anciens et des Modernes*) raged over what at first might have seemed amusingly inconsequential stakes. The argument broke out in France in 1674 with the publication of Nicholas Boileau's *Art poétique*. Boileau framed what became the "Ancient" position. He held that imitation of the writing of antiquity was the only valid criterion for great literature. In a society as centralized and normalized as France under Louis XIV, this matter bore heavily upon a central register of state hegemony, the value to be attributed to—or discerned upon—cultural objects. Important writers such as La Fontaine and La Bruyère were stalwarts of the Ancient position.

The "Moderns," contrariwise, argued that the human mind had become more mature than it had ever been before (evidenced, for preeminent example, by the pathbreaking genius of Descartes earlier in the seventeenth century). Consequently, to their minds the present offered rich possibilities for surpassing classical writers. This was the position of figures such as Charles Perrault and Bertrand de Fontenelle, who published important contributions to the debate in the 1680s and 1690s. The issue crossed the Channel to England beginning in 1690 and culminated there in Jonathan Swift's *Battle of the Books* in 1704 (Swift supported the position of the Ancients and assailed the British Royal Society for its belief in progress).

This all might seem to have been no more than a zany debate at a retro costume party. But, despite the seeming silliness of its polarization of aesthetic and epistemological criteria, the underlying issue was more disruptive and disturbing. To begin with, the philosophical stakes were instantly politicized because they implicated the structure of cultural preferment in what remained a patronage system itself inscribed within an absolutist hierarchy. So the question of whether there can be a universal criterion for aesthetics, for epistemology, for metaphysics—indeed, for anything—stood in for a more consequential argument about the centralization and the eternalization of authority. On the other side of the controversy lies a view that sees the world as a place where many different things happen simultaneously and require divergent modalities for understanding them. So, looked at closely, the Battle of the Books was not just a matter of local doctrinal difference, implicating nothing more than the immediate content of the slogans flung back and forth. One level higher, the struggle is a model of contention reflecting on *difference* itself and on the power to adjudicate between differences. Thus, it represented an early moment in the effort to understand how to deal with the heteronomy that increasingly characterizes modern existence. At this point it is more evident how much the periwigged seventeenth-century *querelle* has to do with the issues that motivate the debates of Postmodernity.[1]

The language of *querelle* and *battle* is instructive. Think of our own period. In the past few decades, with a melodramatic portentousness that we can presume has been at least partially self-ironic, people have been speaking about "theory wars" and "science wars." In such characterizations a set of bellicose metaphors seem automatically deployed. But, despite the exaggeration of the military figure, such imagery rightly detects *political* objectives in efforts to promote one interpretive model over another. Such efforts do not simply stand up for the rightness of the model they favor. Indivisible from that objective, whether consciously intended or not, they bid for influence or for dominance—ultimately for *power*.

The covert extra-doctrinal motivation that underlies conceptual contention was recognized as early as John Locke's celebrated "Letter concerning Toleration" of 1689. In response to the bloody seventeenth-century religious struggles in England, Locke wrote as follows: "For whatsoever some people boast of . . . the orthodoxy of their faith (for everyone is orthodox to himself): these things, *and all others of this nature*, are much rather the marks of men *striving for power and empire* over one another, than of the Church of Christ."[2] In our

---

1. Significantly, most of the female intellectuals and writers of the time of the Battle of the Books defended the "Modern" position. This gender divergence in the debate helps to uncover the real stakes at issue.

2. John Locke, "Epistola de Tolerantia" (1689), contemporaneously translated as "A Letter concerning Toleration" by William Popple. See Locke, *Political Writings of John Locke*, 390; emph. added. For

own day the struggle in squabbles like the "theory wars" often seems merely a question of symbolic power, to be sure. But since the Enlightenment we have learned and we have been living that power—the power of words, the power that language has, that ideology (or *mentalité*, or Kant's "categories of the understanding") exerts in framing, determining, and changing the world we live in. To understand the unending texture of contention in the realm of cultural understanding, we are constrained to accept that symbols and language *count* and that we fight over them for good reason.

In the cultural disciplines we fight over language. Let's say that politics is the register of everything (at least everything implicating human agency) that has the capacity to constrain human possibilities and determine human lives. In its seeming Idealist intangibility, language might seem to float outside this realm. But, whatever language is, its power is consequentially and irreducibly material. How we think, how we frame and characterize our world, determines the possibilities of our action and the character of our activity. These determinants are not simply voluntarist or optional. They are not quite "facts"—they are looser than that. But neither are they limitlessly negotiable.

There are, of course, other determinants of what we can do and of what happens to us. Earthquakes can cause our houses to fall down upon us. About that there is little the interpretive disciplines can say: these are cases in which *no* negotiation with the "conceptual" seems pertinent. But Postmodernism's foregrounding of the linguistic register of our lives seems right in the awareness it urges of language's escalating predominance in contemporary existence. Today we live in and through words in ways and to degrees that arguably are different from the way other cultural epochs have lived. The deployment of language-power concerns not just "language," then, but "power."

As such, as with all issues of force, coercion, or sway exercised between human beings, the issue of language-power calls us to *ethical* reflection. How we use language, how in particular we produce theories, and how we respond to the other theories cohabiting with ours in the field of conceptual contention raise important questions about how we ought to think about the contention itself and how we ought behave in relation to it. Given the systematic presence

---

a modern scholarly translation of the text, see *A Letter concerning Toleration*, ed. R. Kilbansky, trans. J. W. Gough (Oxford: Clarendon Press, 1968). Virtually all histories of the concept of "toleration" point to Locke's "Letter" as the seminal starting point for discussions. Other pre-Enlightenment figures often mentioned are Jean Bodin, Baruch Spinoza, John Milton, and Bayle. See Craig, *Routledge Encyclopedia of Philosophy*, s.v. "Toleration."

of difference in this realm, we need to reflect upon what modalities are appropriate for conducting ourselves in theory's quarrelsome world.

> Trouvons-nous pourtant quelque fin au besoin d'interpréter?
> [But do we ever reach the end of our need to interpret?]
> —MONTAIGNE, "De l'expérience," *Essais*, bk. 3, chap. 13, 1198

Conflict needs to be thought about in terms not just of its substance or of the power-configuration that frames it but of its *deontology*, of the ethics of its exercise and process. With regard to language our obligation to think about these issues today is greater in proportion to the greater perfusion of the socius by language itself. Here I am concerned with raising questions about how we might most productively understand our activity in the interpretive disciplines. But the interpretive disciplines are not a minor externality in our existence. The social and political importance of interpretive activities has been growing in much of the West (not to speak of other regions of the world) since the decline of interpersonal immediacy, orthodox Christian belief, and centralized power in the early modern period.[3] Against that background thinkers began to assert the social significance of the categories of the people (lawyers, legislators, jurists, philosophers, writers, teachers) who, through their professional command of and activity in language, were centrally involved in conducting such activity. As language increasingly fills and defines the space of social existence, so the interpretive disciplines represent a model for a much broader range of human beings and doings whose character and processes these disciplines seek to illuminate.

I want to sketch what an *ethics of theory* might be under the twin framing conditions—the perfusion of potentiality; the regularity of divergence—which I suggested earlier are foundational. Rather than imagining harmony or hegemony as the normalized case, our first-order assumption might reasonably be that theories *never* agree, that they will *always* be in contention. For any given theory there will be antagonists whose claims are not distinctly less forceful or less widely held. Groups of partisans will form and fight. Here, by the way, the bellicose imagery so familiar to us in the "theory wars" breaks down. Battlefields produce victors. But in the theory world the ontology of "victory" is different. This is the influential proposition that we associate with the work of

---

3. I consider the resonances of this situation in other parts of the world in Terdiman, "Globalization."

figures such as Kuhn and Canguilhem.[4] It fashioned a powerful—and power-fully contested—revision in the way people think about knowledge.

The conventional view of how ideas "win" was seemingly determined by the militarist figuration that, despite a rationalist overlay, floated around it. This model saw scientific ideas subject to what Karl Popper termed "disconfirmation" or "falsification," to the so-called crucial experiment analogous to a "decisive battle"—essentially to defeat by better ideas.[5] This seemed coherent. But as over against it, Kuhn's notion of the "paradigm," so influential today, generalizes to the realm of natural science what people in the interpretive disciplines have *always* experienced. There, what happens in paradigmatic supersession is just as close to the whirligig of taste as it is to any triumph of transcendent or transhistorical rationality.

To assess this seemingly heterodox position, think how few authentic knock-down arguments have *ever* arisen in the interpretive disciplines. In the natural sciences such obliteration of an opposing theory happens regularly. One recent—and, to a Californian, pertinent—example: in the 1950s and 1960s, owing to work by Stanley K. Runcorn and others, the theory of plate tectonics began to make its claims in geology and geophysics.[6] Initially, most earth scientists contemptuously ridiculed Runcorn and his idea that continents could move. But within less than a decade it became virtually impossible for work in geology to situate itself outside the plate tectonics paradigm. Runcorn won. But in contradistinction to this sort of rapid conversion in the natural sciences, in the interpretive disciplines the unanswerable argument that nullifies an opponent's view and leaves it appearing no more than a quaint reminder of the regularity of error virtually never happens.[7]

4. See Kuhn, *Structure of Scientific Revolutions*; and Canguilhem, *Ideology and Rationality in the History of the Life Sciences*; and *Normal and the Pathological*. There is an extensive literature critiquing Kuhn's position, to which he has himself responded. Perhaps the most powerful critique will be found in Feyerabend, *Against Method*. Kuhn replies to his critics in Conant and Haugeland, *Road since Structure*.

5. See Popper, *Conjectures and Refutations*.

6. The theory was based upon speculations first suggested by Alfred Lothar Wegener beginning in 1912. See the United States Geological Service plate tectonics Web site at http://pubs.usgs.gov/publications/text/dynamic.html#anchor10790904.

7. I am not claiming here, of course, that in the interpretive disciplines changes in orthodoxies don't occur. The rise of "Theory" (particularly "French Theory") in the 1960s and afterward itself demonstrates the contrary decisively. But, despite the apparent similarity of the phenomena in scientific versus interpretive disciplines, their causalities and their finalities are divergent. In the United States, for example, French Structuralism replaced various varieties of homegrown Formalism (the New Criticism and similar positions). But it did not *supersede* those older views in the way that plate

The deontological suggestions and speculations in this chapter try to take account of the pattern of disagreement which in *Body and Story* I have tied most centrally to the differences between Enlightenment and Postmodern theories of language and materiality. But more generally what confronts us in the "theory world" is an unremitting pattern counterposing interpretive argument against argument without either position disappearing as a consequence of the unanswerable force of the other. In the interpretive disciplines paradigms always have an answer for their rivals; debate seems never to conclude. In these realms it is much more difficult to imagine what "crucial experiment" could select between competing accounts of phenomena, what new body of evidence could persuade the advocates of a given view that they must abandon it in favor of another, clearly superior model.

I have sought to exemplify this pattern of contention in considering Enlightenment reflection about fiction. I claimed that (among many other things) Diderot's *La religieuse* was an experiment in cultural theory. The novel worked a confrontation between contentious interpretations of the matter. But it could hardly be said to have "disconfirmed" some opposing view about the relation between "fiction" and "truth." Arguably, the novel deepened understanding of both terms of its dialectic. But it only made the paradox of their coexistence and their undecidability more perplexing. Then the argument between Enlightenment conceptions of the language-referent relation and Postmodern competitors today leads to a conclusion of the same form: elucidation perhaps; but victory? emphatically not.

The question is to deepen understanding of what it means for a theory in the interpretive disciplines to "work." Consider a consequential case already referred to in chapter 4. The unconscious is fundamental in psychoanalysis. It could not exist without a censoring function. The censor is the agent that decides what contents of the psyche will be made unconscious. But where in the psyche's topography could such an agent be located? and how could we be unconscious of its action at the same time that it is itself conscious of what it is doing? The paradox is immediate. In *Being and Nothingness* Sartre argued that the notion of an agent such as the censor is incoherent and indefensible.[8]

---

tectonics supplanted static geological paradigms or relativity and quantum mechanics succeeded Newtonian mechanics. Those superseded scientific models are *gone* (or absorbed as local subsets of more capacious and capable theories). But Formalism remains, with its continuing thoughtful claims. In the interpretive disciplines social or disciplinary marginalization is not the same thing as conceptual or experimental obliteration or nullification.

8. "The censor must choose and in order to choose must be aware of doing so. . . . [But] how can we conceive of knowledge which is ignorant of itself?" (Sartre, *Being and Nothingness*, 52–53).

How, then, could any system founded upon a patent error undoing its own fundamental coherence sustain itself in its other analytical and interpretive functions?

The answer is that we go on with Freud—even Sartre himself did. After demolishing what is arguably Freud's central concept, Sartre made Freud one of the principal protagonists of his later work, particularly of *The Family Idiot*, the immense book through which he sought to discover—through Freudian psychoanalysis and Marxian social analysis—what it could mean to "understand" another person.[9]

In the interpretive disciplines theory seems not to be determined by disconfirmation. How can this be? To begin with, in this realm disconfirmation almost never occurs and, then, only concerning the most narrowly constrained indicia—what many call "the facts." You could get a date wrong, though it's hard to imagine a theory based on dates. Outside of these, things float freer and have more latitude. In the language world interpretations are constitutively *underdetermined*. The constraints that some attribute to nature and its "crucial experiments" don't work in the world of concepts. In that world the objects of our description don't reach out from their detachment to call us up short with claims that they have been misconstrued.

That has long been a fundamental theme in the argument for what I have been calling "materialism." Irreducibly, in language there is "play"—in the mechanical sense that in your car the steering might be too loose for safety. Language entails a looseness or slipperiness that never allows for unambiguous interpretation.[10] In science the presumption behind the crucial experiment is that nature will so constrain the interpretation of the data produced in an

---

9. In this case, Flaubert. See Sartre, *Family Idiot*.

10. Decades ago critics talked about various forms of uncertainty and in part rooted the essence of poetry in them. See Empson, *Seven Types of Ambiguity*. Derrida's "dissemination" is a powerful theory of such play or slipperiness or undecidability. Many have wished this weren't so. In *Sketch for a Historical Picture of the Progress of the Human Mind* Condorcet argued for the creation of a language that might avoid the problem of inherent ambiguity and underdetermination: "Perhaps it would be useful today to invent a written language that, reserved exclusively for the sciences, expressing only the combinations of those simple ideas which are the same for every mind, utilized only for logically rigorous reasoning, for the precise and calculated operations of the understanding, could be comprehended by people from every country, translated into every vernacular, and would not have to be transformed, as is now the case, when it passes into general use." Beyond his political and philosophical activity, Condorcet was a distinguished mathematician. His paradigm of universality and univocality seems drawn from mathematics. But it flies in the face of our experience of difference, which is the basis for the political and ethical approach I am taking here. See Condorcet, *Esquisse d'un tableau historique des progrès de l'esprit humain*, 6:17–18; my trans.

encounter with it that the outcome of a properly constructed test will select unmistakably between (say) the theory that holds light cannot be deflected by gravity and the competing one that makes such a prediction.[11]

But today my account of decisive replacement of scientific paradigms by better ones has been considerably complicated. The very physics that predicted starlight would bend when it passed near the sun also led perversely to results that undermined philosophies of science of the Popperian sort.[12] Most nonscientists have heard about the Heisenbergian strand of these developments. "Uncertainty" (perhaps better translated as "indeterminacy") has been taken up by some cultural theorists to support their own notions that social phenomena can in principle never be "empiricized" in the way that classical physics may have suggested might be possible for all knowledge.

Strictly speaking, we need to complicate this view. Uncertainty concerns the accuracy of observations at subatomic levels. It posits an unsurpassable limit to such accuracy owing to the trade-off that occurs when an observing instrument affects the result of the observation—for example, by absorbing light energy emitted from the field observed or injecting photons back into it. On the experiential level of our lives these effects cannot be perceived and can be disregarded.

To my knowledge Heisenberg never sought to extend *uncertainty* to spheres outside of physics. Uncertainty then could only inhabit the interpretive disciplines by analogy and only when the analogy is pretty loose. Social observation can certainly affect the behavior we observe (anyone who has taken a snapshot of someone else knows that effect). But such effects are macroscopic, and it would be hard to call them theoretically irreducible. The physicist *can't* take a picture of her electron without the electron's "knowing" and reacting to the observation. But the photographer could always hide behind a tree. If we transfer Heisenberg's *uncertainty* to the social realm, it risks diffusing into a synonym for the complications of relationship in general and threatens to become conceptually vacuous. It would be preferable to lay out the bases of social inter-

11. In November 1919 the Royal Society announced that its expedition to the Gulf of Guinea had photographed the 29 May solar eclipse and verified the predictions concerning gravity's bending of light which had been made in Einstein's general theory of relativity in 1916. This confirmation was the beginning of Einstein's fame and that of the general theory itself. It also became a primary model for the "crucial experiment."

12. As is well known, to the end of his life Einstein resisted the implications of these latter theories as they concerned the issue of physical determinacy versus indeterminacy. Even in the most hard-edged of the natural sciences, the clash of theory does not seem necessarily to yield entirely to empirical evidence or deductive argument.

activity less obliquely. What we want is to ground in the characteristics of more properly *social* modalities (e.g., language, desire, politics) the effects that produce the play in the system and forestall the certainty and empirical accuracy of our knowledge of the phenomena we investigate. This is the approach that, parallel to Heisenberg's, was suggested by Heisenberg's teacher Niels Bohr. Bohr called his notion "complementarity."

Bohr's view has implications for the ethics of theory. Complementarity bears directly on the sort of battle or quarrel that I claimed is the normal form of competition in social or cultural theory. I want to consider it as the first of several models that might help us capture better how theories relate to one another under the conditions—perfusion of potentiality; regularity of disagreement—which I suggested frame the contemporary organization of theoretical contention.

For nonphysicists complementarity has been brought to wider attention by Michael Frayn's play *Copenhagen*, a semifictionalized account of Heisenberg's visit to Bohr in September 1941.[13] Complementarity was Bohr's theoretical response to Heisenberg's uncertainty—thus instantiating in practice the very point Bohr was making about theory. Bohr developed complementarity in 1927 to account for the paradoxical wave-particle duality—the uncertainty or indeterminacy concerning the character of light which had emerged in quantum theory. Light appears to behave sometimes as wave, sometimes as particles. That is already puzzling. But more problematic still is that these two representations could not (and still cannot) be transcoded into each other through any algebraic or formulaic transformation. The wave equations and the particle equations themselves *don't equate.* They are not just alternative formulations, different versions of the same mathematical or physical relation. No synthesis of them has proven possible; they remain formally irreconcilable. Yet both do good analytical work; both appear "true." Such a situation was baffling to Bohr, and it remains so today. Is reality not one but *multiple?* is light really two *different* phenomena? And how does light know which form to take? Bohr's insight concerning complementarity arose from his question about how these paradoxes could be the case.[14]

13. See Frayn, *Copenhagen.* Paul Lawrence Rose offers the most recent and authoritative account of Heisenberg's mysterious meeting with Bohr in Copenhagen in 1941. See Rose, *Heisenberg and the Nazi Atomic Bomb Project,* 154–66.

14. On the relationship between "complementarity" and the interpretive disciplines, a thoughtful account can be found in Plotnitsky, *In the Shadow of Hegel.*

Richard Rhodes gives a good account of this matter:

The reason that both [particle and wave descriptions] could be accepted as valid is that "particles" and "waves" are words, are abstractions. What we know is not particles and waves but the equipment of our experiments. . . . The solution, Bohr went on, is to accept the different and mutually exclusive results as *equally valid* and stand them side by side to build up a composite picture of the atomic domain. *Nur die Fülle führt zur Klarheit*: only wholeness leads to clarity. Bohr was never interested in an arrogant reductionism. He called instead . . . for "renunciation," renunciation of the godlike determinism of classical physics. . . . The name he chose for this "general point of view" was *complementarity*, a word that derives from the Latin *complementum*, "that which fills up or completes." Light as particle and light as wave, matter as particle and matter as wave, were mutually exclusive abstractions that complemented each other. They could not be merged or resolved; they had to stand side by side in their seeming paradox and contradiction; but accepting that uncomfortably non-Aristotelian condition meant physics could know more than it otherwise knew. . . . In conclusion [Bohr] . . . pointed to complementarity's connection to philosophy. The situation in physics . . . "bears a deep-going analogy to the general difficulty in the formation of human ideas, inherent in the distinction between subject and object. . . ." In the years to come Bohr would extend the compass of his "certain general point of view" far into the world. It would serve him as a guide not only in questions of physics but in the largest questions of statesmanship as well.[15]

Arkady Plotnitsky adds a succinct formulation summarizing Bohr's own account of the concept: "The features of quantum mechanical descriptions are first complementary—mutually exclusive, but both necessary—and second, are *idealizations*, or metaphorical models. Indeed they are symbolizations of idealizations, metaphors of metaphors."[16]

During and after World War II Bohr drew complementarity beyond the realm of photons and quanta and squarely into the interpretive disciplines. For example, based upon complementarity, he developed an explicitly *political* theory concerning the atomic bomb which his own research had helped to bring into being.[17] His theory saw the bomb's existence and effect in terms of this extended

15. Rhodes, *Making of the Atomic Bomb*, 131–33.
16. Plotnisky, *In the Shadow of Hegel*, 31.
17. Bohr's view on the bomb was characteristically complex and multilayered. His research on atomic structure (for which he received the Nobel Prize in 1922) was an indispensable precursor to

theory of meaning. He was one of the first to argue that the terror of the bomb could produce a stability coexisting with its menace at the same time that it contradicted this—an origin of the eerie Cold War doctrine of "mutually assured destruction." In his final years Bohr sought to develop further ways in which, beyond the strict use of the concept in physics, the idea of complementarity could throw light on broader aspects of human life and thought. In a powerful formulation of such capacity for the idea's extension beyond its original domain, in 1961 he wrote, "the complementary nature of the description appearing in this uncertainty is unavoidable already *in an analysis of the most elementary concepts employed in interpreting* [ordinary human] *experience.*"[18]

Complementarity suggests an alternative way of understanding the coexistence of theoretical models that not only do not cohere but which cannot be reciprocally transcoded into each other at all. They bear on the same object. They are both true. But they are *irreconcilable* in fundamental propositions or assumptions. That paradoxical state, I have been arguing, is the *normal* paradigm in the world of interpretive theory. It can lead to theory wars (or to science wars). But in the interpretive disciplines it might also lead to a less polarized practice—and ethics—of theory.

Under the sign of complementarity the clash of theories becomes a matter of differential or differently focused understandings, rather than of logical truth or of quasi-doctrinal—still less, of quasi-martial—conflict. This is because the complementarity model takes the notion of "model" *itself* more seriously and deeply than is implicit in the theory wars mode. The more we move away from a fundamentalist or positivist notion of "truth" inhering in our instrument of understanding or providing unassailable warrant for its result, the easier it is to understand *why other people see things differently*. The metaphors, the figures that Bohr sees in the fundamental operators of his physics, are not the result of some seduction into transdisciplinarity or effort to annex poetry's prestige. They emerged in the encounter with the material itself.

Bohr's position on "theory" is the contemporary philosophy-of-science incarnation of one of the fundamental quarrels that have marked the history of

---

the invention of the bomb. Bohr spent the first part of the war in occupied Denmark, where Heisenberg made his famous visit, but in 1943, under threat of arrest for his resistance activities, Bohr escaped to Sweden and eventually to the United States, where he became part of the Los Alamos group that produced the bomb. But, as early as 1944, he began making arguments against the weapon and its political consequences. In 1957 he won the first Atoms for Peace Award. On Bohr's attitude, see Rose, *Heisenberg and the Nazi Atomic Bomb Project*, 29–30, 83–84.

18. Bohr, *Atomic Physics and Human Knowledge*, 57; emph. added.

theory—in this case the medieval controversy between nominalism and realism. "Realists" believed that concepts were more real than their instantiations. That, roughly speaking, was Plato's view in his theory of the Forms. "Nominalists," on the other hand, held that abstractions (or "universals") lack substantive reality, a quality that can belong only to individual objects. For the nominalists abstractions were not natural kinds or real entities but conceptual *constructions*. Theoretical models and paradigms then fall into the latter case, because such models are necessarily constituted by and dependent upon their reach toward generality. Therefore, they operate at a level different from the one on which we imagine that individual objects exist.[19] Under such a view models tend more in the direction of contingency than of necessity or certainty. They are word and idea constructions. They *figure* the world they take as their object; hence their ontological status is different from that object.

What I want to draw from the nominalist position is this disengagement of theory from the polar categories of immediate sense impression, on the one hand, and a priori or apodictic truth, on the other. Figuration is a *buffer* between thought and action. In just the sense I suggested earlier in this chapter, it is a *looser* relation to what it figures; it allows for play in the system. The knowledge that representation and figuration are my modes of knowing, that my theory is a contingent and limited construction, has the potential to diminish any intransigence in the commitment I have to it and in the range of actions I might undertake in response to disagreement or theoretical conflict. Such knowledge can inflect my belief and behavior concerning competing models. It has *ethical* implications.

There is greater suppleness in metaphors and representations than in real objects—anyone who bangs into a table knows that. It is hard to find language to talk about this, but with acknowledged imprecision perhaps we could say that *objects* don't "mean" in the same way that *theories* do. In our encounters with them objects require of us a more inflexible adherence, and they can be much less forgiving when such adherence does not occur. This problem was Diderot's field of investigation in his *La religieuse* experiment with material, corporeal reality, on the one hand, and what today we would call "fiction," on the other. What *gives?* and what *resists?* For Diderot that question turned out to be a good mean for discriminating between the *story* world and the *body* one. The problem was that in the former realm, language's flexibility and compliance to our

19. Nominalism evolved from Aristotle's thesis that all reality consists of individual things.

wishes could turn against itself—or at least against the person utilizing its expansive and accommodating modality. Then it permitted so much that it appeared to allow virtually *anything*—and consequently left us with hardly any way to choose between what *worked* and what did not.

Bohr's complementarity converges with such a perception. Against the traditional logic of physics, it poses an anti-Positivist disengagement of concepts and models from any simply or singly determined relationship to their experimental or experiential objects. In the lexicon of my discussion *complementarity* is another avatar of the fundamental difference in mode between expansive negotiability and obdurate rigidity. In complementarity concepts may be potentially contingent upon critical experiments, but they are *necessarily* determined by the character of language. Mechanical causality or logical entailment can no longer unanswerably mandate a given conceptualization, or rebut its competitor.

So theories are softer than billiard balls. If we understand them in terms of the medium by and in which they exist, they give more room for *seeing things differently*. The looseness of language and figuration then bears (or at least rightly could bear) upon the allegiance we have to any concept. Such a view would even imply a different attitude toward the positivist position of classical physics itself. The "complementarist" would think: I may not like that other position, and it may seem less supple or inclusive than mine. But in its area, within its inherent limitations (here, its functionality solely on super-atomic, macroscopic levels), *it works*. Such a position gave us Newton and Maxwell. How could anyone be against *them*?[20] Then the ire prosecuted in the opposite direction, on the part of natural science traditionalists against their "science study" challengers, can itself begin to seem unproductively—"uncomplementarily"—parochial.[21]

How to conceive the theory of "theory"? Here is one way. We think about what troubles us. By definition "trouble" is something we haven't yet resolved. This means that no stable way of framing or understanding it exists yet. Whence in

20. Adherence to complementarity emphatically does not mean that no differentiation between the value or applicability of concepts is possible; it does not equate to any form of radical relativism. I will argue this critical point further later.

21. On what some of the participants themselves call the "science wars," see, for example, the Science Wars Web site at http://members.tripod.com/ScienceWars/. Among the most prominent of the protagonists on the "science studies" side of the debate are Sandra G. Harding; see her book *Is Science Multicultural?* and the collection she coedited with Merrill B. Hintikka, *Discovering Reality*; and Donna J. Haraway; see her book *Primate Visions*.

reply a multiplicity of—apparently irreconcilable—lines of attack and proffers for comprehension: *different theories*. These are the elements of complementarity. They are imagination's responses to and representations of difficulty. So, in the perspective of a task to be performed, of a problem to be addressed, contention in the theory realm might better be conceived as the intellect's best chance to see its way clear: rather as *hunt* than as *race*; rather chasing a common objective than battling the other guy. This could lead to more propitious form for reflection on the theoretical wrangles that characterize cultural conjunctures.

Aside from some natural science traditionalists and a few other literalists, we don't find many people—particularly in the interpretive disciplines—who hold to a notion of transhistorical or transcultural truth. Of course, some things seem unarguable. The French Revolution began in 1789. If I don't eat, I'll die. But such propositions generally root in fairly exacting material—in these cases chronological, biological, thermodynamic—determinations. If I became a yogi, perhaps I could train my body to live on fewer calories while in a meditative state. But my heart still needs to beat occasionally, and that will take *some* energy. When the energy runs out, *pfft!*

Then there are conventionalist statements that take the form of "X is Y" where the X's are (say) monarchs whose authority is claimed to be divine; or gender groups whose capacities are claimed to be inferior to those of some other group; and so on. As my examples suggest, conventions change, pulling rugs out from under what may at one time have seemed irrefutable dogmas.

Then there are the things we *wish* or *hope* are true: "Human beings are born free" or "All people are created equal." You might be moved to fight for such propositions. Some have even believed they are "self-evident." But, all things carefully considered, you probably wouldn't credit the notion that they are true in the same way that "starvation produces death" is true.

Finally—admittedly, my typology of possible positions here leaves out significant cases—there are statements of this sort: "Mallarmé was a Symbolist"; or "Derrida is a Postmodernist";[22] or "History is what hurts"; or "there is no outside-the-text." These statements are plausible within an interpretive framework; they don't make much sense outside of one. We could stretch the vocabulary to say that, in that sense, they are *locally* true. But for my argument here the

---

22. But one can disagree: "Derrida, as far as I know, does not see himself as a postmodern, so applying the label to him seems simply to use a term of abuse." See Hoy, "Splitting the Difference," 234.

salient point is that there are *other* local truths, even in the same locality; and ours and theirs may be technically irreconcilable—like Certeau's "Death is an 'outside-the-text'" and other views that I paired with or counterposed against Derrida's dictum in the epigraphs to my introduction. So we're brought back to the pragmatics and to the ethics of such conflictual formulations.

I think the notion of reason pertinent to our period needs to project something I want to call *skeptical truth*. This concept seeks to occupy a mediatory position between radical relativism, one the one hand, and positivism or pure dogmatism, on the other. The standpoint that it urges upon interpretation and epistemology bears the same relationship to these two polar extremes that the third, dialectical, view of the relationship between words and things which I discussed in chapter 5 bears, on the one hand, to faith in the unproblematic adequacy of words to their referents and, on the other, to contemporary "textualist" views denying the possibility of any articulation between them.[23]

This is the spirit in which I take Derrida's own dialectical moves (even though he might repudiate my characterization of them), his skeptical but respectfully informed deconstructive reconsiderations of Marx and Hegel. In thinking them through, Derrida neither signs on to their theses nor renounces his own. Rather, in the spirit both of dialectic and of deconstruction he seeks (as in my Derridean epigraph to this chapter) to hold this complex and knotty material together in tension.

Indeed, it is accurately capturing the characteristics of the tension itself which is the constituting operation in such an analysis. This operation is a model for what I mean here by "skeptical": a form of reason which internalizes just the sort of unresolvable uncertainty that Diderot was exploring in the language experiments of *La religieuse* and his other novels, in *Rameau's Nephew* quintessentially—but *without* conceding to the renunciations of a flattening and internally unarticulated relativism.

Whatever else we might want to say about it, truth seeks to tell us *what is the case*. But since the early modern period the "cases" people encounter in experience have appeared multifarious and slippery. They never model for still photographs; they won't let themselves be captured in a single, simple proposition. The world, Montaigne said, is a perpetual seesaw.[24] But let us understand his charming image not as denoting a flat averaging of standpoints such that each

23. One way of thinking about this would be to see it as undermining what Derrida has slyly deconstructed as the "other's monolingualism"; see *Monolinguism of the Other*.

24. Montaigne, "Du repentir," *Essais*, bk. 3, chap. 2, 899; "On Repentance," *Essays*, 235.

is compressed toward neutrality, as if the seesaw were simply frozen horizontal, but rather as expressing the up-and-down oscillation of our commitment to *any* position, based upon immediate situation and circumstances and upon the transforming movement of time.

Thus, I've described Diderot stretched between his world-*representing* (or world-*transforming*) writing in the *Encyclopédie* and his world-*generating* writing in *La religieuse*. These two views of the pragmatics of language are antagonistic; they resist and undermine each other—particularly in a period that (and for a writer who) had surely not abandoned the project of social *effectiveness* for texts. Diderot holds *both* views about words, language, narrative, and writing in general. But what he finds to be the case here (and in his dialogues, his art criticism, or his aesthetic theory) is a version of what, since early modernity, we *always* find: complementarity. Despite the apparent violation of the law of noncontradiction, language *is* unreliable and duplicitous; and language *is* referentially purposeful and veridical. This "these two" *is* the case: not either/or but both.

In this sense the concepts that might model such a mutable world are always "skeptical." Their purpose, their very being, are unstable. They can't sit still or know for sure. Rather than in the image of the achieved certainties of Descartes' *Discourse on Method*, their existence is figured by the flickering dialectical play of positions in *Rameau's Nephew*. Such concepts cannot *not* entertain and take on the very propositions they simultaneously resist. In a world of tension and change nothing is ever settled; nothing ever stands pat.

For much of Western cultural and epistemological history, stability and mastery have been cardinal and foundational values. Notwithstanding this infrastructural assumption and pushing strenuously against it, the conditions of existence from the Enlightenment to Postmodernity ask us to project and to credit a divergent epistemology and a distinct pragmatics. This conception of a world ceaselessly changing, continuously alienating itself from itself and disseminating its provisional and ephemeral meanings, would be constituted by integrating into our mode of encountering it a practice of *not knowing* which, since the domination of scientific thinking began to take hold of consciousness centuries ago, we have generally thought of as a guilty flaw. Now it may instead have become a prerequisite for subjectivity and for conceptualization. In the Enlightenment, in response to the experience of these new conditions and perceptions, dialectic sought a groundless ground through which a logic of instability might respond to an unstable world. We—and Postmodernists particularly—remain engaged in the effort to produce such models.

Such models must be carefully distinguished, however, from *relativism*. Dialectic registers that the dynamics active in the world are multiple and conflictual. But they are not infinite or stochastic, not carelessly random. Representing them *is* possible. The "state" of things in such a world is not static or frozen, but it is not chaotic either. Analysis seeks to detect and represent a comparatively short list of effective determinants active in any unresolved social situation or cultural representation. Such a depiction may be difficult because things aren't simple, but it can be managed. It exhibits some of the same characteristics that define classical versions of propositional truth: responsiveness to empirical data, qualified falsifiability, social communicability. *Relativism* would be appropriate for a world in which the effective determinants of any action or situation were unlimited, one in which all determinants were equivalent in value and effectiveness, or in which there were no determinants at all. But the world since the Enlightenment has not corresponded to such a description.

"Complementarity" doesn't offer answers, but a way of reconceiving questions. It reframes the understanding of difference so as to credit the claims not only of difference's content, but of its form. It argues a view with which many people are sympathetic, but which has been difficult to integrate into interpretive practice: that differences should be construed with analytical seriousness, not marginalized as dissonance on the way to some version of organic unification. Thus complementarity sees differences as foundational and advantageous. It offers principled support for the evenhanded or egalitarian impulses that encourage us to resist processing differences in such a way that, at the conclusion of our work upon them, they have been covertly normalized, made to fuse with what we already know, and transformed into previously misrecognized versions of the same. Such moves make difference seem illusory. On the other hand, complementarity projects a world that can*not* be sutured or reduced to a logic in which all propositions unfold stably out of self-consistent axioms. For complementarity knowledge can never achieve such low-order unification. Emerging from the realm of science which since the Greeks has taken such unification as a supreme ideal, complementarity reframes epistemology so that knowing is *the knowledge of irreducible heteronomy*—and hence it does not expect that on fuller examination such differences will turn out to have been no more than a provisional defect in our vision.

Philosophical skepticism offers another way of thinking about disagreement which can help frame an ethics for theory. But, before I suggest how, one issue needs a closer look. Earlier in this chapter I sketched a hazy Darwinian model for the generation of theories. In effect I projected spawning a multiplicity of responses to answer unresolved problems. The implication seemed to be that the production of these theories was more or less random—"let's try *this*; now let's try *that*"; in the lingo of flackery, let's run up masses of flags and see if anyone salutes. The presumption of such a model for the generation of models would be that, on the downstream side, experience could be counted upon to "edit" this list, just as happens with mutations in biology. The latter, once they have been generated by random alterations in the DNA, face the test of "real-world" survival—of selection—according to a calculus of beneficial or disadvantageous adaptation.

But in the interpretive disciplines the *production* of these deviant conceptualizations—new theories—is not scattershot in the way of biological mutations. In biology generation is random, but outcome—survival—is determined by the environment. On the other hand, in the interpretive disciplines new theories don't just pop up haphazardly to await their subsequent testing by reality. Of course, that testing does occur. But with such theories there is no moment of *production* which can be separated from the later constraints of *practice*. Production of a theoretical model, rather, could best be figured as the outcome of interdetermination by a continual feedback system.

There are constraints in interpretive or model-constructing experience analogous to the testing of a biological sport through the real-life rigors of selective adaptation. But in the interpretive disciplines the agents that produce the models are conscious. Consequently, determination occurs at every moment of a theory's development—beginning with its originary instant, the inchoate perception that there is something yet or something new to understand. Even in this most primitive of theoretical moments the environment is not just "out there" awaiting the launch of our new decoding of it. The "outside" of any proto-theory, its object and referent, has always already been internalized; the *explanandum* is already present to bear upon the production of its *explanans*.

The process projected here is bidirectional or interdetermining or dialectical. It is homologous with the third paradigm I sketched in chapter 5 for comprehending the relationship between language and referent. That model understood the process as one of complex adjustment and negotiation (what Hegelian Marxists would term "mediation") between words and world, with constraint exerted from both sides of the relationship. So it would be in theory production generally.

But there is a further problem that needs addressing. We need an argument that can make sense of one of the most regular—and puzzling—conditions framing the conflictual world of theoretical positions. Almost always only a *small* number of competing models in the interpretive disciplines claim to give us grasp on a particular realm of existence or experience. Most often these models cluster in groups with few members, frequently in the sets of rival dyads such as the familiar ones—for example, "realist" versus "nominalist"—which I discussed earlier in this chapter. Why should this be so if the world of things and the world of thinking are as unbounded as many contemporary relativists (particularly some Poststructuralists) see them? How could we reconcile their would-be liberatory standpoints (e.g., Lyotard's "incredulity concerning meta-narratives") with the grouping of theoretical positions in numbers of a conspicuously low order?

The world isn't random, so our theories aren't either. That's the heart of my attempt to explain why we don't drown in proliferating explanations, why theories don't expand exponentially as Malthus feared human populations might or as Dukas fantasized in the mushrooming world of *The Sorcerer's Apprentice*. If discourse were stochastic, the notion of explanation itself would have no payoff, and it would have been buried long ago like an unsuccessful mutation in biology. But explanations *work*.

I can't expect that everyone will see the matter in the way I will project it—that, indeed, is my overarching point. But in my projection we are propelled back for explanation to the notion of *constraint* which has threaded through my argument from the outset. Just as in every other phase of our existence *something constrains theory production*; something arrays theories in the low-order clusters I just spoke about—or else we'd have so many of them that our heads would never stop spinning. The only way I can conceive explaining why we do not encounter an inexhaustible number of theoretical positions, as limitless and unclassifiable as the random mutations in DNA which shape the biological world, is to posit that our theories are somehow lined up with their referent and constrained by its finite and determinate character. It might seem a toothless pleonasm, but *determination* is the tool we need to explain why the theory world is not indeterminate.

The Hegelian-Marxian tradition offers a matrix that coheres with the phenomenon I'm discussing. In the notion of *contradiction* we find a structure that parallels the low-order organization of interpretive models. But how do things organize themselves in such a way? Consider an analogy. Many phenomena are essentially continuous. An example would be *race*. People think of races as discrete. But it turns out that the presumed natural divisions by which human-kind has tended to categorize itself are conventional fictions. Real genetically determined characteristics are actually arrayed continuously along vectors with no detectable clustering.[25] A second example would be the sounds in language. In one of his most influential theoretical innovations Saussure pointed out that, while sound production in ("phones") human beings is potentially ar-rayed along the same sort of continuous dimensions as are the genes in human phenotypes, on the other hand, in any population sound production and per-ception clusters in what Saussure famously termed "phonemes," separate fami-lies that in any language define meaningfulness as determinately and discretely as whole notes are defined on a trombone slide.

Contradictions in social existence work like that. The infinite positionalities of potentially continuous phenomena are grouped *by groups themselves*. As I recalled in chapter 2, Georg Simmel drew Vico's celebrated "verum factum"—the idea that we have privileged knowledge of what we ourselves have made—a further step by positing as the condition of possibility of social existence itself the intervention of belief in that very possibility. In other words, as Simmel put it, society is possible because people *think it is*. In effect they theorize society into being.[26]

At some level of abstraction everything in social existence *could* be arrayed along the same continuous dimension as language sounds are in Saussure. But, practically speaking, that never happens. Things come to us already banded together. Consciousness—theory—has already intervened. The structure of con-tradiction in society which Marx believed was the defining force in the course of lives and of history is an instantiation of that fundamental clustering mecha-nism. This is the insight emerging in Marx's notion of the "mode of produc-tion."[27] We could take it today as a means of comprehending the way in which any conjuncture structures the discourses that can respond to and account for it and asserts the demands that theory responds to.

It is probably futile to try deciding which register of reality—the continu-ously distributed particulars in any empirical or perceptual field or the discrete

25. See Cavalli-Sforza, *Genes, Peoples, and Languages*; and Cavalli-Sforza, Menozzi, and Piazza, *His-tory and Geography of Human Genes*.

26. See Simmel, "How Is Society Possible?" 7.

27. See Marx, *Capital*, 1:505, 602, 617. See also Cohen, *Marx's Theory of History*, 79–84. Cohen's account is particularly helpful because of its analytical clarity.

groupings into which consciousness arrays them for intelligibility or practical activation—is more "originary" or fundamental. Perhaps we could understand them as complementary in Bohr's sense of the term. The question is one of perspective and pragmatic purpose. Saussure's phones are real; so are his phonemes. But for whom and under what circumstances?

In the case of language our knowledge of the families into which sounds aggregate for meaningfulness acts as if it derives from outside the system itself. Beside the professionals in linguistics, who "knows" the phonemic system of a language? Only nonspeakers, because they cannot practically operate within a language of whose segmental system they are ignorant. For native speakers this system is just . . . there. Similarly, social contradiction of the classical Marxian type depends upon the objectification and concatenation of a relatively small number of discrete social agents. The "phenotypic" variability among the members of these conflicting families may be great, but for purposes of understanding they can be grouped—they group themselves—into estates, or classes, as elsewhere (we might say, following Renan's analysis in *Qu'est-ce qu'une nation?*) they do into national states, despite the objective heterogeneity among those who become the citizens of such constructed polities.[28]

So, the social real isn't just out there; it's already internalized in us, in the inchoate or nondiscursive concepts and theories that define how people act and how they believe themselves to live. Theories locate themselves in the choices they make in response to the pressures of the real, understood in the sense of what is internalized and effective in human practice. Thereby, theories are embedded in the materiality of existence, as elements that are relatively refractory to transformation by no more than an act of thought.

Some might tax this construction of the problem with guilty capitulation to the real and fault it for being unable to project how, if everything is determined by what already exists, anything might ever be changed. This objection is unpersuasive. Our job is to say what is the case. Hence we'd be irresponsible if we didn't take account of it and of its determinations. But to be determined is not the same as to be forced into blind and thoughtless reproduction of what deter-

28. See Renan, *Qu'est-ce qu'une nation?* Renan's point was that to construct the concepts of a nation and of belonging to it—what Benedict Anderson would much later term an "imagined community"—required considerable work on the raw material of human existence within given borders (as he put it, much remembering and much forgetting), such that, as a result of such conceptual labor, the abstraction of such "national" membership precipitated out and could in turn become internalized.

mines you. You can chime with the dominant discourse, to be sure, and there is inevitably pressure on all of us to do so. But, as many have argued, counter-discourses are another, and quite a cogent, response to hegemony.

Michel de Certeau captured this situation in his mapping of the difference between "tactics" and "strategies." *Strategies* determine their field of play and define the givens of the game. But most of the time we are constrained to the level of *tactics*, obliged to acknowledge the force and the structure of established discourse and to work with them in order to work against them.[29] No one said this would be easy. But, precisely by virtue of its hegemony, a dominant discourse offers itself for subversion, troping, cannibalizing, contradiction, and all manner of alternative means of diminishing, evading, or transforming its pre-existing command of the situation.

Here I use the term *strategy* as a more capacious identifier for the structured ways people react to the situations that confront them. My usage conflates what Certeau meant both by *tactics* and by *strategies*. What then arises in response to any situation, and within any organization of actors, groups, and concepts, is a relatively small number of such strategies for answering the clustered determinants to which response must be made or of which an account must be given. Dominance dominates. But despite its attempt to project seamlessness, it has fissures and leaks. There are gaps in hegemony; there are new experiences it has not yet brought under its control; there are new interests that arise unanticipated in its assumptions. The profuse diversity of the forms of social life prevents any long-term stability in the discourse that attempts to comprehend it. So there is no master-code that already deciphers everything. And just when people think there is, just when the dominant seems to have been fully stabilized, the structures of hegemony are probably about to start shaking. At least that has been the history of experience in the West in the period since the Enlightenment. The European revolutions of 1989 and 1990 are just one striking instantiation of seismic movements that we know will recur, even if we cannot predict where, when, or with what result.

The theories of concern to us, then, are emergent strategies of response to pressures and constraints by which a "fit" of some specifiable kind is projected between the analytic paradigm they offer and some referent that appears to have escaped the control of the dominant discourse, of what everyone already

29. See Certeau, *Practice of Everyday Life*, xix, 35–38. "The place of a tactic belongs to the other" (xix); "A tactic is an art of the weak" (37).

thinks. In the form of a particular set and mix of specific determinants, determination, we might then say, is *invented* by those who experience its force—that is to say, by all of us. It operates in the realm of the imagination: that is, of the structured perceptions and choices that are the locus of signification in experience itself.

But these have always been constrained. This is why theories tend to cluster, whether in convergence with or in opposition to one another, into sets of (often oppositional) strategies. As I suggested earlier, they line up with their referents; they are constrained by its finite and determinate character. To each set of what Adorno termed "domineering institutions," to each configuration of what contradicts them or locus of as yet unmastered tension within them, will correspond a concrete set of strategies for understanding what has not already been integrated into doxa, or for transforming what might seem to most people so unquestionable that no question ever arose—until somebody raised one.[30]

The modes of domination in any historical moment—however internally complex they may be when we examine them analytically—tend to be experienced by individuals and groups as the immediate blockage of aspiration or effort in particular, determinate areas of life. This gives rise to binary or dyadic structures for thinking—on the one hand, about frustrated desire or need; on the other, about the constraints that bear against them. No doubt theoretical systems are a more complex form of response to the unmastered givens of the world in which people—and theorists—live. But at their root they are formed in the same oppositional perception. For that reason the imaginative responses of theoretical construction cluster around a small number of strategies, which in their turn reflexively characterize the unresolved stresses experienced in any moment. Against them they project their resistance and their insurgency.[31]

This argument for the *clustering* of strategies of theoretical and practical response is important because it helps to discern the difference between *philosophical skepticism* and *radical relativism*. Relativism is stochastic. It projects an undifferentiated (and technically meaningless) randomness. No epistemological structure can be derived from a radical relativist position. Skepticism, on the other hand, allows for the uncertainty of knowledge *in relation to* epistemological or social issues. While traditionally skeptics allowed for knowledge of im-

30. Adorno, "Theses upon Art and Religion Today"; cited by Jay, *Dialectical Imagination*, 179.

31. The discussion of "strategies" here revisits issues (and lifts some language) from Terdiman, "Materialist Imagination."

mediate appearance, beyond this supposed immediacy skeptical positions are uncertain because they prescribe an attitude of *speculation* about what is and might be. But such speculation, I want to argue, is *not* undetermined. As I will try to explain in the next portion of this discussion, skeptical positions tend to the same low-order array of possible views which I maintained characterizes the pattern of epistemological and theoretical contention in general. At the limit skepticism projects the dyadic structure of *pour et contre*, of assertion and counter-assertion, which reappears in much medieval European philosophy and later, transformed to a considerable degree in content but not in form, in the dialectic in Hegel and in Marx. Skepticism recognizes that such a structure of opposition constitutes the possibility of *any* position and regulates the stability with which, properly understood, any individual projection of understanding can be credited.

Times of mutability such as the Enlightenment experienced, and such as we are experiencing now, can foster two contrary attitudes toward their uncertainties. One of them seeks to solidify received doctrine and tradition in order to counteract the pressure of the new. Fundamentalisms, dogmatisms, nationalisms, and essentialisms of diverse sorts exemplify such defensive responses to the stresses of transformation.[32] If we see such reactions today, it is because the times are particularly troubled.

The other chief mode of response to troubled times is skepticism. What we could term Socrates' "epistemic modesty" is a prestigious instantiation of this attitude.[33] From Gorgias, Protagoras, and Socrates himself to Montaigne, Locke, Hume, and on to Diderot, Nietzsche, and Derrida, thought-systems that seek to assert the stability of our mode of knowing, particularly of knowing apodictically, run up against forceful strains of principled doubt concerning knowledge's stability and reliability. From Socrates' constantly cited (or mis-cited) "The only thing I know is that I know nothing" to Montaigne's "Que sais-je?" (What do I really know?), the adoption of skeptical standpoints has powerful

---

32. The critique of such national and even theological essentialisms, however, must itself be responsive to specific settings and situations. Not every nationalism is the same. Its bearing must be carefully assessed. Tibet's courageous adherence to Buddhist practice and to the accompanying political tradition making the Dalai Lama the governing primate of what under Chinese occupation has become the delusively named "Tibet Autonomous Region" cannot be comprehended in the same way as neo-fundamentalist nationalisms in India, Pakistan, France, Germany, Austria, or the United States. On Tibet and China, see Isabel Hilton's brilliant book *Search for the Panchen Lama*.

33. See Audi, *Cambridge Dictionary of Philosophy*, s.v. "Skepticism" (738). In this book I spell *skepticism* with a *k*. Yet this too is uncertain. Some people spell it with a *c*.

epistemological and ethical implications.[34] Practicing uncertainty, aporia, or what Nicholas of Cusa termed "learned ignorance" (*docte ignorance*),[35] experiencing and crediting epistemological *otherness*, inherent uncertainty, and difference, means that our whole complex of moral conduct and sociocultural expectation may need to be transformed quite as much as our epistemological activity.

Here, perhaps somewhat scandalously, the link between Enlightenment thinking and Postmodernism's nominal antagonism to it reappears almost as a return of the repressed. What we might think of as *methodological irony* is central to it. Such irony figures that decentering "alongsidedness," that depriviledging of secure and stable identity, which characterizes important aspects of conceptualization and experience since the early modern period. This is what I mean by "skeptical truth." Its Enlightenment emblem might be Montesquieu's devastating re/citational deflation of certainty grounded in national, religious, or cultural doctrine, in his celebrated "Monsieur est Persan? . . . Comment peut-on être Persan?" Or it might express itself in the image of the fretful question the Philosopher in *Rameau's Nephew* asks Rameau himself: "Comment dites-vous tout cela? est-ce ironie, ou vérité?"[36]

Skepticism has existed for many centuries and taken many forms. The meaning of the term has become blurred with diverse usages. The philosophical dictionaries clarify these variations helpfully (the etymology of *skeptic* is suggestive: it means something like "observer" or "seeker").[37] The species of skepticism of particular interest to me here is what the taxonomists term "practical skepticism." This is an attitude that practices the deliberate withholding both of belief and of disbelief. This is not the same as holding that judging is *impos-*

---

34. In *Apology* 21b Socrates—contrasting his own knowledge with that of a reputed wise man—says: "He knows nothing and thinks that he knows; I neither know nor think that I know"; see *Dialogues of Plato*, 1:405. In *Lives of the Eminent Philosophers*, bk. 2, sec. 32, Diogenes Laertius reports Socrates' watchword as: "He knew nothing except just the fact of his ignorance" (1:163). In the "Apologie de Raymond Sebond," his most focused discussion of skepticism, Montaigne refers directly to Socrates' celebrated sentence; see Montaigne, *Essais*, bk. 2, chap. 12, 556–57. Montaigne's "Que sais-je?" ("What do I [really] know?") is also from the "Apologie" (589).

35. See Certeau, "Gaze," 2–38.

36. Montesquieu: "Monsieur is a Persian? But how could anybody possibly be *Persian*?" (*Lettres persanes*, 69; my trans.). Diderot: "How do you mean that? ironically? or straight?" (*Le Neveu de Rameau*, 54; my trans.). On "re/citation," see Terdiman, *Discourse/Counter-Discourse*, 68–70.

37. The *Cambridge Dictionary of Philosophy* is particularly helpful. See Sosa, "Skepticism," 738–41; and Popkin, "Skeptics," 741–42. Popkin is probably the leading contemporary authority on postmedieval skepticism; see *History of Scepticism from Erasmus to Spinoza*; *Scepticism from the Renaissance to the Enlightenment*; and *Scepticism in the Enlightenment*. See also Stroud, *Significance of Philosophical Skepticism*.

sible (an attitude that would be closer to radical relativism). Skepticism remains agnostic on this point. It chooses not to promulgate any proposition with the conviction that it is so true one *must* invest resources—psychological, even physical—to defend it. It is an attitude that has echoed more recently. Think of this passage from Lyotard, which I quoted in chapter 7: "The nineteenth and twentieth centuries have given us as much terror as we can take. We have paid a high enough price for the nostalgia of the whole and the one."[38]

As much as an epistemological position, in this sense skepticism is an *ethical* and *psychological* one. It tells us not what our discourse should be but how we should discourse and engage in discourse. Although Aristotle was opposed to skepticism per se, as I mean it here we could think of skepticism as an element in his *phronesis*, or practical reason.[39] It is a position on how one ought to behave, both inwardly and interpersonally.

Two lines of argument led the Skeptics to their view. The first was epistemological. Skeptics held that for any claim evidence both for and against it can always be offered. Such propositional difference arose from many material and practical differences: disagreement among people; the diversity of experiences; the instability of empirical evidence; the fluctuations in human judgments under differing conditions; even illness or intoxication; and so on. In a willed suspension of judgment skepticism sought to honor the claims of diverse positions. It wanted to reach toward a politics of credence in the good faith and interest even of positions that challenge our own.

The second line of thinking which motivated and sustained skeptical positions was fundamentally psychological. The Skeptics (particularly the followers of Pyrrho, who lived from about 360 to 275 B.C.E.) held that their antagonists the Dogmatists, made categorical statements about the nonevident but then became emotionally disturbed by their inability to demonstrate that these assertions were true. Pyrrhonist Skeptics (who were typically trained as physicians) considered this form of worry a serious but curable mental disorder. The cure was to achieve a balance between contradictory positions, what has been termed "equipollence" (*isostheneia*: creating a balance of equal strength) in relation to them. This stance would lead one to suspend judgment. It had the

38. Lyotard, "Answering the Question: What Is Postmodernism?" 81.
39. The distinction was put clearly in the *Nichomachean Ethics*, written, Aristotle says, "not in order to know what virtue is, but in order to become good." See Aristotle, *Nichomachean Ethics*, bk. 2, chap. 2, 1103b, 26–30.

objective of fostering what the Pyrrhonists termed *ataraxia*: tranquillity, or peace of mind.

The surface paradoxes in such a position are evident (similar ones have been leveled in our own period against philosophers from Nietzsche to Derrida). How can you take a position asserting that you can't take a position? The law of non-contradiction would seem to render such a practice incoherent. The skeptical response was to insist that their attitude went "all the way down." In their view they asserted *nothing*. To be sure there is a *dogmatic* version of skepticism. It asserts that Skeptics doubt; therefore, they disbelieve. Skeptics would not assent to this depiction of their view, for it rules out the possibility of suspended judgment and eliminates the epistemological, ethical, and psychological advantages in such a practice. For the Pyrrhonists skepticism was not a stable or statable theory. Pyrrho himself is not known to have written down anything at all (his teachings were first recorded by his follower Arcesilaus [268–41 B.C.E.], born around the time that Pyrrho died). Rather, Pyrrhonist Skeptics sought to train their minds to an attitude in which they could evade what Bourdieu might have termed the "epistemic violence" that is inherent in *any* assertion.[40] Thus, they sought to cure any internal slippage in the direction of dogmatism.

Their practice for doing this was formalized in a sequence of what they termed "modes," or "tropes," which organized arguments fostering the equipollent suspension of judgment on any matter going beyond immediate appearance. The most widely known of these taxonomies was composed by Sextus Empiricus (fl. third century B.C.E.) in his *Outlines of Pyrrhonism* (*Hypotyposes*) and *Against the Dogmatists*.[41] The *Hypotyposes* disappeared from attention for centuries. But the book's republication in Paris in 1562 had far-reaching effects on European philosophical thought in the Renaissance, on Montaigne particularly.[42]

The modes, or tropes, give a series of tactics for countering tendencies toward monothetic adherence to any argument. One example of the modes, Sextus's tenth trope (*Hypotyposes*, bk. 1, chap. 14), is particularly pertinent to the issues I have been discussing. It recommends juxtaposing the divergent habits, laws, and customary beliefs of one people and one epoch against those

40. Bourdieu's phrase, regarding education, was "pedagogical violence." See Bourdieu and Passeron, *Reproduction in Education, Society, and Culture*, xi.

41. See Sextus Empiricus, *Outlines of Scepticism*.

42. Sextus Empiricus, *Sexti philosophi Pyrrhoniarum hypotyposeon libri III*.

of another, in order to destabilize any ethnocentric certainty.[43] Montaigne reproduces it exactly in "De l'expérience" ("On Experience") when, with delight at the absurd incongruity, he describes the irreconcilable sleeping habits of Germans, Italians, and French people: "A German gets sick if you put him on a mattress; an Italian if you put him on a feather bed; and a Frenchman if you make him sleep without bed curtains and a fire."[44]

The influence of the skeptical modes lasted for a long time, powerfully influencing Cicero (who had studied at the Athenian Academy and who incorporated skeptical arguments in *Academia* and *De natura deorum*). In turn, aiming directly at Cicero, Augustine wrote a vigorous denunciation of skepticism in *Contra academicos*. In early modernity, as I suggested, skeptical positions resurfaced influentially in Montaigne's concerted exploration of skepticism in the "Apologie pour Raymond Sebond" (1580) in book 2, chapter 12, of the *Essais*; and in Pierre Bayle's *Historical and Critical Dictionary*, published in 1697. Bayle's *Dictionary* earned condemnation both by the Reformed Church of the Netherlands and the French Catholic Church. It was one of the most widely sold books in the early eighteenth century.[45]

The influence of the tenth mode's strategic anti-ethnocentric move in the Renaissance and after is incalculable. It begins with Montaigne's "On Cannibals" (*Essais*, bk. 1, chap. 31) and continues through Pascal's argument about the divergence of belief on the two sides of the Pyrenees and Cyrano's startling deflation of humanity's claims to exceptionality in *Histoire comique des états et empires de la lune* and *Histoire comique des états et empires du soleil* (published posthumously in 1656 and 1662, respectively). Then the tactic of the tenth Pyrrhonian trope bursts into extraordinary prominence and pertinence in the Enlightenment.[46] It is foundational in Montesquieu's *Lettres persanes*, in Voltaire's *Lettres philosophiques* and *Candide*, in Diderot's *Supplément au voyage de Bougainville*, and in many other texts.

It is easy to speculate about the conditions under which skepticism becomes pertinent to people, and many have done so. Augustine obviously felt an im-

43. See Laursen, *Politics of Skepticism in the Ancients*, 108. Beyond the Enlightenment the tenth mode provides a significant basis for the epistemological and ethical decenterings and displacements of modern social constructionism. Concerning the Pyrrhonian "modes" in general, see Annas and Barnes, *Modes of Scepticism*, chap. 3.

44. Montaigne, *Essais*, bk. 3, chap. 13, 1213.

45. See Popkin, "New Views on the Role of Scepticism in the Enlightenment," 163.

46. This is what Roger Caillois, in the introduction to his edition of Montesquieu, termed the "sociological revolution" (preface to Montesquieu, *Oeuvres complètes*, 1:5).

perative need to repudiate Cicero's indecision concerning the gods. Christianity (we could say without intending any disrespect) is the primary European form of dogmatism in the postclassical period. It is fundamental to Christian theology to place *certainty* at its epistemological heart. Augustine figures this in the celebrated narrative in the *Confessions* of his own Pauline conversion experience. So long as Christianity dominated thinking through the medieval period, we should not be surprised to see philosophical skepticisms so marginalized as to be virtually invisible.

But the Reformation transformed that inhibition. The humanism of the Renaissance enabled renewed access to classical texts. But it was the struggle between Reform and Counter-Reformation, the destabilization of Catholic doctrine, and the violence materialized most pertinently in the religious wars in France which occupied virtually the entire second half of the sixteenth century—the carnage concluded with the Edict of Nantes in 1598—which made classical skepticism practically and philosophically pertinent. Probably no one doubts that decline of theological warrant for certainty during and after the sixteenth-century religious wars had profound resonances in thinking in the early modern period and after.

With slightly tongue-in-cheek teleologism and a wink toward Hegel, we might say that Montaigne (who lived from 1533 to 1592) came along at the right time. The brutality of his period and his immediate environment, the thousands killed in the fighting, made a philosophy that fostered toleration particularly apposite and attractive. And it made the substance of such toleration, as Montaigne articulated it, more compelling than would have been an attitude of vague dissociation, disengagement, or nonchalance. The hecatombs of Montaigne's period were not *just* theoretical, but their violence was rooted in what became (despite Christian charity and humility) a vicious combat of doctrine and dogma.[47] In Montaigne's writing philosophical skepticism becomes the heart of a gentle wisdom whose humanist luminousness exemplifies what I am seeking to frame in this discussion of the ethics of theory. This is *active* toleration.

In Enlightenment writing the argumentative equipollence that the skeptics sought to practice is fundamental—for example, in Diderot's dialogues, par-

47. See Horkheimer, "Montaigne und die Funktion der Skepsis," 2:201–59. Those who promulgate views concerning the violence supposedly peculiar to or inherent in Islamic sectarianism might usefully remember the carnage in sixteenth-century Christian Europe. I've already referred to Locke's "Letter concerning Toleration" (1689), written under parallel conditions in Britain.

ticularly *Rameau's Nephew*. In Plato the purpose of the *elenchus* is to bring Socrates' interlocutor to a knowledge Socrates already has. The same is even truer in the dialogues of Bishop Berkeley (1685–1753), whose *Three Dialogues between Hylas and Philonous* were published in 1713. The objective of Berkeley's dialogues was for Hylas—and Berkeley's readers—to learn the truth (in this case of solipcism) that Philonous possesses. Not so in Diderot. In *Rameau's Nephew* both characters vehemently *know*. But their knowledge is irreconcilable, and neither gives an inch. Rather than a scoring a knockdown or inducing an epistemic conversion experience in the interlocutor, the arguments of Rameau and the Philosopher unceasingly parry and block each other. The *form* of this contention creates yet a *different* argument, in favor of a gentle skepticism.[48] Despite the intensity of its interpersonal agon, *Rameau's Nephew* ends with the evocation of a mild, ironic *laughter*.

Our theories dialogue with each other in an analogous way. By virtue of their multiplicity and heteronomy they make an argument against totalizing *any* argument. They represent a practical demonstration of the partiality and contingence of *any* position. Skepticism can illuminate the bearing of such a practical realization. It enacts a respect for forms of difference, beginning with the form of my ability (if I am honest and competent in my thinking) to counter *my own* most passionate argument with a divergent one just as deeply felt. In that sense skepticism lives life in complementarity. Skeptical *ataraxia* would then be the internal experience of what, on the outside, in intellectual, social, and political terms, we would call toleration.

In our own period we find versions of such principled skepticism. Think of Lyotard's resonant repudiation of doctrinal or metatheoretical dogmatism and his celebrated definition of *Postmodern* (mentioned earlier) as "incredulity concerning metanarratives."[49] Consider Derrida's stirring (if somewhat tentative) endorsement of humanist attitudes and values regularly denigrated since Althusser's notorious promulgation of what he termed "theoretical antihumanism."[50] In these interventions the virtue of toleration of difference and

48. On the paradoxical but strategic *fragility* of certain Enlightenment conceptions of "reason," see Tonelli, " 'Weakness' of Reason in the Age of Enlightenment," 36. Diderot himself wrote the article on Pyrrhonism in the *Encyclopédie* ("Pyrrhonienne ou Sceptique Philosophie"); *DFPV* 8:138–60.

49. Lyotard, *Postmodern Condition*, xxiv.

50. This reappropriation of "humanism" and the humanist ideal needs to be brought into contact with the notion of "theoretical anti-humanism" first formulated by Louis Althusser and through him propagated somewhat confusedly to many other thinkers and theorists. There is no opposition between these two ideas. Theoretical anti-humanism has nothing to do with opposition to respect for

disagreement toward which Enlightenment thinking was itself trying to think its way seems to anticipate the ethical attitude and practical conduct that might respond to the pressures of Postmodernity's registration of difference of all kinds.

> Tout cela ne va pas trop mal.
> [All that seems perfectly fine.]
> —MONTAIGNE, "Des cannibales," *Essais*, bk. 1, chap. 31, 253

In the interpretive disciplines theory proliferated astonishingly in the period beginning with the Structuralist uprising in the 1960s. The "Structuralist controversy" initiated a challenge to methodological indifference which continues today.[51] That habit of paradigmatic self-reflexivity, that programmatic epistemological and representational monitoring, is what in the interpretive disciplines we call the enterprise of theory to begin with. In France a vaguely positivist philologism, biographism, and naive source and theme criticism had sustained belletristic critical practice since the days of Sainte-Beuve and Lanson.[52] All that changed vertiginously in the 1960s. The Structuralist controversy asked us to think of ourselves as interpreters and to think about what we *do* when we work on texts or on any object that needs interpretation. It wanted to make what we do a *discipline*.

But the theory upsurge has had an unintended, perhaps a paradoxical, consequence. There has been an astonishing sea change in the interpretive disciplines, in which even undergraduate theory courses have now become indispensable in curricula in a way that is astonishing for those who fought the early theory battles beginning in the mid-1960s. Then, people lost their jobs for "doing theory." But today, so many theories! so many institutional reflexes of the intensity with which theoretical positions are held: journals, newsletters, Web sites and discussion groups, professional conferences of all sorts.

---

persons. The position was stated most clearly in Althusser's 1964 essay "Marxism and Humanism," 229. Althusser's notion arises in his effort to undermine belief in the individual subject as the determinant of history. As is well known, Althusser conceived the latter as a "process without a subject"; see *Lenin and Philosophy*, 122, 124. For Althusser the worth attributed to persons is distinct from inflation of the importance of individual agency, desire, or power in determining the course of history. The latter is what he criticizes in his anti-humanism.

51. See Macksey and Donato, *Languages of Criticism and the Sciences of Man*; Dosse, *History of Structuralism*; Cusset, *French Theory*.

52. See Wellek, *History of Modern Criticism*, esp. vol. 4, "The Later Nineteenth Century"; and vol. 8, "French, Italian, and Spanish Criticism, 1900–1950."

We move in schools, and we tend to passion about our critical and theoretical engagements. But hang on a second. If one of these many and proliferating theories was *right*, word would have gotten around. If we were to take a few steps back to look at the *pattern* of our contention, however principled and well intended, I think it might pull many of us in the direction of a more peaceable assessment of what it means to have and to do theory and of how to engage with people whose theories contest our own.

This book began by fomenting a contention between the Enlightenment and Postmodernity, on the grounds of how *language* and *materiality* can "be" with each other. I want to conclude it with an argument for principled toleration for methodological divergence and diversity—just as we have learned to tolerate (and even to celebrate) diversity in many other realms and registers of social existence. Indeed, it is this increasing diversity and perceived complexity of the socius since World War II which has underlain, sustained, and I think necessitated our turn toward fascination with theory. We think about whatever is a problem. Theories—particularly their recent upsurge—come from that ultimately practical reflection. Today this is where many of the problems—the unresolved and the challenging, the unaccommodated in thinking—locate themselves. But it would be reasonable to think that we should not put our bodies on the line—still less put our students' or our younger colleagues' bodies on the line—over what isn't surely true to begin with. A modesty before the complications of existence would suggest a more generous consideration even for that with which we think we disagree.

In this effort I want notions such as complementarity and orientations such as philosophical skepticism to model for the disposition that I believe we should entertain in the face of a proliferation of theoretical ventures and proffers. That is how I hope we might feel our way into a different orientation toward the intensities of theoretical difference. These differences can only grow denser and more intense as the dynamics of all forms of communicative interconnection penetrate farther into existences—in the West and virtually everywhere else in the world. These developments will confront us with objects and behaviors, beliefs and ideologies, texts and representations, which our understanding won't crack, which our theories won't open. Indeed, they have already been doing so for decades. What disposition might we have toward these challenges and toward this unknown?

We need to practice a sophisticated *not knowing for sure*. I call this "toleration." No ethical system is absolutely transcendent. Its prescriptions and proscriptions, its recommendations and disinclinations, emerge from the patterns and stresses of practical experience and respond to those exigencies. We need to assess those tensions. Two extremes seem unpropitious. In the face of Hitler or Stalin it's not time for toleration. In such situations human values that appear to most of us non-negotiable contend, and there is real threat. Among these values is belief in the worth of persons, in their right to self-development, in their right to deliberate together. These are commitments that we have inherited from the Enlightenment, and vigorous contention is the right response when they are put in jeopardy. On the other hand, I want to distinguish my argument for toleration from what some call pure "situationism." Situationism's time compass seems too short and volatile. It recommends attitudes responding to the immediate moment. Such a view leads to a lability without sufficient constraint, to ethics for the instant only. But most practical challenges are more durable, or refractory, than that. I want to assume that there will be ongoing controversy, and I want to project an ongoing disposition appropriate to the contentions of such a world. I surely do not mean simply be blasé in the face of difference, disagreement, and challenge.

The best measure of the ethical stance I am exploring here is one of the fundamental forms of our communication. I mean *pedagogy*. Pedagogy isn't just for students. To the extent that two people in communication always possess differential quantities, qualities, and organizations of knowledge (as the skeptics constantly maintained), we teach each other every time we talk. That sort of modest and slow life-inflecting conversation seems to me the horizon of theory's field and its purpose.

So, how might we teach? and how think about teaching? First of all, our thought must assume—and our practice celebrate—that we disagree. That is when toleration becomes important. There is no need to tolerate positions with which we are in harmony or toward which we are indifferent. The notion of toleration means sanctioning expression of beliefs, attitudes, or practices that, at the limit, the tolerator would prefer did not exist.[53] Why would we do that? To begin with, to enact a commitment to our own inherent perspectival and

---

53. As Voltaire may—or may not—have said in the dictum often attributed to him which has become toleration's most famous emblem, "I disagree with what you say, but I will defend to the death your right to say it."

experiential limitation. And to confirm a deep engagement with the ideal of deliberation and non-autocratic decision making, an ideal that particularly attracts us whenever we think about—or experience—the contrary.

John Stuart Mill's *On Liberty* (1859) is probably the most sustained argument for toleration that we have. Mill believed toleration was an essential element of the defense of liberty. He argued for toleration on two principal grounds. First, he asserted that social and intellectual progress requires it. Second, he believed that individuals' development and flourishing are fostered by it. Mill argued for the human *difficulty* and the reciprocal human *worth* of toleration. In effect he saw it—*avant la lettre*—as a rationally applied discipline, in effect a remedy for Freud's notorious "narcissism of minor differences."[54]

Toleration is more than mere acquiescence or resignation. It involves a principled recognition that there can be truth even in what we ourselves suspect or believe to be wrong. This sort of "double-think" might seem counter-intuitive to the point of being self-disabling. In Orwell's lexicon the term *double-think* meant a guilty acceptance of what one otherwise knew to be false. That is the attitude depicted so movingly in Václav Havel's "The Power of the Powerless." In prerevolutionary Czechoslovakia toleration for the conditions under which life had to be lived required inflection by a deep and conscious irony.[55]

But under more tolerable conditions toleration seeks to reverse the valence of double-thinking's self-deception. It projects a *salutary* form of the exercise: not now duplicitous but generous and imaginatively charitable and—most important of all—epistemologically sophisticated. For it recognizes that the situatedness of truth (in any social realm at least) means that *her* version, rooted in a system of concepts and perceptions that may diverge from *mine*, has claims upon me in the same way that my own view has claims on her. The vocation of such thinking is to credit the value of consequential difference. The ethic of toleration is thus based upon and in its turn determines an epistemology—the enactment of the conviction concerning "skeptical truth"—which I am arguing has animated much influential reflection since the period in the Enlightenment when the notion of toleration itself became an emblem and a sociopolitical rallying cry.

54. See Mill, *On Liberty*, 18:213–310, esp. sec. 12. Freud's expression first appeared in "Taboo of Virginity," 199; it recurs in *Group Psychology and the Analysis of the Ego*, 18:101; then reappears in a celebrated discussion in *Civilization and Its Discontents*, 21:114.

55. Havel, "Power of the Powerless," 36–122. Havel describes how all shopkeepers in the former Communist Czechoslovakia kept photographs of the leader in their shop windows, while at the same time feeling entirely disengaged from the representation of such respect.

So, what will our teaching each other entail? First of all, we need to learn to break out two differential moments in our discourse about theory (this is what the most effective and productive of our theory teachers have always done). The first of these moments is *exposition*. We need to train ourselves to give an even-handed and sophisticated account of the positions we discuss—the more the position we are accounting for seems to us *un*-congenial, the more sympathetic an account we need to conceive. This is a fundamental element of intellectual discipline in an age of proliferating, competing theories. Its importance cannot be overstated.[56]

The second moment is the one to which we have been solicited since the Enlightenment—and to which we have become so accustomed that sometimes we speed to it immediately, skipping over the first, necessary, expositional and comprehending moment. This second moment is the exercise of *critique*. At this stage our divergence from the position we analyze is not only honored but honoring. It enacts the dialectic that, through long experience, we know can illuminate—if not resolve—differences. It is the fundamental enactment of respect for persons and for their ideas.

Differences exist; they even proliferate. But this does not mean that we cannot expect to better understand the motivations, the explanatory strengths, and the areas of limitation of any theoretical model, including, at the limit of the exercise, even our own. Theorists of theoretical relativism are right to maintain that there is no neutral place from which hierarchies of models can be objectively ordered. And it is true that many arguments—often near-polemics—about whether one theory is better than another are badly formed and unproductive.

But this doesn't mean that assessing the differential productivity of different theories is out of bounds. This need not—and should not—be done polemically. We need to find and articulate the ground of commensurability that could make possible relative judgments of a model's range and bearing and of its effectiveness. This means paying greater attention to the instrumental *means* and the analytic *objectives* of models than has often been the case in the theory wars.

To put this differently, we need to restore and to foreground *agency* and *pragmatics* in the making of our paradigms. We need to articulate what they really try to do—and *can* do—before we castigate them for not being able to do

56. Its model might well be Fredric Jameson's remarkable essay on Lacan, "Imaginary and Symbolic in Lacan," reprinted in *Literature and Psychoanalysis, the Question of Reading*, 338–95. In its first part the essay offers an exposition of Lacanianism as cogent as any that has appeared. In the second part Jameson provides a powerful contestation of Lacan's theory.

something different. And we need always to recall that, being models, they cannot exhaust universal truth, only more or less capably frame some aspect of the world. It's possible to see the implications of such an attitude for pedagogy, even the pedagogy in the curricular settings of those undergraduate classes and "introductory theory" graduate seminars that many of us teach. The conception likewise projects a practice of *writing* about theory, or about *that* theory, which might help to make our criticism communicative and productive.

Models always imply choices; a theory is always constructed. But, as I have argued, these effects are not the stochastic result of fluke or of caprice. Here a randomizing or arbitrary Saussurian paradigm simply won't work. At the origin the attribution of reference to any given phoneme may be unmotivated; there may be no cognizable reason that English call it *cow* while French call it *vache*. But this structure of random connection is a dreadful paradigm for understanding how models of social or cultural interpretation work. To say that no material or social referent can determine the theory that accounts for it is *not* the same thing as to claim that every theory has equal status, range, or effectiveness in the marketplace or before the law of paradigmatic existence.

The reason is that a theory's referent isn't the only actor in the process. A theory and its productivity are inevitably *situated* in a field of facts, interpretations, assumptions, ideologies, and—above all—questions.[57] As the product of theoretical labor that works in the way all labor does, a model arises within a web of intentions and determinations. It emerges neither from revealed truth nor from random "model-generativity." The choices that form it are motivated and selective; they are responsive to a network of determination and shaping needs and forces. The choosing that constructs the model thus needs to be brought to light; the consequences of these choices need to be explained.

And once a choice of analytical paradigm has been made, then we must ask: what are the range and the strength of the model it determines, and, inevitably, what are its areas of blindness or underdevelopment? For there will always be such areas of blindness—unhappily, even in our *own* theory. Theories are inevitably reductive. They have no choice; they cannot evade this consequence of their own ontology. As I began arguing in my introduction, the map is never

---

57. My notion converges here with Sartre's concept of "situation," a figure for the totality of constraints and pressures acting on an individual—or, we might say, a theoretical formation—in a specific conjuncture. (There is no significant connection here between this concept and the "situationism" I briefly considered earlier.)

the territory; if it were, it would be of no use to us, we could never carry it around with us. Any theory chooses some aspects of the world to foreground and neglects or ignores others. As in everything else we do, we pay an opportunity cost for selecting our models.

But then, if for social or ethical reasons we think it is imperative to focus investigation upon what a given theory blurs, that need itself becomes the basis for a critique of any model that veils such aspects of reality.[58] So, for example— to consider the case that has been central to me in *Body and Story*—if our bodily experience of *difficulty* and *resistance* interests us crucially or seems to us fundamental to representation of the world, then it is likely Postmodern paradigms will not help us much. For they have little power to model such experiences, since they are based in a mode of human activity—language. The world seen from the angle of the *body* and *materiality* can never be subsumed in the vision that bases itself in *story* and in *language*. For reasons reciprocal to their area of strength, language models are more or less unproductive in this *other* register of our existence.

Ultimately, toleration is an effect and an act of imagination. For those of us in the interpretive disciplines, imagination is our business. We seek to understand how people understand—how they construe, how they represent, how they project the meanings and the limitations that constitute social existence. To be thoughtful about imagination means understanding your own construction and conduct, seeing it as unrolling, as it has been developed and will be developing—not simply as it presents itself and its own self-evidence.

Applying that act of imagination to constructions, positions, dispositions, and even actions with which we do not agree, which appear to us misguided or even unconscionable, is what the ethics of theory in an age of multifarious and heteronomous constructions of the world solicits us to do. The demands of theory are first of all to recognize that theories are partial, that at best they are complementary, that they can never be exhaustive.[59]

58. From a quite different perspective, Alan Garfinkel comes to convergent conclusions in *Forms of Explanation* (see esp. chaps. 5–6). Garfinkel argues that in our discourse about the social world there is always what he terms an "ethics of explanation": "Choosing one explanatory frame over another has value presuppositions and value consequences" (156). Despite the liberations of textuality, these presuppositions and consequences are what we are *not* free *not* to bring to light and expose to principled critique.

59. Some of the material in this section was first discussed in Terdiman, "Subject of the Other," 27–47. Reprinted in Geyer and Schmitz-Emans, *Kritische Theorie des Subjekts*, 51–64.

> The serious objections to textualism, I think, are not epistemological but
> moral.   —RORTY, *Consequences of Pragmatism*, 156

Many will see a relationship between the view I predicate here and the general orientation of American Pragmatism, most forcefully brought into intellectual debate in recent decades in the work of Richard Rorty. But Rorty's vision depends upon a reduction in criteria of veridicality so radical that it reminds one of the univocal reductionisms of what Rorty himself called the "textualist" position.

Pragmatists believe that knowledge is instrumental. It acts to organize experience, and we judge it according to criteria of satisfactoriness. Explanations— what Rorty calls "redescriptions"—seek a fit between cognition, representation, and pragmatic effectiveness. Concepts, in turn, codify habits of belief or rules of action. Truth can only be judged in relation to *goals*, and values are always conjunctural. By nature such projections are always fallible.

This is not a bad background for fostering toleration of other people's views, since it is inevitable that their construction of situations must differ—in experience, in belief, in disposition—from our own. Rorty wants to discredit tendencies toward metaphysical guarantees and transcendental warrants—toward thinking of thinking *sub specie aeternitatis*. But his counter-discourse is so driven by its anti-foundationalism that it produces an almost entirely ephemeral model of thinking, *sub specie momenti*, as we might say—so malleable, so fluid, as to slip free even of the fundamental constraints of self-consistency across time. It's not interesting to say that in Rortyan pragmatism "anything goes." The standard of what "goes" is what explains best. But, as reality in his projection is constantly and fundamentally heteronomous, so the discourse that might prove best at construing it, by adopting that very heteronomy as its time-scale, loses its privilege at the very moment that it asserts it.

This is a bad consequence for paradigms that seek to make sense. There's no point in teaching a way of construing things if it might well turn out inapplicable in the next second. If Rorty's view were right, we'd probably have to conclude that the game is over. The trick would be to build back a more durable time-scale into pragmatism's openness to the multifariousness of explanations that cannot simply be transcoded one into another or absorbed one by another. This time compass arises in the general and sometimes excruciating homeostasis of experience, in the reality of constraint and of the refractory—such that the game is no longer up for grabs at every instant. Nothing in Rorty theoretically resists such a construction. But he does not particularly enable it.[60]

An ethics of theory would need to find an equipoise that could honor the divergent demands, on the one hand, of theory's multifariousness and heteronomy, on the other, of its need to incorporate into its projection of the world the sort of inertia, of weight difficult to move, habit difficult to change, neurosis difficult to cure, which materialism has sought—sometimes without full consciousness of its own potentialities—to project.[61] Change is neither stochastic, nor is it eradicable. Our construction of the world might well react to both of the dynamics of demand that the world willy-nilly projects upon us. Conceptions of materiality, conceptions of language—of body and of story—have been the surrogates for these demands for a long time.

This book began considering a single text. It has—absurdly perhaps—attempted to unfold out of Diderot's La religieuse a fascination, followed over several centuries, with the potency and vertiginousness of language. And it has sought to double that story with another, about the substance that language and stories can't adequately capture or communicate—the material, often the corporeal referent, which occupies language's thought at the same time that it eludes its modality.

The binarism of the impulses Body and Story has had at the back of its mind from the outset was already present in La religieuse. The passion of Diderot's commitment to reform situates at the heart of precisely in the field I have been describing in this chapter. It pushes against a constituted pattern of existence. It is furious with the real. But at the same time the vehicle of this compelling reformist intensity is also an intent anatomy of unresolvable ambivalence.

What links body and story in La religieuse is not a tension, for in a sense the two registers never touch. But they map a world. In their very irreconcilability, in their complementarity, they enact, they practice, a fundamental skepticism about the possibility of any single theory being able to totalize experience. Diderot seeks to honor these claims, but he can only do so, as we might put it,

60. See Rorty, Consequences of Pragmatism.
61. This is the weight of what in an earlier book I called "present past" and attributed to the homeostatic inertia of the memory function fundamental to human identity and activity. See Terdiman, Present Past.

paratactically: by allowing two disparate impulses to cohabit within his text. Such a situation so scandalously violates the prescriptions of "organic form" which were emerging just around Diderot's own period that the generosity of its enactment seems to alternate with pure ineptitude as an explanation for the bizarre divergent—even incoherent—energy of the novel.

The forms of the dialectic, from Socrates' *elenchus* to Diderot's dialogism, Hegel's *Logic*, Marx's "contradiction," and perhaps even Derrida's "deconstruction," stand in close relationship to epistemological and social situations in which the encounter with difference defines and drives the development of experience. In its more authoritarian avatars, as I recalled, "dialectic" has been the bête noire of influential versions of Postmodern thinking. And there is a basis for such a view, since any mode of thinking bent on resolution may fail to recognize and to leave room for elements of difference which do *not* resolve— for Bataille's excess or Derrida's supplement. Dialectic has been seen as reason's means for achieving totalitarian domination over the less powerful, for ensuring the arrest of history.

But alongside this we need to recognize the potentiality for termlessness that is just as present in the dialectic and that I argued was one of the twin dynamics in Hegel's own dialectical mode (even if in understanding of his work it has often been swamped by its finalist opposite). If we credit that ambivalence—if, in other words, we credit the form of Diderot's unending dialectic as well as Plato's more conclusory version—then dialectic can enact complementarity itself. It has the capability to respect the insights of the skeptical view, without, however, shutting down the possibility of productive exchange, even of transformation. In the ethical and epistemological sense I am outlining here, dialectic may turn out already to have projected the frame in which postmodern subjects can encounter the conditions of their heteronomous, speculative, and unresolved existence.

Theory isn't unbound. It responds to demands. We could take the discourse of the Enlightenment to be a particularly penetrating—and prestigious—exemplar of such convergence around real problems. But if we do so, we ought not to omit the conditions that make the Enlightenment's problems—the worth of individuals, their right to self-development, the reasonableness of collective deliberation concerning collective problems—propagate forward to us. The stochastic quality of postmodern celebrations of uncompassable and limitless languaging is symptomatic of a moment just *before* our angle of vision widened, before our gaze opened itself beyond the developed North and West, to the realities of a much more refractory globalizing world. This is where these fundamental problems reproduce themselves in, and become pertinent for, a considerably larger population in a world that is itself much broader than the Enlightenment philosophes were able to imagine.

Today we not only imagine this world; we confront it daily in all the technological, commercial, intellectual, modes of our existence. Our notion of theory is striving, rushing, to catch up with the materiality of our transformed experience. The claims of this materiality—of the body without which we *aren't*, and of all the other bodies in the world—challenge us. We need to honor these claims.

Works Cited

Works by Diderot: Unless otherwise specified, I cite Diderot's works from *Oeuvres complètes*, ed. Herbert Dieckmann, Jean Fabre, Jacques Proust, and Jean Varloot. Paris: Hermann, 1975–. There have been twenty-two volumes published to date. I identify this edition with the abbreviation *DFPV*.

Citations from the *Encyclopédie*: Since many research libraries do not possess an edition of Diderot's *Encyclopédie*, I have chosen to cite from the *Encyclopédie* as follows: for entries authored by Diderot, I cite from *DFPV*. For *Encyclopédie* entries by other authors, I cite from the CD-ROM edition, which is now widely available: Diderot, Denis and Jean Le Rond d'Alembert, eds., *Encyclopédie de Diderot et d'Alembert, ou dictionnaire raisonné des sciences, des arts et des métiers*. CD-ROM ed. Paris: REDON, 2002.

Works by Freud: I cite from *The Standard Edition of the Complete Psychological Works*. Trans. and ed. James Strachey, Anna Freud, Alix Strachey, and Alan Tyson. 24 vols. London: Hogarth, 1953–74. I identify this edition with the abbreviation *SE*.

Abbott, Edwin. *Flatlands: A Romance of Many Dimensions*. London: Seeley, 1884.

Adam, Barbara. *Time and Social Theory*. Cambridge: Polity Press, 1990.

Adorno, Theodor W. *Hegel: Three Studies*. Trans. Shierry Weber Nicholsen. Cambridge: MIT Press, 1993.

———. *Minima Moralia: Reflections from a Damaged Life*. Trans. E.F.N. Jephcott. London: Verso, 1978.

———. *Negative Dialectics*. Trans. E. B. Ashton. New York: Seabury, 1973.

———. "Theses upon Art and Religion Today." *Kenyon Review* 7, no. 4 (Fall 1945): 677–82.

Allen, Woody. "The Kugelmass Episode." In *Complete Prose of Woody Allen*, 347–60. New York: Wings Books, 1991.

Althusser, Louis. "Ideology and Ideological State Apparatuses (Note towards an Investigation)." In *Lenin and Philosophy and Other Essays*, 127–86. New York: Monthly Review, 1971.

———. "Marxism and Humanism." In *For Marx*, 219–47. New York: Vintage, 1969.

Anderson, Benedict. *Imagined Communities: Reflections on the Origin and Spread of Nationalism*. Rev. ed. London: Verso, 1991.

Annas, Julia, and Jonathan Barnes. *The Modes of Scepticism: Ancient Texts and Modern Interpretations*. Cambridge: Cambridge University Press, 1985.

Arendt, Hannah. *Between Past and Future: Eight Exercises in Political Thought*. Harmondsworth: Penguin, 1993.

Aristotle. *Nichomachean Ethics*. Trans. Terence Irwin. Indianapolis: Hackett, 1985.

———. "On the Soul [*De Anima*]." In *Complete Works of Aristotle: The Revised Oxford Translation*, ed. Jonathan Barnes, 641–93. Princeton: Princeton University Press, 1984.

Armstrong, Nancy. *Desire and Domestic Fiction: A Political History of the Novel*. New York: Oxford University Press, 1987.

Ashcroft, Bill, Gareth Griffiths, and Helen Tiffin. *The Empire Writes Back: Theory and Practice in Post-Colonial Literatures*. London: Routledge, 1989.

Auerbach, Erich. *Mimesis: The Representation of Reality in Western Literature*. Trans. Willard R. Trask. Princeton: Princeton University Press, 1953.

Bakhtin, M. M. *The Dialogic Imagination: Four Essays*. Trans. Caryl Emerson and Michael Holquist. Austin: University of Texas Press, 1981.

Bannet, Eve Tavor. *Structuralism and the Logic of Dissent*. Urbana: University of Illinois Press, 1989.

Barguillet, Françoise. *Le roman au XVIIIe siècle*. Paris: Presses Universitaires de France, 1981.

Barthes, Roland. " 'Longtemps je me suis couché de bonne heure.' " In *Le bruissement de la langue: Essais critiques IV*, 333–46. Paris: Seuil, 1984.

———. " 'Longtemps je me suis couché de bonne heure.' " In *The Rustle of Language*, 277–90. Trans. Richard Howard. New York: Hill and Wang, 1986.

———. *Le plaisir du texte*. Paris: Éditions du Seuil, 1973.

———. *The Pleasure of the Text*. Trans. Richard Miller. New York: Hill and Wang, 1975.

Bataille, Georges. *The Accursed Share: An Essay on General Economy*. Trans. Robert Hurley. New York: Zone, 1988.

———. "The Critique of the Foundations of the Hegelian Dialectic." In *Visions of Excess: Selected Writings, 1927–1939*, 105–15. Minneapolis: University of Minnesota Press, 1985.

———. *Inner Experience*. Trans. Leslie Anne Boldt. Albany: State University of New York Press, 1980.

———. "The Notion of Expenditure." In *Visions of Excess: Selected Writings, 1927–1939*, 116–29. Minneapolis: University of Minnesota, 1985.

———. *Visions of Excess: Selected Writings, 1927–1935*. Trans. Carl R. Lovitt Allan Stoekl, and Donald M. Leslie Jr. Minneapolis: University of Minnesota Press, 1985.

Baudrillard, Jean. *Simulations*. New York: Semiotexte, 1983.

Bender, John, and David E. Wellbery, eds. *Chronotypes: The Construction of Time*. Stanford: Stanford University Press, 1991.

Benjamin, Walter. "Theses on the Philosophy of History." In *Illuminations*, trans. Harry Zohn, 253–64. New York: Schocken, 1969.

Benrekassa, Georges. *Concepts et savoir de la langue*. Paris: Presses Universitaires de France, 1995.

Berger, John. *Pig Earth*. New York: Pantheon, 1979.

Bernstein, Richard J. "An Allegory of Modernity/Postmodernity: Habermas and Derrida." In *Working through Derrida*, ed. Gary B. Madison, 204–29. Evanston, Ill.: Northwestern University Press, 1993.

Bohr, Niels. *Atomic Physics and Human Knowledge*. Cambridge: Cambridge University Press, 1961.

Borges, Jorge Luis. *Ficciones. Collected Fictions*. Trans. Andrew Hurley. New York: Viking, 1998.

Bourdieu, Pierre. *The Logic of Practice [Le Sens Pratique]*. Trans. Richard Nice. Stanford: Stanford University Press, 1990.

———. *Outline of a Theory of Practice*. Cambridge: Cambridge University Press, 1977.

Bourdieu, Pierre, and Jean-Claude Passeron. *Reproduction in Education, Society, and Culture.* 1970. Reprint. Trans. Richard Nice. London: Sage, 1977.

Braudel, Fernand. *The Identity of France,* vol. 2: *People and Production.* Trans. Sian Reynolds. New York: HarperCollins, 1990.

Brewer, Daniel. *The Discourse of Enlightenment in Eighteenth-Century France: Diderot and the Art of Philosophizing.* Cambridge: Cambridge University Press, 1993.

Brink, André. *The Novel: Language and Narrative from Cervantes to Calvino.* New York: New York University Press, 1998.

Brown, Anthony Cave. *Bodyguard of Lies.* New York: Bantam Books, 1975.

Buchanan, Ian. *Deleuzism: A Metacommentary.* Durham, N.C.: Duke University Press, 2000.

Burge, Tyler. "Individualism and the Mental." In *Midwest Studies in Philosophy,* vol. 4, ed. P. A. French. Minneapolis: University of Minnesota Press, 1979.

Butler, Judith. *Bodies That Matter: On the Discursive Limits of Sex.* New York: Routledge, 1993.

———. "A Questionable Patrilineage: (Post-)Hegelian Themes in Derrida and Foucault." In *Subjects of Desire: Hegelian Reflections in Twentieth-Century France,* 177–86. New York: Columbia University Press, 1987.

———. *Subjects of Desire: Hegelian Reflections in Twentieth-Century France.* New York: Columbia University Press, 1987.

Cajuerio-Roggero, Maria Amalia. "Dîner chez les Dambreuse: 'La réaction commençante.'" In *Histoire et langage dans "L'éducation sentimentale,"* ed. Maurice Agulhon. Paris: Société d'Édition d'Enseignement Supérieure, 1981.

Callinicos, Alex. *Against Postmodernism: A Marxist Critique.* New York: St. Martin's Press, 1989.

Canguilhem, Georges. *Ideology and Rationality in the History of the Life Sciences.* Trans. Arthur Goldhammer. Cambridge, Mass.: MIT Press, 1988.

———. *The Normal and the Pathological.* Trans. Carolyn R. Fawcett and Robert S. Cohen. New York: Zone Books, 1989.

Caplan, Jay. *Framed Narratives: Diderot's Genealogy of the Beholder.* Minneapolis: University of Minnesota Press, 1985.

Cavalli-Sforza, Luigi. *Genes, Peoples, and Languages.* Trans. Mark Seielstad. New York: North Point Press, 2000.

Cavalli-Sforza, Luigi, Paolo Menozzi, and Alberto Piazza. *The History and Geography of Human Genes.* Princeton: Princeton University Press, 1994.

Certeau, Michel de. *The Capture of Speech.* Trans. Tom Conley. Minneapolis: University of Minnesota Press, 1997.

———. "The Gaze: Nicholas of Cusa." *Diacritics* 17, no. 3 (Fall 1987): 2–38.

———. *L'écriture de l'histoire.* Paris: Gallimard–Bibliothèque des Histoires, 1975.

———. *L'étranger; ou, l'union dans la différence.* Paris: Desclée de Brouwer, 1968.

———. "The Politics of Silence: The Long March of the Indians." In *Heterologies: Discourse on the Other,* 225–33. Minneapolis: University of Minnesota Press, 1986.

———. *Practice of Everyday Life.* Trans. Steven F. Rendall. Berkeley: University of California Press, 1984.

———. *The Writing of History.* Trans. Tom Conley. New York: Columbia University Press, 1988.

Chamayou, Anne. *L'Esprit de la lettre, XVIIIe siècle.* Paris: Presses Universitaires de France, 1999.

Chartier, Roger. *The Cultural Origins of the French Revolution.* Trans. Lydia G. Cochrane. Durham, N.C.: Duke University Press, 1991.

Cohen, G. A. *Marx's Theory of History: A Defence.* Princeton: Princeton University Press, 1978.

Coleridge, Samuel Taylor. *Biographia Litteraria.* 2 vols. London: Routledge and Kegan Paul, 1983.

Condorcet, Jean-Antoine-Nicolas de Caritat, Marquis de. *Esquisse d'un tableau historique des progrès de l'esprit humain.* Ed. A. Condorcet O'Conner and M. F. Arago. Vol. 6 of *Oeuvres de Condorcet.* Facsimile of 1847–49 Paris ed. Stuttgart–Bad Cannstatt: Frommann, 1968.

———. *Sketch for a Historical Picture of the Progress of the Human Mind.* (1794.) 1955. Reprint. Westport, Conn.: Hyperion Press, 1979.

Cook, Elizabeth H. *Epistolary Bodies: Gender and Genre in the Eighteenth-Century Republic of Letters.* Stanford: Stanford University Press, 1996.

Cooper, Barry. *The End of History: An Essay on Modern Hegelianism.* Toronto: University of Toronto Press, 1984.

Craig, Edward, ed. *Routledge Encyclopedia of Philosophy.* 10 vols. London: Routledge, 1998. (Cited from CD-ROM ed.)

Culler, Jonathan. *Flaubert: The Uses of Uncertainty.* Ithaca: Cornell University Press, 1985.

———. *Structuralist Poetics: Structuralism, Linguistics, and the Study of Literature.* Ithaca: Cornell University Press, 1975.

———. "The Uses of Madame Bovary." In *Flaubert and Postmodernism,* ed. Naomi Schor and Henry F. Majewski, 1–12. Lincoln: University of Nebraska Press, 1984.

Cusset, François. *French Theory: Foucault, Derrida, Deleuze et les mutations de la vie intellectuelle aux États-Unis.* Paris: La Découverte, 2004.

Darnton, Robert. *The Great Cat Massacre.* New York: Basic Books, 1984.

———. *The Literary Underground of the Old Regime.* Cambridge: Harvard University Press, 1982.

Debord, Guy. *Society of the Spectacle.* Detroit: Black and Red, 1970.

Deleuze, Gilles, and Félix Guattari. *Anti-Oedipus: Capitalism and Schizophrenia.* Trans. Mark Seem, Robert Hurley, and Helen R. Lane. New York: Viking, 1977.

De Man, Paul. *Allegories of Reading: Figural Language in Rousseau, Nietzsche, Rilke, and Proust.* New Haven: Yale University Press, 1979.

Derrida, Jacques. "Cogito and the History of Madness." In *Writing and Difference,* 31–63. Chicago: University of Chicago Press, 1978.

———. "Cogito et histoire de la folie." In *L'écriture et la différance,* 51–97. Paris: Seuil, 1967.

———. "Deconstruction and the Other." In *Dialogues with Contemporary Thinkers: The Phenomenological Heritage,* ed. Richard Kearney, 105–26. Manchester: Manchester University Press, 1984.

———. *De la grammatologie.* Paris: Minuit, 1967.

———. "Différance." In *Marges de la philosophie,* 3–29. Paris: Minuit, 1972.

———. "Différance." In *Margins of Philosophy,* 3–27. Chicago: University of Chicago Press, 1982.

———. "Discours." In *Jacques Derrida: Doctor Honoris Causa Universitatis Silensius,* ed. Tadeusz Rachwał. Katowice, Poland: Wydawnictwo Uniwesytetu Sląskiego, 1997.

———. *La dissémination.* Paris: Seuil, 1972.

———. *Dissemination.* Trans. Barbara Johnson. Chicago: University of Chicago Press, 1981.

——. *L'écriture et la différance*. Paris: Seuil, 1967.

——. "An Idea of Flaubert: 'Plato's Letter.' " *MLN* 99, no. 4 (1984): 748–68.

——. *Marges de la philosophie*. Paris: Minuit, 1972.

——. *Margins of Philosophy*. Trans. Alan Bass. Chicago: University of Chicago Press, 1982.

——. "Marx & Sons." In *Ghostly Demarcations: A Symposium on Jacques Derrida's Specters of Marx*, ed. Michael Sprinker, 213–69. London: Verso, 1999.

——. *Monolinguism of the Other, or, The Prosthesis of Origin*. Trans. Patrick Mensah. Stanford: Stanford University Press, 1998.

——. *Of Grammatology*. Trans. Gayatri C. Spivak. Baltimore: Johns Hopkins University Press, 1974.

——. "La question du style." *Nietzsche aujourd'hui*, 220–35. Paris: 10/18, 1968.

——. *Specters of Marx: The State of Debt, the Work of Mourning, and the New International*. Trans. Peggy Kamuf. London: Routledge, 1994.

——. *Writing and Difference*. Trans. Alan Bass. Chicago: University of Chicago Press, 1978.

Dews, Peter. *Logics of Disintegration: Post-Structuralist Thought and the Claims of Critical Theory*. London: Verso, 1987.

Dick, Philip K. "How to Build a Universe That Doesn't Fall Apart Two Days Later." In *The Shifting Realities of Philip K. Dick: Selected Literary and Philosophical Writings*, ed. Lawrence Sutin, 259–80. New York: Vintage, 1995.

Diderot, Denis. "Art." In *DFPV*, 5:395–509.

——. "Bas." In *DFPV*, 6:27–126.

——. "Éléments de physiologie." In *DFPV*, 17:263–574.

——. *Éloge de Richardson*. In *DFPV*, 13:181–208.

——. *Est-il bon? est-il méchant?* Ed. Jack Undank. Geneva: Institut et Musée Voltaire, 1961.

——. *Jacques le fataliste et son maître*. In *DFPV*, 23:1–291.

——. *Lettre sur le commerce de la librairie* (1767). Paris: Librairie Fontaine, 1984.

——. *Le neveu de Rameau*. Ed. Jean Fabre. Paris: Droz–Textes Littéraires Français, 1963.

——. *Le neveu de Rameau*. In *DFPV*, 12:31–196.

——. *Pensées sur l'interprétation de la nature* (1753–54). In *DFPV*, 9:1–111.

——. *La religieuse*. In *DFPV*, 11:1–294.

——. *Salon de 1767*. In *DFPV*, 16:1–525.

Dieckmann, Herbert. *"Le Philosophe": Text and Interpretation*. Language and Literature, n.s. 18. St. Louis: Washington University Studies, 1948.

Diogenes Laertius. *Lives of the Eminent Philosophers*. Cambridge: Harvard University Press, 1942–.

DiPiero, Thomas. *Dangerous Truths and Criminal Passions: The Evolution of the French Novel, 1569–1791*. Stanford: Stanford University Press, 1992.

Dosse, François. *History of Structuralism*. Trans. Deborah Glassman. Minneapolis: University of Minnesota Press, 1997.

Ducrot, Oswald, and Tzvetan Todorov. *Encyclopedic Dictionary of the Sciences of Language*. Trans. Catherine Porter. Baltimore: Johns Hopkins University Press, 1979.

Eagleton, Terry. *The Illusions of Postmodernism*. Oxford: Blackwell, 1996.

Eco, Umberto. *A Theory of Semiotics*. Bloomington: Indiana University Press, 1976.

Elias, Norbert. *Time: An Essay*. Trans. Edmund Jephcott. Oxford: Blackwell, 1992.

Ellmann, Maud. *The Hunger Artists: Starving, Writing and Imprisonment*. Cambridge: Harvard University Press, 1993.

Ellrich, Robert J. "The Rhetoric of *La Religieuse* and Eighteenth-Century Forensic Rhetoric." In *Diderot Studies 3*, ed. Otis E. Fellows and Gita May, 129–54. Geneva: Droz, 1961.

Emerson, Ralph Waldo. "Ode, Inscribed to W. H. Channing" (1847). In *Collected Poems and Translations*, ed. Harold Bloom and Paul Kane, 50–51. New York: Library of America, 1994.

Empiricus, Sextus. *Outlines of Scepticism*. Ed. Julia Annas and Jonathan Barnes. New York: Cambridge University Press, 2000.

Empson, William. *Seven Types of Ambiguity*. 3d ed. 1930. Reprint. New York: New Directions, 1966.

Engels, Friedrich. *Herr Eugen Dühring's Revolution in Science (Anti-Dühring)*. Trans. Emile Burns. 1939. Reprint. New York: International Publishers, 1966.

Eribon, Didier. *Michel Foucault*. Trans. Betsy Wing. Cambridge: Harvard University Press, 1991.

Erlich, Victor. *Russian Formalism: History, Doctrine*. New Haven: Yale University Press, 1965.

Ermarth, Elizabeth Deeds. *Sequel to History: Postmodernism and the Crisis of Representational Time*. Princeton: Princeton University Press, 1992.

Evans, Gareth. *The Varieties of Reference*. New York: Oxford University Press, 1982.

Fanon, Frantz. *The Wretched of the Earth*. Trans. Constance Farrington. New York: Grove Press, 1968.

Fanuzzi, Robert. *Abolition's Public Sphere*. Minneapolis: University of Minnesota Press, 2003.

Favret, Mary A. *Romantic Correspondence: Women, Politics, and the Fiction of Letters*. Cambridge: Cambridge University Press, 1993.

Feyerabend, Paul. *Against Method: Outline of an Anarchistic Theory of Knowledge*. London: Verso, 1975.

Finder, Joseph. *The Moscow Club*. New York: Viking, 1991.

Flaubert, Gustave. *Correspondance*. Ed. Jean Bruneau. 4 vols. Paris: Gallimard-Pléiade, 1980–98.

Forero, Juan. "As Bolivian Miners Die, Boys Are Left to Toil." *New York Times*, 24 March 2003, A:3.

Foucault, Michel. *The Archaeology of Knowledge*. Trans. Alan Sheridan. New York: Pantheon, 1972.

———. "Mon corps, ce papier, ce feu." In *Histoire de la folie à l'âge classique*, 583–603. Paris: Gallimard, 1972.

———. "My Body, This Paper, This Fire." Trans. Geoff Bennington. *Oxford Literary Review* 4, no. 1 (Fall 1979): 9–28.

———. *Power/Knowledge: Selected Interviews and Other Writings, 1972–1977*. New York: Pantheon, 1980.

Frank, Joseph. *The Idea of Spatial Form*. New Brunswick, N.J.: Rutgers University Press, 1991.

———. "Spatial Form in Modern Literature." In *The Widening Gyre*, 3–62. New Brunswick, N.J.: Rutgers University Press, 1963.

Fraser, J. T. *Time: The Familiar Stranger*. Amherst: University of Massachusetts Press, 1987.

Fraser, Nancy. "The French Derrideans: Politicizing Deconstruction or Deconstructing the Political." In *Working through Derrida*, ed. Gary B. Madison, 51–76. Evanston, Ill.: Northwestern University Press, 1993.

Frayn, Michael. *Copenhagen*. London: Metheun, 1998.

Freud, Sigmund. *Civilization and Its Discontents*. (1930). Trans. James Strachey. *SE*, vol. 21.

———. *Group Psychology and the Analysis of the Ego*. (1921). Trans. James Strachey. *SE*, vol. 18.

———. *Interpretation of Dreams*. Trans. James Strachey. *SE*, vol. 4.

———. "Note upon the 'Mystic Writing Pad.'" In *SE*, 19:227–34.

———. "Project for a Scientific Psychology." *SE*, vol. 1.

———. *Psychopathology of Everyday Life*. *SE*, vol. 6.

———. "The Taboo of Virginity" (1918). *SE*, vol. 11.

Friedlander, Saul, ed. *Probing the Limits of Representation: Nazism and the "Final Solution."* Cambridge: Harvard University Press, 1992.

Gallagher, Catherine. *Nobody's Story: The Vanishing Acts of Women Writers in the Marketplace, 1670–1820*. Berkeley: University of California Press, 1994.

Garfinkel, Alan. *Forms of Explanation: Rethinking the Questions in Social Theory*. New Haven: Yale University Press, 1981.

Gautier, Théophile. *Albertus, ou L'Ame et le péché*, in *Poésies complètes*, ed. René Jasinski. Paris: Nizet, 1970.

———. *Mademoiselle Maupin*. Paris: L'Imprimerie Nationale, 1979.

Gay, Peter. *The Enlightenment, an Interpretation: The Rise of Modern Paganism*. New York: Vintage, 1968.

———. *Freud: A Life for Our Time*. New York: Anchor, 1988.

Giard, Luce. "Biobibliographie." In *Michel de Certeau: Cahiers pour un temps*, ed. Luce Giard, 245–53. Paris: Éditions du Centre Pompidou, 1987.

———. "Mystique et politique." In *Histoire, mystique et politique: Michel de Certeau*, ed. Luce Giard, Jacques Revel, and Hervé Martin, 9–45. Grenoble: Jérôme Millon, 1991.

Ginzberg, Carlo. *History, Rhetoric, and Proof*. Hanover, N.H.: University Press of New England, 1999.

Goldhammer, Arthur. "Man in the Mirror: Language, the Enlightenment, and the Postmodern." In *Postmodernism and the Enlightenment: New Perspectives in Eighteenth-Century French Intellectual History*, ed. Daniel Gordon, 31–44. New York: Routledge, 2001.

Goldin, Frederick, ed. *Lyrics of the Troubadours and Trouvères*. Garden City, N.Y.: Anchor, 1972.

Gordon, Daniel. "On the Supposed Obselescence of the French Enlightenment." In *Postmodernism and the Enlightenment: New Perspectives in Eighteenth-Century French Intellectual History*, ed. D. Gordon, 201–21. New York: Routledge, 2001.

———. *Postmodernism and the Enlightenment: New Perspectives in Eighteenth-Century French Intellectual History*. New York: Routledge, 2001.

Gosden, Christopher. *Social Being and Time*. Oxford: Blackwell, 1994.

Goulemot, Jean-Marie. *Forbidden Texts: Erotic Literature and Its Readers in Eighteenth-Century France*. Trans. James Simpson. Philadelphia: University of Pennsylvania Press, 1994.

Green, Alice. "Diderot's Fictional Worlds." *Diderot Studies* 1 (1949): 1–26. Ed. Otis E. Fellows and Norman Torreys. Syracuse: Syracuse University Press, 1952.

Guilleragues, Gabriel Joseph de Laverne. *Lettres portugaises*. Ed. Frédéric Deloffre and Jacques Rougeot. Geneva: Droz, 1972.

Habermas, Jürgen. *Autonomy and Solidarity: Interviews*. Ed. Peter Dews. London: Verso, 1986.

——. *Dialectic of Enlightenment*. Trans. John Cumming. London: Verso, 1979.

——. *The Philosophical Discourse of Modernity: Twelve Lectures*. Trans. Frederick G. Lawrence. Cambridge: MIT Press, 1987.

——. *Theory of Communicative Action*. Trans. T. McCarthy. 2 vols. Boston: Beacon, 1984, 1987.

Haraway, Donna J. *Primate Visions: Gender, Race, and Nature in the World of Modern Science*. New York: Routledge, 1989.

——. "Situated Knowledges." In *Feminism and Science*, ed. Evelyn Fox Keller and Helen E. Longino, 249–63. Oxford: Oxford University Press, 1996.

Harding, Sandra G. *Is Science Multicultural? Postcolonialisms, Feminisms, and Epistemologies*. Bloomington: Indiana University Press, 1998.

——. "Rethinking Standpoint Epistemology." In *Feminism and Science*, ed. Evelyn Fox Keller and Helen E. Longino, 235–48. Oxford: Oxford University Press, 1996.

Harding, Sandra G., and Merrill B. Hintikka, eds. *Discovering Reality: Feminist Perspectives on Epistemology, Metaphysics, Methodology, and Philosophy of Science*. Boston: D. Reidel, 1983.

Havel, Václav. "The Power of the Powerless." In *Living in Truth*, ed. Jan Vladiska, 36–122. London: Faber and Faber, 1986.

Hayes, Julie Candler. *Reading the French Enlightenment: System and Subversion*. Cambridge: Cambridge University Press, 1999.

Hegel, G.W.F. *Hegel's Philosophy of Right*. Trans. T. M. Knox. Oxford: Oxford University Press, 1952.

——. *Lectures on the Philosophy of World History*. Trans. H. B. Nisbet. Cambridge: Cambridge University Press, 1975.

——. *Logic: Part One of the "Encyclopedia of the Philosophical Sciences."* Trans. William Wallace. Vol. 1. Oxford: Oxford University Press, 1970.

——. *Phänomenologie des Geistes. Werke*, vol. 3. Ed. Eva Moldenhauer and Karl Markus Michel. Frankfurt am Main: Suhrkamp, 1986.

——. *Phenomenology of Spirit*. (1807). Trans. A. V. Miller. Oxford: Clarendon Press, 1977.

——. *The Philosophy of History* (1822–31). Trans. J. Sibree. New York: Dover, 1956.

Hilton, Isabel. *Search for the Panchen Lama*. New York: Norton, 1999.

Hirschman, Albert O. *The Passions and the Interests: Political Arguments for Capitalism before Its Triumph*. Princeton: Princeton University Press, 1977.

Hobson, Marian. *The Object of Art: The Theory of Illusion in Eighteenth-Century France*. Cambridge: Cambridge University Press, 1982.

Horace. *Epistles*. Ed. Roland Mayer. Cambridge: Cambridge University Press, 1994.

Horkheimer, Max. "Montaigne und die Funktion der Skepsis." In *Kritische Theorie*, ed. Alfred Schmidt, 201–59. Frankfurt: S. Fischer, 1968.

Horkheimer, Max, and Theodor W. Adorno. *Dialectic of Enlightenment*. Trans. John Cumming. London: Verso, 1979.

Hoy, David Couzens. "Splitting the Difference: Habermas's Critique of Derrida." In *Working through Derrida*, ed. Gary B. Madison. Evanston, Ill.: Northwestern University Press, 1993.

Hulbert, James. "Diderot in the Text of Hegel: A Question of Intertextuality." *Studies in Romanticism* 22 (1983): 267–91.

Hume, David. *An Enquiry concerning Human Understanding* (1739–40). Ed. Anthony Flew. La Salle, Ill.: Open Court, 1988.

——. "Of National Characters." In *Essays, Moral and Political*, 197–215. Indianapolis: Liberty Classics, 1985.

Jakobson, Roman. "Closing Statement: Linguistics and Poetics." In *Style and Language*, ed. Thomas A. Sebeok, 350–77. Cambridge: MIT Press, 1960.

James, C.L.R. "The Black Jacobins." In *The C.L.R. James Reader*, ed. Anna Grimshaw, 67–111. Oxford: Blackwell, 1992.

Jameson, Fredric. "Architecture and the Critique of Ideology." In F. Jameson, *Ideologies of Theory: Essays 1971–1986*, 2:35–60. Minneapolis: University of Minnesota Press, 1988.

——. *Fables of Aggression: Wyndham Lewis, the Modernist as Fascist*. Berkeley: University of California Press, 1979.

——. *The Ideologies of Theory: Essays 1971–1986*. 2 vols. Minneapolis: University of Minnesota Press, 1988.

——. "The Ideology of the Text." In F. Jameson, *Ideologies of Theory: Essays 1971–1986*, 1:17–71. Minneapolis: University of Minnesota Press, 1988.

——. "Imaginary and Symbolic in Lacan: Marxism, Psychoanalytic Criticism, and the Problem of the Subject." In *Literature and Psychoanalysis, the Question of Reading: Otherwise*, ed. Shoshana Felman, 338–95. Baltimore: Johns Hopkins University Press, 1982.

——. "Marxism and Historicism." In F. Jameson, *Ideologies of Theory: Essays 1971–1986*, 2:148–77. Minneapolis: University of Minnesota Press, 1988.

——. "Marx's Purloined Letter." *New Left Review* 209 (1995): 75–109.

——. *The Political Unconscious: Narrative as a Socially Symbolic Act*. Ithaca: Cornell University Press, 1981.

——. *Postmodernism, or the Cultural Logic of Late Capitalism*. Durham, N.C.: Duke University Press, 1991.

——. *The Prison-House of Language*. Princeton: Princeton University Press, 1972.

——. *The Seeds of Time*. New York: Columbia University Press, 1994.

——. "Transformations of the Image in Postmodernity." In *The Cultural Turn: Selected Writings on the Postmodern, 1983–1998*, 93–135. London: Verso, 1998.

——. "The Vanishing Mediator: Or, Max Weber as Storyteller." In F. Jameson, *Ideologies of Theory: Essays 1971–1986*, 2:3–34. Minneapolis: University of Minnesota Press, 1988.

Jay, Martin. *The Dialectical Imagination: A History of the Frankfurt School and the Institute of Social Research, 1923–1950*. 1973. Reprint. Berkeley: University of California Press, 1996.

Jenson, Deborah. *Trauma and Its Representations*. Baltimore: Johns Hopkins University Press, 2001.

Kant, Immanuel. *Critique of Pure Reason*. 1781. Trans. Norman Kemp Smith. New York: St. Martin's, 1965.

——. *Critique of Pure Reason*. 1781. Ed. and trans. Paul Guyer and Allen W. Wood. Cambridge: Cambridge University Press, 1998.

——. *Observations on the Feeling of the Beautiful and Sublime*. Trans. John Goldthwait. Berkeley: University of California Press, 1991.

——. "What Is Enlightenment?" In *"Foundations of the Metaphysics of Morals" and "What Is Enlightenment?"* New York: Macmillan, 1990.

Kaufmann, Walter. "The Hegel Myth and Its Methods." In *Hegel's Political Philosophy*, ed. Walter Kaufmann, 137–171. New York: Atherton, 1970.

——. Introduction. In *Hegel's Political Philosophy*, ed. Walter Kaufmann, 1–9. New York: Atherton, 1970.

Kavanagh, Thomas M. *Enlightenment and the Shadows of Chance: The Novel and the Culture of Gambling in Eighteenth-Century France.* Baltimore: Johns Hopkins University Press, 1993.

Keller, Evelyn Fox, and Helen E. Longino, eds. *Feminism and Science.* Oxford: Oxford University Press, 1996.

Knox, T. M. "Hegel and Prussianism." In *Hegel's Political Philosophy*, ed. Walter Kaufmann, 13–29. New York: Atherton, 1970.

Kojève, Alexandre. *Introduction to the Reading of Hegel: Lectures on the "Phenomenology of Spirit."* Ed. Allan Bloom. Trans. Raymond Queneau and James H. Nichols Jr. Ithaca: Cornell University Press, 1980.

Kosseleck, Reinhart. *Futures Past: On the Semantics of Historical Time.* Trans. Keith Tribe. Cambridge: MIT Press, 1985.

Kristeva, Julia. "Mémoire." *L'infini* 1 (Winter 1983): 39–54.

Kuhn, Thomas S. *The Road since Structure: Philosophical Essays, 1970–1993.* Ed. James Conant and John Haugeland. Chicago: University of Chicago Press, 2000.

———. *The Structure of Scientific Revolutions.* 2d ed. Chicago: University of Chicago Press, 1970.

Lacan, Jacques. "Le séminaire sur 'La Lettre Volée.' " In *Écrits*, 11–61. Series "Le champ freudien." Paris: Editions du Seuil, 1966.

LaCapra, Dominick. *Representing the Holocaust: History, Theory, Trauma.* Ithaca: Cornell University Press, 1994.

Lange, Frederick Albert. *The History of Materialism and Criticism of Its Present Importance.* Trans. Ernst Chester Thomas. 3d ed. London: Routledge and Kegan Paul, 1925.

Laursen, John Christian. *The Politics of Skepticism in the Ancients, Montaigne, Hume, and Kant.* Leiden: E. J. Brill, 1992.

Lewis, David. *On the Plurality of Worlds.* Oxford: Blackwell, 1986.

Locke, John. *A Letter concerning Toleration.* Trans. J. W. Gough. Ed. R. Kilbansky. Oxford: Clarendon Press, 1968.

———. *Political Writings of John Locke.* Ed. David Wooton. New York: Mentor-Penguin, 1993.

Longino, Helen. "Subjects, Power, and Knowledge: Description and Prescription in Feminist Philosophies of Science." In *Feminism and Science*, ed. Evelyn Fox Keller and Helen E. Longino, 264–79. Oxford: Oxford University Press, 1996.

Lough, John. *The "Encyclopédie."* New York: David McKay, 1971.

Loy, J. Robert. *Diderot's Determined Fatalist: A Critical Appreciation of "Jacques le fataliste."* New York: King's Crown, 1950.

Lukács, Georg. "Reification and the Consciousness of the Proletariat." In *History and Class Consciousness: Studies in Marxist Dialectics*, 83–222. Cambridge, Mass.: MIT Press, 1971.

Lyotard, Jean-François. "Answering the Question: What Is Postmodernism?" In *The Postmodern Condition: A Report on Knowledge*, ed. and trans. Geoff Bennington and Brian Massumi, 71–82. Minneapolis: University of Minneapolis Press, 1984.

———. *La condition postmoderne.* Paris: Éditions de Minuit, 1979.

———. *The Inhuman: Reflections on Time.* Trans. Geoffrey Bennington and Rachel Bowlby. Cambridge: Polity, 1991.

———. *The Postmodern Condition: A Report on Knowledge.* Trans. Geoff Bennington and Brian Massumi. Minneapolis: University of Minnesota, 1984.

Macherey, Pierre. *Theory of Literary Production*. Trans. Geoffrey Wall. London: Routledge and Kegan Paul, 1978.

Macksey, Richard, and Eugenio Donato, eds. *The Languages of Criticism and the Sciences of Man: The Structuralist Controversy*. Baltimore: Johns Hopkins University Press, 1972.

Mallarmé, Stéphane. "Un coup de dès." In *Oeuvres complètes*, ed. Henri Mondor and G. Jean-Aubry, 459–77. Paris: Gallimard-Pléiade, 1945.

———. "Crise de vers." In *Oeuvres complètes*, ed. Henri Mondor and G. Jean-Aubrey, 360–68. Paris: Gallimard-Pléiade, 1945.

———. "Faits divers." In *Oeuvres complètes*, ed. Henri Mondor and G. Jean-Aubrey, 1577–79. Paris: Gallimard-Pléiade, 1945.

———. "Or." In *Oeuvres complètes*, ed. Henri Mondor and G. Jean-Aubrey, 398–99. Paris: Gallimard-Pléiade, 1945.

Marongiu, Jean-Baptiste. "Le partage, l'infini et le jardin [interview with Jean-Luc Nancy]." *Libération*, 17 February 2000, section "Livres," 3.

Marx, Karl. *Capital: A Critique of Political Economy*. Trans. Ben Fowkes. Vol. 1. Harmondsworth: Penguin–New Left Books, 1976.

———. *Contribution to the Critique of Political Economy*. Trans. S. W. Ryazanskaya. New York: International Publishers, 1970.

———. "Economic and Philosophical Manuscripts (1844)." In *Writings of the Young Marx on Philosophy and Society*, ed. and trans. Lloyd D. Easton and Kurt H. Guddat, 284–337. New York: Doubleday-Anchor, 1967.

———. "On the Jewish Question." In *Karl Marx: Early Writings*, ed. T. B. Bottomore, 1–40. New York: McGraw-Hill, 1964.

Marx, Karl, and Frederick Engels. *The Communist Manifesto: A Modern Edition*. London: Verso, 1998.

———. *The German Ideology*. 3d ed. Moscow: Progress, 1976.

———. *Selected Letters*. Boston: Little, Brown, 1980.

May, Georges. *Le dilemme du roman au XVIIIe siècle*. Paris: Presses Universitaires de France, 1963.

McKeon, Michael. *The Origins of the English Novel, 1600–1740*. Rev. ed. Baltimore: Johns Hopkins University Press, 2002.

Merleau-Ponty, Maurice. *Phénoménologie de la perception*. Paris: Gallimard, 1945.

———. *Phenomenology of Perception*. Trans. Colin Smith. New York: Humanities Press, 1962.

Mill, John Stuart. *On Liberty* (1859). Ed. J. M. Robson. *Collected Works of John Stuart Mill*, 18:213–310. London: Routledge, 1991.

Miller, Nancy K. *French Dressing: Women, Men, and Ancien Régime Fiction*. New York: Routledge, 1995.

Montagu, Ewen. *The Man Who Never Was*. Philadelphia: J. B. Lippincott, 1954.

Montaigne, Michel Eyquem de. "Apologie de Raimond Sebond." In *Essais*, ed. Albert Thibaudet, bk. 2, chap. 12, 481–683. Paris: Gallimard-Pléiade, 1950.

———. "Des cannibales." In *Essais*, ed. Albert Thibaudet, bk. 1, chap. 31, 239–53. Paris: Gallimard-Pléiade, 1950.

———. "Du repentir." In *Essais*, ed. Albert Thibaudet, bk. 3, chap. 2, 1899–914. Paris: Gallimard-Pléiade, 1950.

———. *Essays*. Trans. J. M. Cohen. Harmondsworth: Penguin, 1958.

———. *Lettres persanes*. Ed. Paul Vernière. Paris: Classiques Garnier, 1960.

———. "On Repentance." In *Essays*, 235–50. Harmondsworth: Penguin, 1958.

Montesquieu, Charles de Secondat. *Oeuvres complètes*. Ed. Roger Callois. 2 vols. Paris: Gallimard-Pléiade, 1949–51.

Morson, Gary Saul. *Narrative and Freedom: The Shadows of Time*. New Haven: Yale University Press, 1994.

Mowitt, John. *Text: The Genealogy of an Antidisciplinary Object*. Durham, N.C.: Duke University Press, 1992.

Mukařovský, J. "Standard Language and Poetic Language." In *A Prague School Reader*, ed. P. Garvin. Washington, D.C.: Georgetown University Press, 1964.

Mulcaire, Terry. "Public Credit; or, the Feminization of Virtue in the Marketplace." *PMLA* 114, no. 5 (October 1990): 1029–42.

Mylne, Vivienne. *The Eighteenth-Century French Novel: Techniques of Illusion*. 2d ed. Cambridge: Cambridge University Press, 1981.

Nancy, Jean-Luc. *La communauté désoeuvrée*. Paris: Christian Bourgois, 1986.

———. "Exscription." In *The Birth to Presence*, trans. Brian Holmes, 319–40. Stanford: Stanford University Press, 1993.

———. *The Inoperative Community*. Trans. Lisa Garbus, Peter Connors, Michael Holland, and Simona Sawhney. Minneapolis: University of Minnesota Press, 1991.

Nietzsche, Friedrich. "On the Truth and Lies in the Nonmoral Sense." In *Philosophy and Truth: Selections from Nietzsche's Notebooks of the Early 1870s*. Trans. Daniel Breazeale, 79–97. Atlantic Highlands, N.J.: Humanities Press, 1979.

Norris, Christopher. *What's Wrong with Postmodernism: Critical Theory and the Ends of Philosophy*. Baltimore: Johns Hopkins University Press, 1990.

Nussbaum, Martha C. *Love's Knowledge: Essays on Philosophy and Literature*. New York: Oxford University Press, 1990.

Offen, Karen. "Reclaiming the European Enlightenment for Feminism; or Prolegomena to Any Future History of Eighteenth-Century Europe." In *Perspectives on Feminist Thought in European History*, ed. Tjitske Akkerman and Siep Stuurman, 85–103. London: Routledge, 1998.

Pascal, Blaise. *Pensées*. Ed. Zacharie Tourneur and Didier Anzieu. 2 vols. Paris: Armand Colin, 1960.

Plotnitsky, Arkady. *In the Shadow of Hegel: Complementarity, History, and the Unconscious*. Gainesville: University Press of Florida, 1993.

Pocock, J.G.A. *Politics, Language and Time: Essays on Political Thought and History*. New York: Atheneum, 1971.

———. *Virtue, Commerce and History: Essays on Political Thought and History, Chiefly in the Eighteenth Century*. Cambridge: Cambridge University Press, 1985.

Pomeau, René. Introduction to Jean Jacques Rousseau, *Julie, ou la nouvelle Héloïse*, i–xliv. Ed. R. Pomeau. Paris: Garnier–Classiques Garnier, 1960.

Popkin, Richard H. *History of Scepticism from Erasmus to Spinoza*. Rev. ed. Berkeley: University of California Press, 1979.

———. "New Views on the Role of Scepticism in the Enlightenment." In *Scepticism in the Enlightenment*, ed. R. H. Popkin, E. de Olaso, and G. Tonelli, 157–72. Dordrecht: Kluwer, 1997.

———. "Skepticism." In *The Cambridge Dictionary of Philosophy*, ed. Robert Audi, 738–41. New York: Cambridge University Press, 1995.

Popkin, Richard H., Ezequiel de Olaso, and Georgio Tonelli, eds. *Scepticism in the Enlightenment*. Dordrecht: Kluwer, 1997.

Popkin, Richard H., and Charles B. Schmitt, eds. *Scepticism from the Renaissance to the Enlightenment.* Wiesbaden: Otto Harrassowitz, 1987.

Popper, Karl R. *Conjectures and Refutations: The Growth of Scientific Knowledge.* New York: Basic Books, 1962.

——. *The Open Society and Its Enemies.* Princeton: Princeton University Press, 1950.

Proust, Jacques. "De l'*Encyclopédie* au *Neveu de Rameau.*" In *Recherches nouvelles sur quelques écrivains des Lumières*, ed. Jacques Proust. Geneva: Droz, 1972.

Proust, Marcel. *À la recherche du temps perdu.* Ed. Jean-Yves Tadié. 4 vols. Paris: Gallimard-Pléiade, 1987–89.

——. *In Search of Lost Time.* Trans. Terrence Kilmartin, C. K. Scott Moncrieff, and J. D. Enright. 6 vols. New York: Modern Library, 1998–99.

——. *Sodom and Gomorrah.* Trans. Terrence Kilmartin, C. K. Scott Moncrieff, and J. D. Enright. *In Search of Lost Time*, vol. 4. New York: Modern Library, 1999.

——. *Swann's Way.* Trans. Terrence Kilmartin, C. K. Scott Moncrieff, and J. D. Enright. *In Search of Lost Time*, vol. 1. New York: Modern Library, 1992.

Putnam, Hilary. *Mind, Language, and Reality.* Cambridge: Cambridge University Press, 1975.

Renan, Ernest. *Qu'est-ce qu'une nation?* Paris: Calmann Lévy, 1882.

Rhodes, Richard. *The Making of the Atomic Bomb.* New York: Simon and Schuster, 1986.

Ricoeur, Paul. *Time and Narrative.* Trans. Kathleen McLaughlin and David Pellauer. 3 vols. Chicago: University of Chicago Press, 1984–88.

Rilke, Rainier Maria. "Die Aufzeichnungen des Malte Laurids Brigge." In *Sämtliche Werke*, ed. Ruth Sieber-Rilke and Ernst Zinn, vol. 6. Wiesbaden: Insel-Verlag, 1966.

Rorty, Richard. *Consequences of Pragmatism: Essays, 1972–1980.* Minneapolis: University of Minnesota Press, 1982.

——. "The Contingency of Language." In *Contingency, Irony, and Solidarity*, 3–22. Cambridge: Cambridge University Press, 1989.

——. "Method, Social Science, and Social Hope." In *Consequences of Pragmatism (Essays: 1972–1980)*, 191–210. Minneapolis: University of Minnesota Press, 1982.

——. "Nineteenth-Century Idealism and Twentieth-Century Textualism" (1980). In *Consequences of Pragmatism (Essays: 1972–1980)*, 139–59. Minneapolis: University of Minnesota Press, 1982.

——. *Philosophy and the Mirror of Nature.* Princeton: Princeton University Press, 1979.

——. "Remarks on Deconstruction and Pragmatism." In *Deconstruction and Pragmatism*, ed. Chantal Mouffe, 13–18. London: Routledge, 1996.

Rose, Paul Lawrence. *Heisenberg and the Nazi Atomic Bomb Project: A Study in German Culture.* Berkeley: University of California Press, 1998.

Roth, Michael S. *Knowing and History: Appropriations of Hegel in Twentieth-Century France.* Ithaca: Cornell University Press, 1988.

Rousseau, Jean Jacques. *Julie, ou la nouvelle Héloïse.* Ed. and intro. René Pomeau. Paris: Garnier–Classiques Garnier, 1960.

Sade, Marquis de. *Philosophy in the Bedroom.* Trans. Richard Seaver and Austryn Wainhouse. In *Three Complete Novels.* New York: Grove Press, 1965.

Sartre, Jean-Paul. *Being and Nothingness: An Essay in Phenomenological Ontology.* Trans. Hazel Barnes. New York: Philosophical Library, 1956.

——. *The Family Idiot: Gustave Flaubert, 1821–1857.* Trans. Carol Cosman. 5 vols. Chicago: University of Chicago Press, 1981–93.

———. *What Is Literature?* Trans. Bernard Frechtman. Bloomington: Indiana University Press, 1978.

Saussure, Ferdinand de. *Cours de linguistique générale.* Ed. Charles Bally and Albert Sechehaye. 3d ed. Paris: Payot, 1964.

———. *Course in General Linguistics.* Trans. Roy Harris. Ed. Albert Sechehaye, Charles Bally, and Albert Riedlinger. La Salle, Ill.: Open Court, 1986.

Scarry, Elaine. *The Body in Pain: The Making and Unmaking of the World.* New York: Oxford University Press, 1985.

Sedgwick, Eve Kosofsky. "Privilege of Unknowing." *Genders* 1 (Spring 1988): 102–24.

Ségur, Louis-Philippe, Comte de. *Mémoires, ou souvenirs, et anecdotes,* 3 vols. 3d ed. (Paris: A. Eymery, 1827).

Sen, Amartya. *Human Rights and Asian Values.* New York: Carnegie Council on Ethics and International Affairs, 1997.

Shermer, Michael, and Alex Grobman. *Denying History: Who Says the Holocaust Never Happened and Why Do They Say It?* Berkeley: University of California Press, 2000.

Simmel, Georg. "How Is Society Possible?" In *On Individuality and Social Forms,* ed. Donald L. Levine, 6–22. Chicago: University of Chicago Press, 1971.

———. *The Philosophy of Money.* Trans. Tom Bottomore and David Frisby. London: Routledge and Kegan Paul, 1978.

Simon, Julia. *Mass Enlightenment: Critical Studies in Rousseau and Diderot.* Albany: State University of New York Press, 1995.

Smith, Adam. *An Inquiry into the Nature and Causes of the Wealth of Nations.* Ed. Kathryn Sutherland. Oxford: Oxford University Press, 1993.

Smith, Adam [pseud. for George J. W. Goodman]. *Supermoney.* New York: Random House, 1972.

Spitzer, Leo. *Linguistics and Literary History.* New York: Russell and Russell, 1962.

Spivak, Gayatri C. "Il faut s'y prendre en s'en prenant à elles." In *Les fins de l'homme: À partir du travail de Jacques Derrida,* ed. Jean-Luc Nancy and Philippe Lacoue-Labarthe, 505–15. Paris: Galilée, 1981.

———. *In Other Worlds: Essays in Cultural Politics.* New York: Methuen, 1987.

———. "Limits and Openings of Marx in Derrida." *Outside in the Teaching Machine,* 97–119. New York: Routledge, 1993.

Stroud, Barry. *The Significance of Philosophical Skepticism.* New York: Oxford University Press, 1984.

Surya, Michel. *Georges Bataille: La mort à l'oeuvre.* Paris: Seguier, 1987.

Taylor, Charles. *Hegel and Modern Society.* Cambridge: Cambridge University Press, 1979.

Terdiman, Richard. "Afterword: Reading the News." In *Making the News: Modernity and the Mass Press in Nineteenth-Century France,* ed. Jeannene Przyblyski and Dean de la Motte, 351–76. Amherst: University of Massachusetts Press, 1999.

———. "Cultural Studies in a Traditional Frame." In *Dialogues on Cultural Studies: Interviews with Contemporary Critics,* ed. Fengzhen Wang and Shaobo Xie, 233–51. Calgary: University of Calgary Press, 2002.

———. *Discourse/Counter-Discourse.* Ithaca: Cornell University Press, 1985.

———. "Globalization: Ideology and Materiality." In *Rethinking Globalism,* ed. Manfred B. Steger, 107–20. New York: Rowman and Littlefield, 2003.

———. "The Marginality of Michel de Certeau." *South Atlantic Quarterly* 100, no. 2 (Spring 2001): 397–419.

——. "Materialist Imagination: Notes toward a Theory of Literary Strategies." *Helios* 7, no. 2 (1980): 27–49.

——. "On the Dialectics of Post-Dialectical Thinking." In *Community at Loose Ends*, ed. James Creech, 111–20. Minneapolis: University of Minnesota Press, 1991.

——. *Present Past: Modernity and the Memory Crisis*. Ithaca: Cornell University Press, 1993.

——. "The Response of the Other." *Diacritics* 22, no. 2 (Summer 1992): 2–10.

——. "The Subject of the Other: From Alterity to Heterology." *Comparative Literature East and West* 2, no. 2 (Winter 2000): 27–47.

——. "The Subject of the Other: From Alterity to Heterology." In *Proteus im Spiegel: Kritische Theorie des Subjekts im 20. Jahrhundert*, ed. Paul Geyer and Monika Schmitz-Emans, 51–64. Würzburg: Königshausen und Neumann, 2003.

Timpanaro, Sebastiano. *On Materialism*. Trans. Lawrence Garner. London: NLB, 1975.

Tomashevsky, Boris. "Thematics." In *Russian Formalist Criticism: Four Essays*, ed. Lee T. Lemon and Marion J. Reis, 61–95. Lincoln: University of Nebraska Press, 1965.

Tonelli, Georgio. "The 'Weakness' of Reason in the Age of Enlightenment." In *Scepticism in the Enlightenment*, ed. Richard H. Popkin, Ezequiel de Olaso, and Georgio Tonelli, 35–50. Dordrecht: Kluwer, 1997.

Undank, Jack. "A New Date for *Jacques le fataliste*." *MLN* 74 (1959): 433–37.

United States Geological Service Web Site. http://pubs.usgs.gov/publications/text/dynamic.html#anchor10790904.

Vance, Eugene. *Reading the "Song of Roland."* Englewood Cliffs, N.J.: Prentice-Hall, 1970.

Vidal-Naquet, Pierre. *Assassins of Memory: Essays on the Denial of the Holocaust*. Trans. Jeffrey Mehlman. New York: Columbia University Press, 1992.

Warner, William B. *Licensing Entertainment: The Elevation of Novel Reading in Britain, 1684–1750*. Berkeley: University of California Press, 1998.

Wartofsky, Marx. "Diderot and the Development of Materialist Monism." In *Diderot Studies 2*, ed. Otis E. Fellows and Norman Torreys, 279–329. Syracuse: Syracuse University Press, 1952.

Weber, Max. *Economy and Society: An Outline of Interpretive Sociology*. Ed. Guenther Roth and Claus Wittich. Berkeley: University of California Press, 1978.

——. "Science as a Vocation." In *From Max Weber: Essays in Sociology*, ed. H. H. Gerth and C. Wright Mills. New York: Oxford University Press, 1946.

Wellek, René. *A History of Modern Criticism, 1750–1950*. 8 vols. New Haven: Yale University Press, 1955–92.

Whitrow, G. J. *Time in History: Views of Time from Prehistory to the Present Day*. Oxford: Oxford University Press, 1989.

William IX, Duke of Aquitaine. "Un vers de dreyt nien." In *Lyrics of the Troubadours and Trouvères*, ed. Frederick Goldin. Garden City, N.Y.: Anchor, 1972.

Williams, Raymond. "Base and Superstructure in Marxist Cultural Theory." In *Problems in Materialism and Culture*, 31–49. London: Verso-NLB, 1980.

——. *Marxism and Literature*. Oxford: Oxford University Press, 1977.

Woolf, Virginia. *The Common Reader: First Series*. Ed. and intro. Andrew McNeillie. 1953. Reprint. San Diego: Harcourt Brace Jovanovich, 1984.

——. "Mr. Bennett and Mrs. Brown" (1924). In *Collected Essays*, 319–37. New York: Harcourt, Brace, and World, 1966.

Index

Printed in the United States
64099LVS00013B/85-108